SOCIAL WORK SKILLS

A PRACTICE HANDBOOK

Pamela Trevithick

Open University Press
Buckingham · Philadelphia

D0281527

Open University Press
Celtic Court
22 Ballmoor
Buckingham
MK18 1XW

email: enquiries@openup.co.uk
world wide web: www.openup.co.uk

and
325 Chestnut Street
Philadelphia, PA 19106, USA

First Published 2000
Reprinted 2001 (twice), 2002 (twice)

Copyright © Pamela Trevithick, 2000

All rights reserved. Except for the quotation of short passages for the purpose of criticism and review, no part of this publication may be reproduced, stored in a retrieval system, or transmitted, in any form or by any means, electronic, mechanical, photocopying, recording or otherwise, without the prior written permission of the publisher or a licence from the Copyright Licensing Agency Limited. Details of such licences (for reprographic reproduction) may be obtained from the Copyright Licensing Agency Ltd of 90 Tottenham Court Road, London, W1P 0LP.

A catalogue record of this book is available from the British Library

ISBN 0 335 20699 9 (pb)   0 335 20700 6 (hb)

Library of Congress Cataloging-in-Publication Data Available

Typeset by Type Study, Scarborough
Printed in Great Britain by Biddles Ltd, www.biddles.co.uk

CONTENTS

for
Charlie Beaton

ACKNOWLEDGEMENTS

The suggestion that I write a book came several years ago when, quite unexpectedly, I was approached by a stranger after a talk I had given at a National Association for Mental Health (MIND) conference on women and mental health. The stranger was Jo Campling, a well-known editor in the world of social work publishing, to whom I owe special thanks. Without Jo's encouragement, this text would not have been started – nor found its way to Jacinta Evans at Open University Press. I am grateful to Jo for so much, particularly her gentle reminders to finish the text. I am also indebted to Jacinta for the skilful way she steered the text to publication, and for the thoughtfulness I have experienced from the staff at Open University Press. In particular, I would like to thank Kate Tadman, Maureen Cox and Janet Howatson for their editorial skills and impressive attention to detail, and Clara Waissbein and Tanya Sellars for their patience in addressing my queries. The comments I received from the external reviewers, Joyce Lishman and Michael Preston-Shoot, were enormously valuable and helped make the text more accessible. I am especially grateful to Michael for his detailed comments and encouragement, and for sharing his knowledge so generously. However, all errors are mine.

My greatest thanks go to my friends, Judy Carver and Robert French, without whom this work could not have been completed. Their belief in me, and this text, has sustained me through dark, dismal days when nothing seemed possible. The devoted way they ploughed through different chapters will remain with me always. I would also like to thank my son, Tom, for allowing me to disappear for hours on end without complaint, and Bridget for her help at a crucial time. Tom and Bridget have grown up with this book, and their love has been deeply sustaining. The support given by Charlie Beaton and Donald Branch over the years has been particularly important to me, especially during the final weeks of writing. A special thanks goes to Jane Dennis for her practical help and dependability, and Julie Selwyn for her inspired comments at a moment that mattered.

I would also like to thank other colleagues and friends who helped make this book possible including: Charlotte Ardizzone, Moira Bakehouse, Rosemary Baragwanath, Bill Beaumont, Chryselle Brown, Brian Caddick, Terrell Carver, Roger Clark, Mark Cox and his computer team (Paul Croft, Dave Hurst, David Midwinter, James Watson), Joy Dalton, Marie-Laure Davenport, Jon Doble, Rosemary Evelyn, Elaine Farmer, Eileen Gambrill, Maureen Hanscomb, Mrs Harris, Mushroom Hamilton, Anna Harvey, James Hennefeld, Elaine Kreiger, Hilary Land, Jos Large, Tony Lewis, Kate Lyon, Geraldine Macdonald, Gill McGill, Rachel Mirress, Shailen Nandy, Jean Neumann, Phyllida Parsloe, Rose Perrson, David Quinton, Rosie Tomlinson, Ann Shabbaz, Sue Pollock, Jane Stacey, Chris Stephens, Peter Walker, Liz Wilson and Norma Wilson. I owe a particular thanks to the service users I have worked with over the years, whose stories continue to fuel in me a sense of outrage and an enduring belief in the importance of fairness. Finally, I want to thank my students, particularly my tutees, for their comments on the social work skills unit I taught for nine years, on which this text is based.

INTRODUCTION

... there are no easy remedies in social work, especially
when we are confronted daily with oppression and
deprivation . . .

(Coulshed and Orme 1998: 3)

The context of social work is changing rapidly. However, one fundamental element remains the same, namely that social work is located within some of the most complex problems and perplexing areas of human experience, and for this reason, social work is, and has to be, a highly skilled activity. The purpose of this text is to describe this skilled activity by providing an account of 50 skills commonly used in social work, and to identify how these skills can be used in practice to enhance our effectiveness and help bring about positive outcomes. It attempts to bridge a gap that currently exists in relation to texts written specifically on the theme of social work skills. This gap has also been noted in relation to skills teaching. According to research undertaken by Marsh and Triseliotis (1996), 51 per cent of students interviewed stated that there was too little social work skills training on their courses. In a list of recommendations, Marsh and Triseliotis conclude that 'much greater attention [needs to be] paid to the teaching of social work skills using concrete practice situations' (1996: 219). This should include 'better and more applied teaching of psychology' (p. 220).

In order to develop these skills – a 'toolbox' of interventions – we need to have a sound theoretical and research base from which to begin to understand people and their situations, and to formulate plans of action appropriate to the circumstances encountered. This involves understanding how experiences are perceived, understood and communicated by people, and how this impacts on behaviour and life situations, both positive and negative. To some extent, this understanding will always be incomplete and uneven because, in the realm of human experience, life is unpredictable and some uncertainty is inevitable (Marris 1996). Improving our practice skills, based on current research and the 'best' evidence available, is a difficult task and one that daunts other professionals in this field, as this quotation from a report from the Cabinet Office notes:

While there is plenty of research available in areas such as education, social services and criminal justice, the coverage is patchy and there is little consensus amongst the research community about the appropriateness of particular methodologies or how research evidence should be used to inform policy and practice.

(Major 2000: 1)

The complex nature of social work is due, in part, to the fact that it involves working across differences of class, race, gender, age, disability, sexual orientation, religion, culture, health, geography, expectations and outlook on life. Differences can be seen in the different ways that problems are presented, communicated and perceived by individuals and in terms of the solutions sought. There are also differences in the way other disciplines and professions analyse and work with problems.

It is not always easy for people seeking help to state their needs or put words to their thoughts and feelings, particularly when these are tangled amid feelings of confusion, fear, humiliation, anger and despair. Then it can be hard for people to remember their strengths and abilities; the courage and determination that have enabled them to get this far. Within this tangled mass of jumbled experiences misunderstandings can easily occur, sometimes with tragic consequences, as the inquiries into the deaths of children known to social services attest (DHSS 1982; Gough 1993). As practitioners we still have more to learn about how to work with people in ways that are clear: ways that shine a torch on what is happening and why, that illuminate possible ways to move things forward and provide evidence of effectiveness or otherwise.

This learning is an ongoing process and never complete. Indeed, one way to view every interaction is as a learning experience for both parties. As practitioners we may be learning how to pose questions in ways that offer the greatest chance of being given open and honest responses. Or we may be learning to listen creatively to what is being said, or not said. At the same time, through the process of actually putting words to thoughts, feelings and experiences, service users may be ordering events and emotions, and learning more about their strengths and limitations, and their capacity to cope, or not, when faced with too much strain. They may be using this opportunity to come to terms with experiences that have been unbearable up to that point and, in this difficult process, may be learning how to trust again. Other service users test our skills in different ways, particularly those who 'have no interest in being helped', 'who are not motivated to change' or who have a different value base (Trotter 1999: 1).

This text emphasizes the central importance that communication and interviewing skills play within social work practice. As human beings we are, in fact, always communicating something, although this may not be intelligible to ourselves or to others. It may require some deciphering, which can be likened to learning a different language or, more precisely, a new dialect. As practitioners, to achieve an understanding about what is being communicated means using everything at our disposal in order to come alongside the experiences of the people with whom we work. From this perspective I do not believe that it is possible to be an effective practitioner without being an effective communicator. This, in turn, implies that, for effective communication to be possible, we have to know ourselves (Dominelli 1998: 10; Lishman 1998: 94). That is, we have to know the boundary of our own thoughts, feelings and experiences and to use these as a basis for understanding others, but without becoming merged, or so distant that we cannot empathize with another person (Thorne 1997: 181–2). This involves being able to take in and communicate what we think and feel using reading, writing, speaking and listening (Smith 1986: 246). The focus for this text is primarily on speaking and listening, although writing and recording skills are covered in Chapter 7.

To understand what is happening and why is, I believe, essential if change is to be a possibility. It is also important to be able to enable others to help themselves, which involves practitioners being comfortable in the role of *helper*. This is not easy to achieve when there is so much confusion and ambivalence within social work about helping others (England 1986: 65; Lishman 1994: 4). The emphasis placed on encouraging people to 'help themselves', with all the ambiguity this implies, can leave those people adrift who feel unable to care for themselves, for whatever reason. If we offer *help*, what are our intentions? Does helping others imply that as practitioners we are stuck in 'compulsive caregiving' (Braye and Preston-Shoot 1995: 129) or in a compulsive need to feel superior or to exercise power and control over others? These are central issues within social work because our intentions and actions are important and the people we work with have different capabilities. This makes our work, and the concept of empowerment and partnership, a complex undertaking (Thoburn *et al.* 1995), and more difficult to achieve than is sometimes suggested.

Similarly, good communication involves being able to hear how others gather and form their thoughts and feelings, and the meaning they give to particular experiences. This requires being able to establish a rapport and to form a relationship so that the information gained and experience shared can be consolidated and, hopefully, used to open up new avenues and inform future action. All points of contact and connection can have a profound impact, although we may never know their full significance. As practitioners struggling to balance different demands and tasks, it can be difficult to recognize how important we are to the people we work with.

By developing relationships that take account of our importance to each other, and the reciprocal nature of our connection, we are attempting to avoid adding ourselves to the pile of disappointing experiences, failures and 'let downs' that many service users have endured. By remaining within clear professional boundaries, being true to our word, keeping to the commitments we have made, never promising more than we can deliver and responding as closely as possible within agency constraints to the needs identified by the individual, we are offering the possibility of a new and different experience. If all goes well, this can increase confidence and form a basis from which to explore other relationships and possibilities. Within the confines of inner city or rural neglect or decay, these possibilities may be few and hard to identify but every experience, positive or negative, carries with it the possibility of influencing the next stage in a person's life (Salzberger-Wittenberg 1970: 162). The challenge here is a formidable one, namely how to sort out and work through the barriers within the individual and their social environment that inhibit progress, so that these experiences can be turned into opportunities for growth and change.

Positive experiences engender hope and trust, and convey a comforting sense of being understood and accepted. As human beings we have a deep-seated wish to be understood, to be accepted for who we are, and for our lives to have meaning and purpose (Howe 1996: 94). This desire is as true for people who come from deprived sectors of the population, who form the vast major-ity of social work service users, as it is for people who come from other, more advantaged sectors. Although at times this desire for meaning and under-standing may elude us, nevertheless most of us continue to yearn for someone who can bring this sense of understanding and meaning into our lives and with it the transformation that this possibility offers. Some find this through religion, while others turn to their families or friends to fulfil this need. Another, smaller cross-section are forced to look to professionals to fulfil these needs, perhaps because they are not loved enough or because the capacity to adapt or to give and take, which is central to the task of relating, has already broken down and needs to be addressed.

On the other hand, negative experiences can reaffirm old suspicions and doubts, deepen mistrust, shatter hope and produce even greater despair. Too often service users arrive into the situation with too much negativity and with too little belief in the possibilities that change can offer. Try as we may, we cannot avoid the fact that some service users pose a threat to themselves (Huxley 1997: 133) and/or to others, whether unintentionally (Issac *et al.* 1986) or not (Hester *et al.* 1996). These risks have to be acknowledged in any assessment or evaluation process. As far as possible, all judgements, whether positive or negative, should be backed by evidence.

If, as practitioners, we can involve ourselves in the experience of relating to another human being, what we ourselves gain from this involvement is that we too can develop and learn from the encounter, about ourselves and about other people. That is our ultimate reward. To be invited to enter another person's world, if only for a brief time and in a limited way, can in itself be a mark of trust and hope and, from this place, so much can happen. The small gains that some service users achieve can feel to them, and to us, like major successes and act as a reminder that some people can travel a long way on a little, while others need much more in order to move their lives forward. That is not to idealize poverty and the sense of shame and social exclusion that can haunt the lives of poor people but it is important to remember that, as human beings, we are complex and unique individuals and always more than our suffering (Angelou 1994).

The context of social work

The diverse nature of social work has been made more complex since the 1980s because of the changes that social work has had to embrace, some of which have given rise to confusions and uncertainties (Lishman 1998: 91). The election of the Labour government in 1997 has given rise to other changes. Devolution has resulted in different policies being implemented in England, Wales and Scotland. For example, the Social Work Council envisaged for England is different from the one planned for Scotland. Again, changes put forward for probation services in England and Wales are different from those planned for offender services in Scotland.

One philosophy behind some of these changes is a commitment to reduce health and social inequalities through the establishment of national standards and objectives in relation to health and social services and a framework for assessing performance and effectiveness (Huber 1999: 2). These objectives can be seen in initiatives stemming from *Quality Protects* (DoH 1998a) and *Modernising Health and Social Services* (1998b) and in the government's commitment to a 'what works is what counts' approach to service delivery (DoH 1998b: 93). Improvements in the quality of care will be overseen through the establishment of a proposed regulatory body, the General Social Care Council, which is due to be established in 2001. To achieve these aims, a collaboration between health and social services and interdisciplinary approaches to social care are seen as essential, although this may take different forms in various parts of the United Kingdom. Although the current framework of social work education and training was only established in 1995, it is about to be changed again. The introduction of changes will be linked to the setting up of the Social Work Council and development of the new Code of Conduct for social workers. These changes and proposals, together with the linking of *Quality Protects* grants with quality of services, will continue to have a profound impact on social work and the range and quality of services provided. If the crisis in recruiting and retaining social workers continues, it is difficult to see how these changes can be implemented without incentives to improve staff morale and performance.

Changes in the law

Since the late 1980s, there have been three major pieces of leglisation affecting social work practice (Ball 1996: xviii), namely the National Health Service and Community Care Act 1990; the Children Act, England, 1989 and the Criminal Justice Act 1991. The last has been substantially amended and superseded by subsequent legislation (Criminal Justice Act 1993, Criminal Justice and Public Order Act 1994 and Crime and Disorder Act 1998). In addition, there is now a considerable amount of case law emanating from interpretations of the Children Act 1989. The introduction of the Family Law Act 1996, particularly its provisions for addressing domestic violence, is an important development for social workers and probation officers. (Legislation closely modelled on the Children Act, England 1989 includes the Children Act, Scotland, 1995 and the Children (Northern Ireland) Order 1997).

In support of legislation listed above, codes of practice and guidance are drawn up by the government. These are important because they state government's expectations of local authorities in relation to good practice. For example, guidance issued under section 7(1) of the Local Authority Social Services Act 1970 means that, should local authorities fail to act in accordance with the guidance, a complaint can be made to the ombudsman or it may count as evidence against them in legal proceedings. The difference between regulations, codes and guidance is described as follows:

> One might sum up the differences between the requirements of these various official documents like this: Regulations say *'You must/shall'*; codes say *'You ought/should'*. When guidance explains regulations, it reaffirms the *'You must'* messages. However when it goes beyond regulation setting out good practice, it conveys the message that *'It is highly desirable to . . .'* or *'Unless there is good reason not to, you should . . .'* rather than, *'You must'*.
> (Department of Health 1989: 2)

I have described these differences in some detail because familiarity with the requirements of government, including the law, could be an important basis from which to argue for certain services to be provided and to 'endorse anti-discriminatory practice' (Braye and Preston-Shoot 1995: 66). Some commentators have suggested that the European legislation when implemented, such as the Human Rights Act, may help service users to secure relevant services.

Outline of the text

In the first section of this book I look at the theoretical underpinnings to practice. In Chapter 1 I look at how we can use theory and research to enhance our practice skills. In particular I explore what we mean when we use different theoretical terms and identify ten practice choices, giving a case example of their use in practice. In Chapter 2 I give an overview of key psychological concepts. These provide a framework to help us understand other theories and human behaviour. In Chapter 3 I bring theory and practice into closer dialogue by looking at communication, listening and assessment skills, and how we can evidence effectiveness.

In the second section I explore how these theoretical concepts relate in practice. I describe 50 skills used within social work on a regular basis, giving a name to many of the skills practitioners already use but may not have categorized. Other core skills are included, but not described separately. These include communication, interviewing, observation, listening, assessment and decision-making skills, bringing the total number to roughly 56 skills. Since beginning the book, I have encountered other skills worthy of mention but it was not possible to include them all without changing the nature of the book. Some readers may be disappointed not to find certain skills included, such as those associated with particular practice approaches like cognitive-behavioural or client-centred approaches. However, whenever possible I have tried to give references to further reading. Every skill has a theoretical underpinning but the emphasis in this text is on the use of skills in practice, rather than explaining the theoretical root of each skill. That would require a book in its own right, which, hopefully, will one day be written.

The perspective I stress throughout this section, and the text as a whole, is that every intervention should have a purpose and, as much as possible, that purpose should be identified clearly and openly as part of the agreement we establish with service users and other key individuals and professionals involved. If we fail at the outset to find agreement or to identify a *common purpose* this omission is likely to emerge as a difficulty later on. This emphasis on being clear and specific in areas makes our contact with service users more purposeful and also allows us to assess the appropriateness of specific social work methods, approaches, perspectives, interventions and skills in terms of their effectiveness in bringing about desired and agreed outcomes. The focus of this book is on work with individuals, because the individual is located in other social formations, namely the family, group and community. However, the skills described are transferable and can be related to other practice orientations, and to work with service users in different settings.

Some points of clarification about the text are worth noting. Throughout, I have described people who come within the remit of social work as *service users*. This term is not ideal, but nor are others (Stevenson and Parsloe 1993: 6). This dilemma is made more complicated because, in my experience, none of the terms used – service users, consumers, recipients of services or clients – draw on a language commonly used by people in receipt of social work services. The suggestion that the word *client* should refer to 'those who have social work imposed upon them' and *service users* to denote 'recipients of social work intervention voluntarily entered into' is an interesting differentiation (Wise 1995: 116) but not always an easy distinction to draw. Nevertheless, Wise's conceptualization is helpful because it highlights the importance of language, and its limitations. Changing the words we use, while introducing a climate of hope and the chance for a fresh start, cannot in itself ensure that we have fundamentally altered the stigma and oppression that travels with certain oppressed groups. Nor can it ensure that those people are treated better, both within social work and outside. Also on the subject of language, it is remarkable to note, given the historic and present day dominance of women in social work, both as service users and practitioners, how many authors use the male pronoun *he*. On occasion I have chosen to highlight how inappropriately this pronoun is used by adding the adverb *sic*.

The interventions identified do not solely refer to work with service users, but can include any other people we encounter during the course of our work (England 1986: 25). Sometimes our colleagues, managers or other professionals need to be supported and challenged in ways that are similar to our interactions with service users. Indeed, Wootton suggests that rather than focusing our attention on service users, many of whom lack the power and resources to change their lives, 'would not caseworkers do better to get their hands on some of our world's rulers?' (Wootton 1959).

Although I am an academic-practitioner, the pronoun *we* refers to the fact that I have written this text as a practitioner. As a result, most case examples tend to describe my experience of working with children and families, which may not feel satisfactory for practitioners working in other fields of social work. I apologize for this. In the case examples all names and other identifiable characteristics have been changed to protect service users' identities. In relation to this text, unless stated to the contrary the reader can assume that the situations described refer to service users who have sought our help on a voluntary basis.

1 USING THEORY AND RESEARCH TO ENHANCE PRACTICE

> ... to practice without a theory is to sail an uncharted sea;
> theory without practice is not to set sail at all ...
>
> (Susser 1968)

In this chapter I begin by looking at the tension that exists within social work in the relationship between theory and practice. I analyse how different terms are defined and, drawing on these definitions, identify ten practice choices, using a case example to describe how these choices might be used in practice.

The dialogue between theory and practice

To be an effective practitioner requires that we have a sound theoretical base. This is not easy to achieve. In the past, there has been a reluctance among some practitioners to embrace theory and research. The stereotypical view is one where theory and research are considered to be irrelevant, obscure, abstract and untranslatable in terms of direct practice. Some practitioners feel that to refer to theory is to lose touch with the realities of social work practice, and likely to be deskilling experience if it leaves us questioning our 'innate' skills, particularly our ability to relate to others. From this perspective it is easy for the split between theory and practice to be reinforced because practitioners have not experienced the benefits and clarity that theory can bring to practice situations.

But take, for example, a practitioner working with a distressed child who is struggling to settle into a new placement. This practitioner may find a useful link between theory and practice in Bowlby's (1980) theory of attachment, particularly his concept of *separation response* (protest, despair and detachment). This may help to illuminate the practitioner's understanding of this child and, in turn, help foster carer(s) and parent(s) to understand and to tolerate certain behaviours. We can, no doubt, choose to look at different writers in this field (Vygotsky 1932; Piaget 1959; Stern 1985; Wolff 1989; Lindon 1993; Bee 1995) or update our knowledge by referring to more recent research on attachment theory (Murray and Cooper 1994; Holmes 1997; Howe and Fearnley 1999) and relevant texts (Fahlberg 1991; Rutter 1991; Howe 1995; Brandon *et al.* 1998; Howe 1999). However, I would argue that our practice is impoverished without reference to those theories that attempt to bring together a range of explanations, including current research findings, because these have a bearing on the strategies or interventions that we might choose, or wish to learn about, in order to help children and parents overcome the dilemmas they face (Department of Health 1995a).

Similarly, in direct work, we are more likely to recognize key issues or reactions if we have a knowledge base to draw on. The concern that knowledge can 'be used to gain power over others' (Payne 1997: 30) can be addressed in relation to service users by finding ways to share our knowledge with them, so that they have access to the same understanding – and the sense of confidence and resilience that knowledge can give. From this perspective, the value of a given theory and research lie in their usefulness in relation to practice and the degree to which they illuminate our understanding and future action (Payne 1998: 124). If any theory can achieve this it has an important contribution to make, even if its value is limited or has to be adapted to fit different settings. In the example given above, attachment theory provides a theoretical framework from which to hypothesize and analyse the behaviour of the child in question. References to present and past research findings attempt to test out those hypotheses – put flesh on the bone – by looking for evidence for and against the hypothesis put forward, and to develop new hypotheses or theories based on that evidence.

The anti-intellectual stance within social work

This mistrust of theory has been described as an 'anti-theoretical or a theoretical stance' (Coulshed 1991: 2), as an 'anti-intellectualism' or an 'intellectual purge' (Jones 1996: 204). It is seen when practitioners ignore or dismiss research findings as irrelevant, unrepresentative and too abstract, sometimes because research fails to confirm the unquestioned assumptions and 'common-sense' notions that some practitioners have learned to rely on. This antagonism, however, cannot be explained only in terms of how practitioners have reacted. Jordan suggests that at times academics and researchers have gone about the task of linking theory to practice quite insensitively, sometimes dictating to practitioners 'not only how they should work, but also what rationale they should follow' (Jordan 1990: 13). Also, a degree of wariness is understandable given the fact that some research findings have been critical of practice, and more positive accounts of social work successes tend to be ignored (Cheetham *et al.* 1992: 2). Others suggest that practitioners fail to see the important part that theory can play because of a confusion about what constitutes a theory, which leads to the mistaken belief that they do not have or need to have theories when, in fact, we all use theory to inform practice:

> it is psychologically impossible not to have theories about things. It is impossible at a basic perceptual level, at a cognitive and at an emotional level. The search for meaning, as a basis for predicting behavioural success and avoiding danger, appears to have been 'wired' into our brains by evolution.
>
> (Sheldon 1995: 8)

These theories or explanations of human behaviour or events may, however, be expressed in quite obscure ways. For example, some writers refer to 'practice wisdom' (Hardiker and Barker 1981: 2; Dominelli 1998: 4): that is, skills based on personal experience of 'what works' in practice. The difficulty here is that some of these 'wisdoms' are not always ordered in such a way that they can be identified or differentiated from more common-sense notions, described by Pinker as 'an anecdotal ragbag of folk remedies' (1990: 64). As a result we have no reliable way of knowing in what ways these 'practice wisdoms' contribute to our stock of knowledge nor how applicable or transferable these wisdoms are across different situations. Instead, much of this knowledge remains beyond any evaluative process.

One important reason why these practice wisdoms are difficult to identify is because they are sometimes on-the-spot responses to complex dilemmas for which practice is ahead of theory. For example, for some time there was little information for practitioners to draw on with regard to the impact of drug abuse, particularly solvent abuse, in relation to young people. A similar gap in our knowledge once existed in relation to the impact of sexual abuse (Bagley and King 1990: 37). No doubt similar gaps will come to light as different social and emotional problems emerge and are acknowledged. On the other hand, there is no shortage of statistics or research in relation to the impact of poverty among people from more deprived sectors of the population, yet in recent years this knowledge has not influenced practice to any marked degree (Jones 1998: 124). For example, although it is well documented that not all claimants receive their full benefit entitlement (Walker and Walker 1998: 47), we are still not at a point where all practitioners engage in benefit checks as a matter of course.

This selective use of what we know has to be seen in a wider context than the practice orientation of particular social workers. For example, Jones locates this hostility to the 'peculiarities' of British social work education in a passage that is worth quoting at length:

> British social work education is also unique in its anti-intellectualism and its hostile stance to the social sciences. Since 1975 there has been an ongoing process of theoretical stripping out of the social work curriculum. In its place students are increasingly confronted with a mish-mash of methods, skills and values teaching, often lacking in any coherence. Values in particular have come to occupy a strangely central position, with

CCETSW [Central Council for Education and Training in Social Work] appearing to believe that they can be a substitute for knowledge and understanding. There is no comparable system of social work education in the world which is so nationally uniform, uninspired and tailored so closely to the requirements of major state employers.

(Jones 1996: 190–91)

These points are important and, given such obstacles, it is more than ever crucial that we remain intellectually and emotionally alive to the complexities that social work presents; that we keep hold of a critical faculty or an 'intellectual scrutiny and rigour' (Coulshed 1991: 1): 'Good social work rests upon the process of criticism, a process of experience and understanding, of analysis and comparison. A critical faculty is integral to the very practice of social work, to enable the worker to evaluate his client's and his own communications' (England 1986: 125).

Certainly, one way that this aliveness could be inspired would be if social work texts and research findings could be presented in ways that are more visually appealing, relevant and interesting, so that they provide 'the possibility of a good read' (England 1986: 205). Also, as practitioners we need to work in a learning culture where curiosity, enquiry and exploration are encouraged and where opportunity, encouragement, time and resources to update our knowledge are seen as priorities. This would, hopefully, encourage many more practitioners to write and to engage in research and this, in time, may provide the link that is needed in the theory–practice divide.

Competence based approaches

Some of this tension between theory and practice, and the lack of clarity about what social workers' knowledge base should be, is exposed in the debate about the value, or otherwise, of a competence based approach to teaching and learning within social work. CCETSW categorizes the knowledge base that social workers are required to have in order to qualify for the Diploma in Social Work under the following six headings:

- communicate and engage
- promote and enable
- assess and plan
- intervene and provide services
- work in organizations
- develop professional competence

It is not possible to do justice to the wide ranging debate that has taken place since CCETSW first introduced competences into the new Diploma in Social Work in Paper 30 (CCETSW 1989; 1991; 1995b). What is striking is the degree of agreement among social work academics in their criticisms of the appropriateness of this approach within social work. These include the criticism that teaching the 'mechanics' or 'techniques' produces technicians rather than professionals (Hayman 1993: 181) and that this process misses all that is complicated in the interaction between social worker and service user (Cheetham 1997: 264). Competences are also described as constraining a reflective approach to practice (Payne 1998: 122) and seen to ignore the central importance that process plays within a given interaction (Adams *et al.* 1998: 258). Furthermore, competences are accused of being inconsistent with the development of anti-oppressive practice and a more values based approach to social work (Dominelli: 1998: 9). Howe generalizes the concerns expressed: 'Such an outlook seeks to establish routines, standardized practices and predictable task environments. It is antithetical to depth explanations, professional integrity, creative practice, and tolerance of complexity and uncertainty' (Howe 1996: 92).

The major advantage of a competence based approach lies in its emphasis on outcomes and on the importance of social workers being able to demonstrate the appropriate use and effectiveness of designated skills in relation to practice. This includes a requirement that students and social workers are familiar with the law and how this relates in practice, and that students and practitioners should take 'responsibility for their continued learning and development' beyond the acquisition of a professional qualification (CCETSW 1995a: 19). I believe that the emphasis on students being able to demonstrate that they have acquired certain knowledge is essential to good practice. For a helpful summary of the main advantages and disadvantages of a competence based approach, see Thompson (1995: 101–4).

Transferability of skills

The transferability of skills involves students and practitioners being 'able to explain in a coherent, comprehensive and convincing manner how their practice is informed by their knowledge base, and being able to apply their knowledge and learning to new situations through appraising what is general and what is particular in each situation' (CCETSW 1995a: 19). However, for skills to be reliable and enduring across different, often difficult, situations they have to be based on a sound theoretical understanding of human beings in their particular social contexts. This includes an understanding of theories in relation to human behaviour: 'The final factor for skill development which is reliable and transferable is an understanding of theories of human behaviour so that skills are related to individual clients and not just routine behaviour' (Parsloe 1988: 8).

For example, if confronted with a situation where a service user is being aggressive or threatening, I would be very cautious before using interventions that are challenging or confrontational unless my purpose was to bring matters to a head. This kind of evaluative process requires that we have a body of knowledge to draw on in order to help us to explore what was happening and why. Establishing a relationship between theory and practice in this way means that both are constantly in dialogue, each informing the other in ways that illuminate different aspects of our work and that 'invigorate, fascinate and professionally uplift' (Howe 1997: 175).

Key questions

Much is asked of social workers, and the use of theory and research can be helpful markers when we find ourselves overwhelmed by the intractable nature of the problems presented. They can help us to address the key question posed throughout this text, namely 'what can I and others say or do to make a difference?' In addressing this question, theory can illuminate our understanding of people and their circumstances in five key areas:

1 Observation: it tells us what we see and what to look out for
2 Description: it provides a conceptual vocabulary and framework within which observations can be arranged and organized
3 Explanation: it suggests how different observations might be linked and connected; it offers possible causal relationships between one event and another
4 Prediction: it indicates what might happen next
5 Intervention: it suggests what might be done to bring about change
(Howe 1997: 171)

It is necessary to draw on theories or to 'borrow' knowledge (Payne 1997: 44) from a range of other disciplines, particularly sociology and psychology, including social psychology (Howe 1997: 172). To this list Hardiker and Barker add organizational theory as a 'foundation knowledge' (1981: 29). However, borrowing from other disciplines in this way has given rise to considerable controversy about what constitutes a useful theory for social work. This controversy has been described by Payne as 'theory wars'. One of the best examples of this can be seen in the way that psychodynamic theory was misrepresented and discounted within social work in the 1970s and 1980s and, to some extent, continues to be attacked today.

Some of this controversy has been played out in relation to whether knowledge is primarily drawn from sociology or psychology, because these two disciplines look across at people and their social situations in different ways. In addition, different schools within these disciplines take up different emphases. The polarized way that psychology and social factors have been represented within social work denies that both are important. It should be clear that our interest in one discipline does not automatically cancel out our interest in the other. However, at different times, it may be necessary to focus on one more than the other. For example, a woman who asks for help in order to enable her to leave a violent relationship will need help and understanding from different sources (Hague and Malos 1998). To have the courage to think through the emotional consequences involved in, say, leaving her home and moving to a new area, perhaps to a women's refuge, will require our focusing on feelings and the meaning given to experiences. At the same time, in order to make it possible for this woman to leave, it may be essential to focus on her housing needs and on ensuring that she knows her legal rights and where to go for help. Or again, where poverty is likely to be an issue, we may focus our work on trying to ensure that she is in receipt of the right benefit and so forth. The list of possible tasks is endless but cannot be fully embraced unless we can bring social and psychological considerations into an intellectual climate where both can be recognized. Some of the tension between individual and social causation can be found in the current debate about the purpose of social work and the role of a social worker (Dominelli 1998; Clark 2000: 49–62).

Practice terminology: the absence of a common language

The tension between theory and practice within social work is not helped by the different way that authors use terms such as theory, hypothesis, method, model, practice approach, perspective, intervention, and skills. Given this confusion, it is important to identify these differences and to define how these terms are used within this book.

Theory

The knowledge base of social work derives from many sources. However, what constitutes a *theory*, particularly in relation to what constitutes a *social theory*, is subject to some debate (Marshall 1994: 532). One way to define a theory would be as: 'A group of related hypotheses, concepts, and constructs, based on facts and observations, that attempts to explain a particular phenomenon' (Barker 1995: 336). Every attempt to try to make sense of the world or particular events constitutes a theory since one characteristic of a theory is that it goes beyond the descriptive to include explanations of why things happen (phenomena). This places theory and theorizing at one end of a spectrum as something accessible; something that we all do, whether intentionally or not. It is sometimes referred to as *informal* theorizing.

At the other end of the spectrum, the validity of *formal* types of theory tend to be based on scientific criteria. Sheldon (1995) leans towards this more formal use of theory in his breakdown of the 'qualities possessed by theories', which should have built in:

- potential refutability ('at greatest risk of potential refutation by stating clearly what ought not to occur')
- riskiness of prediction
- testability
- logical consistency
- clarity of expression
- applicability
- simplicity

- the potential to attempt to address 'important things not yet known'
  or those 'circumstances in which there is no convincing explanation
  available'.

(Sheldon 1995: 10)

The difficulty in relation to formal theories of this kind is that they run the
risk of dismissing explanations that cannot easily be tested by more objective
measures, which means it is possible to miss vital clues or to misread situations. Also, there is now growing agreement that all theories are influenced
to varying degrees by the role, behaviour, values and assumptions of those
involved in theorizing, including researchers (Kuhn 1970). A final way theory
has been categorized is through differentiating between *grand* and *middle-range*
(micro-level) theories, with grand theories attempting to explain more or
less everything in society (e.g. Marxism, psychoanalysis) and middle-range
theories attempting to explain only a limited range of phenomena (e.g.
inequalities, oppression) (Thompson 1995: 23).

Whether social work can lay claim to any distinct theories in its own right,
independent of other disciplines, is debatable and if it can, it is not clear what
a social work theory would consist of in terms of its distinct characteristics
(Payne 1997: 34). My own view is that it is possible for social work to have its
own unique theory base, built on knowledge-in-practice (Schön 1991), which
identifies how certain theories are applied and adapted to specific practice situations, and then to use the findings of practice as a basis for new hypotheses
to be developed and further theory-building. In this process, the term theory
is used within this text to include formal and informal, grand and middle-
range concepts that attempt to *explain* phenomena.

Hypotheses

In between theory and practice lies the activity of formulating and testing
working *hypotheses*. The dictionary definition of a hypothesis is 'a suggested
explanation for a group of facts or phenomena, either accepted as a basis for
further verification (working hypothesis) or accepted as likely to be true. An
unproved theory' (Hanks 1979). Formulating hypotheses in this way marks an
attempt to define, explain and predict certain events with a view to increasing
our understanding in order to arrive at an agreed course of action. One way to
see hypotheses is as a type of 'informal' theory-making, 'based on testable
hypotheses' (Pinker 1990: 24). For example, in a case of non-attendance at
school, we might formulate a variety of hypotheses: that the child is absent
from school because s/he is looking after a parent; s/he may be being bullied;
s/he finds the teacher frightening; s/he finds the culture of school bewildering,
and so forth.

Having formulated these hypotheses, which forms an important part of
Schön's notion of *reflection-in-action*, the task is to 'test' against evidence that
either confirms or refutes each hypothesis (Schön 1991: 146) 'by showing that
the conditions that would follow from each hypothesis are not the observed

ones' (Schön 1991: 143). The importance of seeking verification has to be stressed and is consistent with an evidence based approach to practice. The use of unclarified or unconfirmed data based on intuition or common-sense notions alone is not enough (Coulshed 1991: 24).

Method or practice orientation

Again, confusion surrounds the use of the term *method*. One way that method is used, particularly in the USA, is to identify the four general forms of practice (Haynes and Holmes 1994). These are:

- work with individuals (sometimes involving counselling)
- groupwork (sometimes called social groupwork)
- family work (including family counselling and family therapy)
- community work (sometimes called community organization or community development).

Method is also used to describe specific types of interventions. For example, Pinker uses the term to include task-centred and problem-solving methods and also to describe what I would call *practice approaches*, namely 'crisis intervention and behaviour modification methods of intervention' (Pinker 1990: 24). It describes a 'way of doing things, of working with facts and concepts in a systematic fashion' (Reber 1985: 439). Or again, sometimes method is used interchangeably with the term *intervention*, as a way of formulating an appropriate plan of action.

Disagreement about the definition of social work methods, and how these should be categorized, particularly in relation to case work and community work, formed part of the argument of the Barclay Working Party and the Barclay Report (1982). Since confusion still surrounds its use, within this text I use the term *practice orientation* to describe the four general types of practice (work with individuals, groups, families and communities) and *practice methods* to describe the application of *specific practice interventions* that form part of a particular *practice approach*. For example, I would include *unconditional positive regard* as a specific practice intervention in a client-centred approach; *modelling* as an example in cognitive-behavioural approaches; *impact* as specific practice terminology used in crisis intervention; *circular questioning* as a specific practice intervention in family therapy (systems theory) and *interpretation* and *insight* for psychosocial approaches. Given the lack of consistency that exists among different authors about how they use the term social work methods, in this text I have avoided using this word except in a general sense or when quoting other authors.

Models

Howe, like Hardiker and Barker (1981), differentiates between a *model* and a theory, and does so by identifying a model as a *description* rather than an explanation of phenomena, acting not as a perfect representation but as an initial attempt to order, or simplify, information by illuminating the pattern of relationships or phenomena observed: 'Models, acting as analogies, can be used to order, define, describe phenomena. They do not explain the things seen, but they do begin to impose some low level order on what is otherwise a jumble of information. Models act as bricks in theory building' (Howe 1987: 10). However, the word model is used differently within certain disciplines or by certain authors. For example, the *medical model* is closer to a grand theory. Others use the word model to describe what I would call a practice approach or perspective (Payne 1998: 136), or to describe both a theory and perspective, such as the *social model of disability* (Oliver 1990, 1996). Finally, England uses the word model to include client-centred, task-centred and unitary 'theory', which he differentiates from theories because they do not include explanations.

Given the confusion that surrounds the use of the word, it is not my intention to use model within this text.

Practice approach

The term *practice approach*, sometimes called *theoretical approach*, is used within the text to describe a systematic approach to practice, which draws on a distinct body of theory and, as a result, has its own specific practice terminology and interventions (see the practice methods listed under the heading *method* or *practice orientation*). Although more could be listed, the main practice approaches used within social work include:

- client-centred approaches (this often takes the form of counselling)
- cognitive-behavioural approaches
- task-centred work
- crisis intervention
- psychodynamic or psychosocial approaches
- systemic family therapies.

Task-centred work, although important, is not included as a practice approach because it does not adhere to any distinct theory base. Instead, it describes a 'set of activities' rather than a 'theoretically-based approach from which a set of activities flows' (Marsh 1997: 195). Thus, focusing on *tasks* could form part of other practice approaches (see the Appendix for a brief account of the main social work approaches and concepts).

An eclectic approach

Eclecticism can be seen as a response to the diversity and complex nature of many of the problems social work embodies (Cheetham *et al*. 1992: 51) and has important advantages: 'Eclecticism enables different ideas to be brought to bear, helps to amalgamate social work theories when they make similar proposals for action, deals better with complex circumstances and allows workers to compensate for inadequacies in particular theories' (Payne 1998: 130). Although many practitioners describe themselves as being 'eclectic', not all can identify the particular practice approach or specific practice terminology and interventions they actually use, and why they use them. In fact, eclecticism can tend to confuse rather than clarify what is actually involved in practice because, in reality, few practitioners have the expertise to be able to dip into a range of practice approaches, which means that this 'pick-and-mix' approach may be less flexible or adaptable than is sometimes implied (Thompson 1998: 304). Social work will always involve a degree of eclecticism, and some practitioners may indeed draw on a range of practice approaches and methods in the way this term describes. However, I have not included it as a distinct approach because too often the term eclecticism is used too loosely and not in a way that denotes an approach to practice based on an identifiable knowledge base. Given the lack of vigour that surrounds the use of the word, it is not my intention to refer to eclecticism as a distinct practice approach within this text.

Perspective

The word *perspective* is often used but rarely defined in social work texts. One way to define it would be as a 'view of the world' (Payne 1997: 290), but often a partial view. In this text, I use the term perspective to denote a partial but important way of thinking about, observing and ordering phenomena and how they relate to society as a whole.

In the framework I am describing, perspectives are differentiated from practice approaches because, although they order and make sense of experiences and events from the particular and partial viewpoint, they are not linked to a particular theory and practice method in the way that the five practice approaches identified are linked. For example, while *consciousness raising* may be a term associated with a feminist perspective, other perspectives may also lay claim to raising awareness in similar ways.

Again, others could be added to this list but the main perspectives relevant to social work include:

- an anti-discriminatory perspective
- an anti-oppressive perspective
- an anti-racist perspective
- a feminist perspective
- a user's or a survivor's perspective
- a radical social work perspective.

These perspectives are frequently called upon to do more than deepen our understanding because they influence practice in a more direct way. For example, some are, in fact, political perspectives (Langan and Lee 1989: 176), such as an anti-oppressive perspective, which, for some authors, describes a specific type of practice (anti-oppressive practice), designed to deliver an anti-oppressive service (Dominelli 1998: 8). This terminology denotes Dominelli's desire to incorporate what I would define as a practice approach, practice method and perspective into one 'new practice paradigm', namely anti-oppressive practice (Dominelli 1998: 7). Other perspectives described in social work texts explore how the world looks through the eyes of minority or disadvantaged groups: from a children's perspective, a disabled or older person's perspective or a lesbian/gay perspective. Other perspectives look at the details and facts from a specific viewpoint or angle, such as an ethical, values, agency or economic perspective.

Not enough is known about the ways in which particular perspectives influence practice and how effective this work is in bringing about desired change, but it seems to be the case that most practitioners undertake assessments from one perspective or another and that at times, different perspectives can clash. For example, a user perspective may clash with an agency perspective (Lishman 1994: 87). Also, the partial nature of any perspective can mean that there is the risk that an individual's perception of events is 'blinkered' and prone to generalizations or bias.

Intervention

Intervention in social work 'is analogous to the physician's term *treatment'* (Barker 1995: 195) and is defined as taking 'a decisive or intrusive role in order to modify or determine events or their outcome' (Hanks 1979). It is direct action, or a specific social work input, based on our understanding of the situation or problem presented, and can involve providing direct services or trying to effect change in the social environment, including organizations, in order to change 'the balance of forces in the social environment in the client's favour' (Kadushin 1990: 14). This may involve acting as an advocate or a mediator on behalf of a service user.

Whether, when and how to intervene is a complex issue. It requires that we are clear beforehand that we have a mandate to do so, particularly where the request for our intervention does not come from the person for whom the help is being sought. We also need to be sure that our involvement is justified at that time (Doel 1994: 24). This should be based on how we, the service user and others judge the situation, based on a consideration of the following factors:

1 the urgency of the problem;
2 the consequences of not alleviating the problem;
3 the chances of success in alleviating the problem;
4 the ability of the worker and agency to help with the problem;
5 the motivation of the client to work on the problem;
6 the support which the client will receive from other people; and
7 the specific nature of the problem.

(Doel 1994: 27)

Skills

O'Hagan, citing a different dictionary definition, writes of *skills* as 'practical knowledge in combination with ability . . . cleverness, expertise, . . . knowledge or understanding of something' (O'Hagan 1996: 13). However, what constitutes a social work skill is difficult to define because it is used inter-changeably with other terms, such as intervention, competence, practice and techniques (O'Hagan 1996: 12). This can create confusion, but is understand-able given the fact that they very much belong to the same family. For example, CCETSW describes *competent practice* as practice conducted in a 'skilled manner'(CCETSW 1995a: 3), although it is not clear what constitutes a 'skilled manner'.

In this book, skill denotes the degree of knowledge, expertise, judgement and experience that is brought to play within a given situation, course of action or intervention. This can involve several factors. For example, it can involve arriving at a sound judgement in relation to the choice of practice setting and how best to work within a particular environment: the level of intensity that the work requires and over what period. It can also involve formulating a judgement about the level of skill that the work requires and what the practice emphasis should be, particularly at the beginning, middle or end of a piece of work or course of action. Part of this decision-making process involves being able to use supervision effectively and creatively and also being able to pursue (and argue for) additional consultation, training and support when required. These skills are described in greater detail in the ten practice choices that follow.

Relating theory to practice: ten practice choices

The following breakdown describes ten common choices that arise in direct work with service users. Not all decisions will involve all ten choices but many will include having to explore, in consultation with the service user, options that include the following.

Practice orientation

This involves making a choice in relation to the most appropriate orientation across four options:

- work with individuals
- family work
- groupwork
- community work.

Practice approach

The main approaches include:

- client-centred (this often takes the form of counselling)
- cognitive-behavioural
- crisis intervention
- systemic family therapies

- psychodynamic/psychosocial approaches
- others.

Perspective

The main perspectives that illuminate factors from a particular viewpoint include:

- an anti-discriminatory perspective
- an anti-oppressive perspective
- an anti-racist perspective
- a feminist perspective
- others (described earlier in this chapter).

Skills and interventions

These include the fifty generalist practice and interventional skills described in this text:

- planning and preparing for the interview
- creating a rapport and establishing a relationship
- welcoming skills
- empathy and sympathy
- the role of self-knowledge and intuition
- open questions
- closed questions
- 'what' questions
- circular questions
- paraphrasing
- clarifying
- summarizing
- giving and receiving feedback
- sticking to the point and purpose of the interview
- prompting
- probing
- allowing and using silences
- using self-disclosure
- ending an interview
- closing the case and ending the relationship
- giving advice
- providing information
- providing explanations
- offering encouragement and validation
- providing reassurance
- using persuasion and being directive
- providing practical and material assistance
- providing support

- providing care
- modelling and social skills training
- reframing
- offering interpretations
- adaptation
- counselling skills
- containing anxiety
- empowerment and enabling skills
- negotiating skills
- contracting skills
- networking skills
- working in partnership
- mediation skills
- advocacy skills
- assertiveness skills
- being challenging and confrontative
- dealing with hostility, aggression and violence
- providing protection and control
- managing professional boundaries
- record keeping skills
- reflective and effective practice
- using supervision creatively.

Practice setting

This includes working in different practice settings such as:

- the workplace
- a person's home
- residential setting
- prison or day centre
- community centre
- hospital
- school
- more natural or spontaneous settings or situation that are appropriate for the particular service user.

Level of intensity

Some referrals require a different level of intensity, depending on the problem(s) presented and the circumstances of the individual. These can roughly be divided into three levels:

- *non-intensive*:   this relates to work that is less intensive, where contact with service users is likely to be fortnightly, perhaps because the work is near to completion and the case is coming to a close or because the work cannot proceed at a quicker pace

- *moderate*:   this is where work is ongoing and contact with the service user, family members and other professionals is likely to occur at least once a week. Providing weekly relationship counselling, family work or individual counselling would normally fall within this level of intensity
- *intensive*:   this is where the work is demanding and the problems presented are multi-faceted, severe, enduring and complex. This may involve two or more points of contact with the service user, different family members and/or other professionals during the course of a week.

Duration

Depending on the problem presented and the individuals involved, the time-span for the work can vary. These will vary according to agency policy and can include involvement that is categorized as:

- short-term (up to 12 weeks)
- medium-term (falling between 12 to 26 weeks)
- long-term (stretching beyond 26 weeks).

Level of skill

The level of skill required can range from:

- *basic skills*:   these relate to those foundation skills that are required in most social work interventions such as empathy, establishing a relationship or a rapport.
- *intermediate skills*:   these relate to the skills required to deal with more difficult situations, such as working with service users who are not easy to engage or seem unresponsive.
- *advanced and specialist skills*:   these skills relate to working in situations that require specialist knowledge, such as training in counselling or family therapy, being able work with problems that are multi-faceted and intractable or in situations involving conflict, hostility or high levels of distress.

Practice emphasis

This can vary depending on whether the work is at the beginning, middle or the end phase. For example, our emphasis at the beginning phase may be on relationship-building; in the middle phase the focus may be on consolidating the relationship and strengthening trust; and at the end it may involve forming links with family members or neighbourhood groups to enable the work to end and progress to continue.

Supervision, consultation, training and support structure

This involves attempting to identify what input we need in order to be effective in our work and to develop our skills and expertise.

Case example

The following chart shows how this decision-making process relates in practice using the example of a young person, Sarah, aged 12, who has been referred by the school because she has recently been found to be self-harming, using a razor blade to score her arm. From the limited information that the school has been able to gather, there is a concern that Sarah may have been the victim of sexual abuse.

Implementation – 10 practice choices

Practice	*Range of choices*	*Decision*
Practice orientation	• Work with individuals • Groupwork • Family work • Community work	Individual work (counselling)
Practice approach	• Client-centred • Cognitive-behavioural • Crisis intervention • Family therapy (systemic) • Psychodynamic • Others?	Client-centred
Perspective	• Anti-discriminatory • Anti-racist • Anti-oppressive • Feminist • User's/survivor's • Children's rights • Others?	• Feminist • Anti-oppressive • Children's/young people's rights
Interventions	(a) Generalist practice skills and interventions (drawn from the list of 50 skills) (b) Specific practice interventions (client-centred)	Assessment skills: information gathering; observation skills; listening skills; judicious use of open and closed questions, etc. Building trust: • congruence • unconditional positive regard; • empathy

Practice	Range of choices	Decision
Practice setting	• Social Services • Own home • School • Family centre • Other?	Play room
Duration	• Short-term (up to 12 weeks?) • Medium-term (12–26 weeks?) • Long-term (26–52 weeks?)	Sexual abuse confirmed. Assessment of the nature of the abuse and degree of trauma. Proposed duration for work – 1 year.
Level of intensity	• Non-intensive (fortnightly/monthly) • Moderate (weekly) • Intensive (twice weekly)	Weekly
Level of skill	• Basic skills • Intermediate skills • Advanced and specialist skills	Advanced and specialist skills
Practice emphasis	• Beginning phase • Middle phase • End phase	Initially to build up trust in order to gain a clearer picture about Sarah and why she harms herself.
Supervision, consultation, training and support structure	• Ongoing and regular supervision • Specialist consultancy? (one-off?) • Training • Peer support (formal?/informal?)	Monthly Consultation from women's therapy centre. Attend training course on working with sexually abused children and adults. Attend peer support group.

The practice choices in this example were chosen for the following reasons. First, in terms of practice orientation (sometimes referred to in texts as method) it was clear from my contact with the school and Sarah's year head that the referral had to be dealt with delicately. Sarah was described as a 'shy' and 'reserved' young woman with few friends. The school was concerned that every effort should be made to ensure that she continued to attend. Had Sarah had a close friendship, I would have considered including that friend in the counselling session if Sarah wanted this.

Having chosen a client-centred approach, the specific practice interventions I used involved empathy, congruence and unconditional positive regard as tools to help Sarah to communicate with me. General interventions involved drawing on a range of skills, such as information gathering and listening skills in order to make an assessment. In particular, I was attempting to identify why

Sarah was drawn to harm herself in this way and its likely impact, both then and in the future. Research on the effects of child sexual abuse indicates that it can lead to low self-esteem, depression, difficulties forming or maintaining relationships, self-injury and emotional disorders (Finkelhor 1990; Corby 1993; Trevithick 1993). I was also aware of Finkelhor's writing on the pre-conditions of abuse and anxious to ensure that Sarah was protected from further harm (Finkelhor 1984).

In choosing a feminist perspective, I was attempting to understand whether Sarah's gender might be playing a part in her self-harming behaviour. Research indicates that girls predominate in statistics in relation to self-inflicted injuries (Coleman *et al.* 1995; Hawton *et al.* 1996). In choosing a children's rights perspective, my aim was to ensure that I remained sensitive to power differences and the difficulties that some young people experience in relating to adults. In terms of the specific interventions chosen, initially these focused on building up trust, as well as attempting to identify risk factors. Working with children who have been abused takes time, patience and sensitivity if the work is to be successful in terms of ensuring that the impact of these painful experiences are worked through (Corby 1993; Doyle 1997; Copley and Forryan 1997). For this reason, the setting for the counselling session needs to be carefully prepared and protected from unnecessary interruptions or distractions. In terms of the time period needed for this work, this depends a great deal on the young person involved. Because of the degree of trauma Sarah exhibited, and the fact that she was still harming herself on occasion, it was agreed that we would work together for a year, but that we would review the situation at three-monthly intervals. In order to provide a 'reparative experience', and for me to track Sarah's progress, we agreed that the counselling sessions should be weekly. As the work progressed, I felt it likely that we would have to address more difficult and painful issues, such as the thoughts and feelings that drove Sarah to harm herself. In terms of the termination of the work, careful planning was needed to ensure that the counselling was drawn to a close in ways that ensured that progress made could be maintained and built upon. Finally, in this case my support and supervision for the work came from my line manager and also from consultation sessions from a women's therapy centre.

This example shows how the ten practice choices might be used to structure the work with Sarah. During the course of the assessment it emerged that problems within the family were contributing to Sarah's distress, so the practice orientation changed in order to include family work. This took place alongside my individual work with Sarah. No changes in direction were implemented without full consultation with Sarah and, as much as possible, with her family, the school and other interested parties.

Conclusion

I have described and defined the use of certain terms within social work in order to demystify these concepts so that they feel more accessible and become ideas that can be explored further. Without this exploration, it is not possible to develop a 'practice-theory for social work' (England 1986: 27), and a common language from which to discuss crucial issues in relation to the effectiveness of different interventions used. From this perspective, abstract knowledge is far less important than developing the skills to *use* that knowledge in practice. More than ever we are being called upon to justify the practice decisions we make, and these cannot be based on our own preferences alone but must include a knowledge of approaches shown to produce better results (MacDonald *et al.* 1992; Hanvey and Philpot 1994: 5; Macdonald and Macdonald 1995). The decisions agreed on must also reflect the preferences that service users express because our likelihood of success depends on how well we invite their involvement and participation.

Turning to theory for guidance should not involve becoming lost in concepts that we strain to understand, nor becoming locked in a professional jargon that sets us apart, but it should result in our acquiring a greater understanding about what constitutes effective practice.

An ongoing criticism focuses on the relationship of social work academics to direct practice. In other disciplines, such as medicine and dentistry, there is an expectation that professors and lecturers will continue to see patients and, through keeping abreast of practice issues, to use their clinical experience to inform their teaching, and to influence discussions on policy and practice. However, the way in which social work careers are structured, particularly promotion, often results in social work managers, academics and policy makers, including staff employed at CCETSW, not being involved in work with service users except indirectly, through supervision, dealing with complaints or similar second-hand points of contact with direct work. This separation reinforces the split that exists between theory and practice with no one experiencing the benefits and clarity that can be the result of a 'marriage' between theory and practice, and practice and theory.

It seems fitting to end this chapter with a quote from the late Veronica Coulshed:

> social work theory should never become an end in itself . . . a truly useful theory would provide guidance towards a more effective practice, giving a measure of confidence so that we do not feel totally at the mercy of our working environment; if we build on and record effective strategies and techniques, then we build transmittable knowledge by directing others to what is common and regularly occurring in human experience.
>
> (Coulshed 1991: 8)

2 UNDERSTANDING HUMAN

BEINGS

My purpose in this chapter is to draw a map of the theories that are relevant and useful in social work today. I aim not to sketch a comprehensive review of different psychological theories but to provide a foundation from which to begin to formulate answers to key questions. Why, for example, do people behave in certain ways, sometimes becoming 'stuck' or locked into 'self-destructive scripts' (England 1986: 16)? What enables people to keep going, sometimes in the face of extreme adversity or demoralizing experiences (Howe *et al.* 1999: 30)? How do these experiences differ, if at all, for people who carry additional oppressions because of their gender, race, class, age, disability, sexual preference, culture, religion and/or health (Clark 2000)? Above all, how can we effectively help people to move their lives forward?

Many of the concepts described in this chapter are based on the belief that emotional development is a continuous process, and that the capacity to develop – to grow and to change – is present in human beings throughout our lives (unless there are biological and neurological conditions to impede this process). The theories outlined here also seek to address a complex issue, that is, to identify the factors – environmental and internal to the individual – that influence the possibilities for growth and development. The study of the 'life-long process of change' (Reber 1985: 195) is usually undertaken within the discipline of developmental psychology. However, this term is often taken to refer to child psychology, rather than an investigation of human development throughout the whole of life from the cradle to the grave. Within this discipline, two major fields of investigation have emerged: stage theory and life span developmental psychology.

Stage theory includes: Freud's stages of psychosexual development; Maslow's hierarchy of needs; Erikson's eight stages of man (Erikson's work is also described as belonging to life span developmental psychology); Piaget's stages of cognitive development and Kohlberg's stages of moral development.

These theories assume that each stage must be completed more or less successfully before the next stage can be negotiated. 'Grand' theories of this kind
have serious shortcomings in terms of whether they can provide a 'complete
explanation of developmental processes' (Rutter and Rutter 1993: 3). Nevertheless, they have contributed a great deal simply by conceptualizing the
different processes and influences involved in development.

Life span developmental psychology argues that continuities and discontinuities both exist within the growth process, and that psychological functioning and development change throughout the course of our lives. 'We are
social beings and our psychological functioning is influenced by the interactions and transactions we have within our social environment' (Rutter and
Rutter 1993: 6). It looks at the effects of people's behaviour, past experiences
and the social structure in shaping experiences and how, for example, risk and
protective factors operate in terms of the developmental process and those factors that influence attachment. It also touches on social learning theory: how
people, particularly children, develop through observing and imitating the
behaviour of others. For further reading on life span psychology, see Sugarman
(1986).

The following is a brief summary of some of the main psychological theories
important within social work. It looks at theories in relation to: need, human
motivation and self-actualization (Maslow); the search to reach our 'true'
potential (Rogers); the learning we can gain from observing human behaviour
(Skinner); the relationship between conscious and unconscious thoughts, feelings and actions (Freud); the impact of life stages on human beings (Erikson);
attachment theory (Bowlby); and the struggle of human beings to achieve
independence (Winnicott). It then looks at other important developments
within psychology, particularly the work of feminists in relation to women's
emotional development and oppression, and explores the issue of change. I
finish the chapter by highlighting the limitations of these theories, particularly in relation to minority groups.

Psychology's three 'forces': humanism, behaviourism and psychoanalysis

Psychology is sometimes described as having three 'forces': psychoanalysis,
behaviourism and the 'third force', humanistic psychology. Psychoanalysis is
based on the belief that as human beings we are born with the capacity for
good and evil and that much of our life is determined by the tension and conflict between these two elements. Behaviourism, on the other hand, is based
on a belief that feelings of distress or neurosis come about through faulty conditioning and that what needs to be changed is maladaptive behaviour. It
stresses the importance of observable, testable, measurable, reproducible and
objective behaviours: we are as we behave. As such, unlike psychoanalysis
and humanism, behaviourism is not primarily concerned with the meaning
and understanding that human beings ascribe to their thoughts and feelings.

Finally, humanistic psychology emphasizes a belief in the essential goodness, wholeness and potential of human beings (Feltham and Dryden 1993: 84). This school of psychology, sometimes described as the 'human potential movement', stresses the importance of individuals exercising freedom of choice in relation to their lives.

Psychoanalysis, behaviourism and humanistic psychology have all had an impact on social work, although psychoanalysis has had a particularly marked influence (Yelloly 1980: v). More recently, behaviourist theories, particularly cognitive-behavioural approaches, have become important, although many social workers gravitate towards humanistic approaches, primarily because of their theoretical accessibility, their 'holistic' approach, their adaptability and the sense of hope they engender.

Humanism

Maslow's hierarchy of needs

Maslow is often described as the founder of humanistic psychology. His quest to understand human behaviour and motivation led him away from psycho-analysis, which he found too absorbed with neurosis and disturbed behaviour, and away from behaviourism, which he found too mechanistic, remarking after the birth of his first child that anyone who had seen a baby born could not be behaviourist. Instead, he put forward the concept of a *hierarchy of needs* where the need for *self-actualization*, that is, the need that human beings have to realize their full potential, can only be fulfilled once other needs have been met. Self-actualization describes an inborn tendency for human beings to grow and to maximize innate talents and potentialities.

According to Maslow (1954), the first level includes basic physiological needs for food, shelter, clothing, and so on. Once these needs have been met, the actualization process creates a momentum for the next level of needs to be realized, namely, for security and safety and to feel free from danger. Again, once these have been met, there is an innate motivation to move on to the next stage, and so forth. This is represented as shown in Figure 2.1.

Maslow's concept has serious limitations. Some people address their needs in ways that do not fall within Maslow's conceptual framework. Creative people have been known to sacrifice basic physiological needs for, say, food and rest, in pursuit of their creativity. Similarly, some people who appear to have satis-fied their basic needs somehow fail to move on to address higher needs. For reasons that this theory cannot explain, they somehow become stuck. How-ever, in his conceptualizaton of a hierarchy of needs, Maslow was one of the first people to analyse human needs and to relate the meeting of needs to a notion of human growth and development, motivation and the maximizing of human potential. As such, 'Maslow's model may provide a rough working generalization about most people in most situations, but it is not really adequate as an explanation of human motivation' (Hayes 1994: 435).

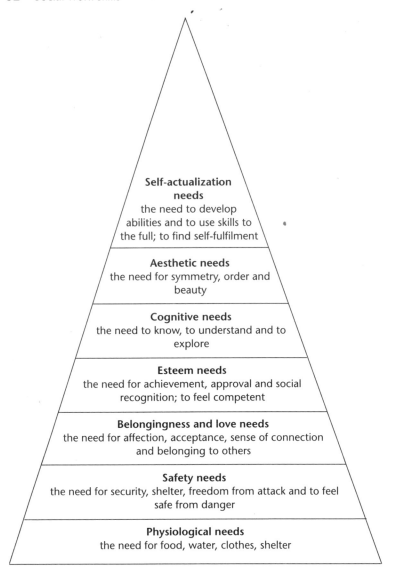

Figure 2.1   Maslow's hierarchy of needs. Fundamental or basic needs must be met or satisfied, at least partially, before other 'higher' needs can be met.

In social work we encounter situations where it appears very difficult for some individuals to move their lives forward beyond the first two levels. The energy spent on trying to survive in the face of adversity necessarily means that emotional resources or energy are not free to be used on other courses of action, such as finding a job, sorting out school problems or meeting other needs. This has important implications for our work because it could mean that providing the right kind of practical or material assistance, or emotional support for service users, could release the momentum and motivation towards self-sufficiency and independence (self-actualization). Without this understanding, we run the risk of providing resources and services into a bottomless pit, where fundamental change does not happen.

Rogers's client-centred approach

Carl Rogers, an American psychologist and founder of client-centred therapy (sometimes called person-centred counselling), shared Maslow's view that human beings have an innate drive or motivation to develop and to maximize their inherited potential. Rogers, described this as an *actualizing tendency*, a term similar to Maslow's terminology. However, unlike Maslow, whose theory is descriptive and speculative and located at the level of ideas, Rogers formulated not only a complex theory of human growth and development, but a practice approach: client-centred therapy (1951). Its aim was to help create the conditions for individuals to overcome the constraints placed on them from the impact and internalization of negative and invalidating experiences and criticisms.

Rogers stressed the need for positive self-regard and noted in detail the impact of adverse conditions on the capacity of individuals to be self direct-ing, to trust their innate abilities and resourcefulness and to be in touch with their own 'locus of evaluation', that is, their ability to trust their thoughts and feelings in relation to decision-making and choosing particular courses of action. For Rogers the actualizing tendency is motivated by the drive for emotional and intellectual growth but this growth is only normally possible in situations where the individual is released or freed from the fear of punish-ment, coercion, inhibiting social pressures and other negative or constraining experiences. Central to Rogers's theory is the belief that individuals know more about themselves and their lives than anyone else and, because of this, are in the best position to deal with personal problems that emerge. The role of the therapist or practitioner is to create the conditions necessary for people to find their way to a new self-concept and self-regard. From this new position, it is hoped that people can develop the capacity to solve their own problems and to function in ways that feel satisfying, so that any opportunities for growth and development that emerge can be explored and maximized.

From this theory of human growth and development, Rogers went on to develop a practice approach to help individuals to overcome these constraints. This involves a therapist or practitioner creating a particular kind of relation-ship using *congruence, unconditional positive regard* and *empathy* in order to understand an individual's subjective experience. The therapist's or prac-titioner's aim is to get alongside the client in ways that show a willingness to enter the world of another human being and to provide an experience and presence that is validating, releasing and restorative. Through this process, individuals are presented with a different way of perceiving and experiencing themselves, so that a new self-concept can emerge and, with this, the capacity to solve their own problems. This is not easy to achieve because it requires a huge level of commitment, skill and discipline on the part of the counsellor. It also requires the individual to recognize and work with the qualities that the counsellor brings to the relationship, so that trust, a particular kind of intimacy and a degree of mutuality can be reached (Thorne 1997: 180). Although not without its critics or shortcomings, Rogers's theory stands out for its profound optimism and belief in the capacity of human beings to embrace difficult experiences, to take hold of their lives and to move forward, and for the important role that others, including social workers, can play within this process (for a more detailed account of Rogers's work, see Thorne 1992).

Behaviourism

The behaviourist school of psychology is based on the theories of Pavlov (1927), Watson (1970), Skinner (1974) and others. It attempts to explain behaviour in terms of observable and measurable responses and starts from the position that behaviours are learned, which means, therefore, that behaviours can be unlearned. Thus, neurosis is considered to be the result of faulty conditioning, which means that when people feel distressed, what needs to be changed is the maladaptive behaviour. This places the focus on the behaviour itself, as opposed to analysing the underlying conflicts or causes. The view is that 'introspection and the unconscious are unscientific hypotheses' (Barker 1995: 34). As a therapy, it is considered to be particularly effective in relation to fears and phobias and also for obsessional states such as compulsive hand-washing.

Most behavioural perspectives share the following characteristics:

- Reliance on empirical findings rather than speculation to inform assessment and intervention
- Identification of personal and environmental resources that can be drawn on to attain desired outcomes
- Description of baseline levels of relevant outcomes and skills
- Clear description of assessment and intervention procedures
- Close relationship between assessment and intervention
- Clear description of desired outcomes
- Concern with evaluation.

(Gambrill 1985: 184)

Behaviourist approaches include four major techniques: systematic desensitization, aversion therapy, operant conditioning and modelling, although therapists may use these interventions differently. Desensitization is often used as an effective means of alleviating fear and anxiety by attempting to weaken the anxiety response to a given stimulus by exposing the individual to a series of similar anxiety-provoking situations until a more relaxed response is reached. Aversion therapy is, in some ways, the opposite of desensitization because it consists of administering unpleasant, painful or punishing stimuli to individuals whose 'unacceptable' behaviour is in some ways felt to be grati-fying, with the intention of altering this reaction and behaviour pattern. The use of this technique on gay men and convicted prisoners has been criticized and, perhaps for ethical reasons, it tends to be less popular than desensitiza-tion. Operant conditioning is a technique where 'the environment has been specifically programmed to support certain behaviours and discourage others' (Sheldon 1995: 62) by altering the consequences that follow. The reinforce-ment may take the form of a reward, such as those found in token-economy schemes. Finally, Bandura (1969) emphasizes the importance of modelling as an effective way to bring about behaviour change. This involves encouraging an individual to acquire behaviour by imitating the actions or behaviour of others. Characteristics which distinguish behaviourist approaches:

According to Gambrill (1985):

> Several characteristics distinguish the behavioural approach from other social work frameworks. A behavioural approach constrains social workers to draw on empirical research in selecting assessment and intervention procedures. For example, if research demonstrates that the observation of behaviour in the natural environment offers valuable information that can complement and correct impressions given by self-reports concerning the interaction between clients and significant others, then this kind of information would be used if feasible and ethical. If the literature shows that one kind of intervention is more effective than another, then within ethical and practice limits, social workers would use this approach regard-less of personal theoretical preferences.
>
> (Gambrill 1985: 185)

It is probably true to say that behaviourism itself has had little impact on social work, although behaviourist theories and practices have had a con-siderable influence, particularly since the 'marriage' that led to the develop-ment of cognitive-behavioural approaches. According to Sheldon, the bringing together of cognitive and behavioural approaches has meant that 'behaviour therapy and applied behavioural psychology have undergone a "cognitive revolution" in the past decade' (1995: xii). As the term implies, cog-nitive-behavioural approaches attempt to link behaviour with how human beings organize and understand their worlds and how these beliefs become known, perceived and understood. Two concepts that link behaviour and thoughts in this way are learned helplessness and locus of control.

Learned helplessness

A particularly valuable concept, based on social learning theory, is learned helplessness (Seligman 1975). This describes the generalized view that help-lessness is a learned state, brought about when individuals are exposed to unpleasant, harmful or corrupting situations where there is no avoidance or escape. Such individuals learn through experience that there is nothing they can do to bring about change or to modify their situation; that is, they become powerless. Seligman's view, and that of cognitive-behaviourists, is that if behaviour can be learned, it can also be unlearned 'in a sympathetic, step-by-step way, by teaching the skills necessary for the reassertion of some control over their unpredictable environments' (Sheldon 1995: 61). Working along-side service users in this way can help to enable them to overcome doubts and fears that they harbour. This concept is particularly useful and adaptable within a social work context because it helps to understand why some people fail to take action or fall victim to events (Cigno 1998: 191).

Locus of control

A different way to conceptualize the degree to which an individual has internalized a sense of helplessness and powerlessness would be to explore the extent to which they believe they can control their destiny and behaviour. This helps to understand where the individual is located in relation to the process of change. The locus of control (Lefcourt 1976) is measured along a scale from a high internal to high external locus. Individuals with a high inter-nal locus of control tend to accept responsibility for their actions and to believe that it is possible to influence or to control ('master') their circum-stances and lives. At the other end of the spectrum, individuals with a high external locus of control believe that control is located elsewhere and that 'things happen to them' – both positive and negative – over which they have little or no control. The usefulness of this concept is that it helps to identify whether, when presented with a new situation or dilemma, individuals will consistently and spontaneously perceive a situation as something over which they can or cannot exercise a degree of control. This has important impli-cations when, as practitioners, we are attempting to assess the degree of responsibility that service users can take on and what role we should play. For a further account of the use of behaviourism within social work, see Hudson and Macdonald (1986) and Cigno (1998) on cognitive-behavioural social work.

Psychoanalysis

Like many writers, Freud described people's tendency for growth and emotional development as innate: as an 'instinctual propelling force' (Freud 1924: 396). Some people have sufficient inner, emotional resources to set in motion this opportunity for growth and development, whereas others do not feel they have enough emotional resources 'inside them', mainly because of depleting experiences in childhood. This means that any movement forward will depend on the quality and nature of help given.

Freud developed his theories from listening to his patients. As a technique, psychoanalysis and some of its theories are not easily applicable to social work. However, Freud's writings on the unconscious (i.e. mental processes of which we are not aware), and concepts such as the superego, ego and id, are important hypothetical constructs that help us to understand human behaviour. Behaviours driven by the id are largely unconscious and describe impulsive behaviours that can lead to all kinds of difficulties, for example, when a young person steals but in explaining their motivation, can only say 'I felt like it'. The ego mediates between the conscious and the unconscious, and it too is partly unconscious. Its primary function is to deal with external reality and to make decisions. Enhancing the capacity of the ego to deal with stress and conflicts is another way to describe our attempts to extend people's capacity to *cope*, which is an important activity within social work. Such strategies are central to ego psychology, popular in the USA (Parad 1958). Finally, the superego is conceptualized as the 'conscience' of the mind, where rules or moral codes are harboured to control behaviours, punishing transgressions by arousing feelings of guilt. Individuals with an over-developed superego can be racked with feelings of guilt, responsibility and blame that are inappropriate to the situation. If the id is concerned with pleasure, and the ego with responsibility and reality, the superego is concerned with idealism, often based on an internalization of parental attitudes.

In order to protect the ego – or the self – from thoughts, feelings or actions that are felt to be too threatening (Jacobs 1988: 78–80), defensive strategies are employed, often unconsciously. For example, events may be forgotten or repressed in order to protect the individual from memories that would produce anxiety or guilt if they became conscious (Reber 1985: 640). Defences can also distort what is remembered, which makes it difficult for the individual or others to gain an accurate picture of experiences and events. On the other hand, defences serve to protect the individual and, as such, it can be counterproductive to confront them head-on or to attempt to break them down. Traditionally, interpretations are used to help individuals to gain insight or to become aware of defensive or unconscious reactions. This is a skill that requires specialist training (McLeod 1993: 27), because if used inappropriately, interpretations can increase defensiveness and inhibit progress.

The importance of the relationship between practitioner and service user lies at the heart of psychoanalytic approaches, not only as a basis for helping people to move forward but as a way of understanding inner conflicts that are unconscious. These are communicated through transference and countertransference reactions, in other words, in the ways we are experienced by service users and what we represent: who we have become for service users or what part we are being expected to play. For example, a mother whose child is refusing to attend school may experience us as being critical (negative transference), where in fact our reaction is deeply sympathetic and uncritical. Or again, we may end an interview feeling despairing, having picked up feelings of abandonment and rejection communicated unconsciously by the service user. Picking up negative or troubling feelings in this way is inevitable; these are the reactions on which 'hunches' or intuition are built. Supervision can help to understand these experiences. However, it is important to stress that being able to work directly with transference and counter-transference reactions, rather than just understanding them as concepts, requires specialist

training. Even with such training, we must always check that we are not bringing our own unresolved feelings into the encounter or into the relationship.
For further writings about the application of psychoanalytic concepts within
social work, see the *Journal of Social Work Practice*.

Erikson's (1965) eight stages of man [sic]

Erik Erikson, a German immigrant to the USA in the 1930s, built on Freud's
theory of psychosexual development (oral, anal, phallic, latency and genital
phases), and the impact of biological and social and cultural influences on
human development. His theory was one of the first to emerge as part of the
discipline of 'life span psychology'. This framework attempts to categorize
human experience from the cradle to the grave and to understand how human
beings operate, find a place and identity and meet the demands placed upon
them within a changing social and cultural context.

Erikson's proposition was that the ego – the self – of the infant is not fixed
at birth, nor during childhood, but that the infant has all the elements necessary for development to take place at different stages. From this basic premise
Erikson saw development being moulded throughout life, as part of a lifelong
response to the demands and challenges placed on individuals. These
demands provoke 'crises', where difficult challenges or problems have to be
confronted and successfully resolved, from which 'vital strength' is gained.
Although it is not essential for each stage to be fully resolved, failure to meet
these challenges can be damaging to development and self-esteem, and can
result in developmental stagnation or a 'stuckness'. This can, however, be
overcome with help.

The eight stages identified by Erikson are not based on clinical or scientific
evidence but they do describe in general the kinds of concerns that human
beings encounter at different points in their lives. They are represented in
Table 2.1.

Erikson's work continues to be influential, particularly in relation to ado-
lescent psychosocial development and the ageing process. For a more detailed
description and critique of Erikson's different stages, see Craib (1989: 84–6);
for the use of Erikson's work in relation to adolescence and the problems of
identity, see Kroger (1996) and for an exploration of how his work has been
adapted within the field of adult development see Levinson (1978, 1996) and
Gould (1999).

Attachment theory

John Bowlby, a British psychiatrist and psychoanalyst, was commissioned after
the Second World War to investigate children orphaned or separated from their
parents as the result of war. In 1951, Bowlby produced a report where his
research concluded that human beings have an innate and fundamental need
to form meaningful attachments with others, particularly in childhood but
throughout life, and that within this process, infants' relationship or 'bond'

Table 2.1   Erikson's eight stages of psychosocial development (eight stages of man)

Approximate age (chronological ages are not always clear)	Stage	Psycho-social crisis	Favourable outcome (potential 'new virtue')
0–1 year	Infancy	Trust v. mistrust	Trust, optimism, hope
1–6 years	Early childhood	Autonomy v. shame and doubt	Sense of control, adequacy, self-confidence
6–8 years	Play age	Initiative v. guilt	Direction and purpose
10–14 years	School age	Industry v. inferiority	Competence in social intellectual and physical skills
14–20 years	Adolescence	Identity v. role confusion	Fidelity; an integrated sense of being a unique individual
20–35 years	Young adulthood	Intimacy v. isolation	Love; ability to form close relationships and to make commitments
35–65 years	Maturity	Generativity v. stagnation	Care and concern for family, society and future generations
65 years +	Old age	Integrity v. despair and disgust	Wisdom; a sense of fulfilment and satisfaction with life and a willingness to face death

with their mothers is of central importance. Bowlby later revised his views on the prominence given to mothers to include other significant adults (Bowlby 1988: 27).

Bowlby's emphasis was on the *affectional bonds* created between the mother and baby, which help to establish a secure base, particularly in the first year of life, where positive and trusted attachment figures foster feelings of confidence and self-worth and act as a source of emotional stability and security (Bowlby 1979: 130). From this secure base, children develop self-confidence, self-reliance, trust and co-operation with others (Bowlby 1979: 117). On the other hand, negative attachment figures who are inaccessible, unreliable, unhelpful or hostile, can result in children feeling anxious, insecure, rootless, mistrustful and lacking in self-confidence. Within this process, Bowlby emphasized the importance of children being able to recognize and to collaborate with attachment figures in ways that feel reciprocal and rewarding (Bowlby 1979: 104), stressing that a healthy personality involves both self-reliance and reliance on others.

He also stressed that the pattern of relationships that are established first will tend to persist throughout life, although therapy can help to bring about change. These models are internalized, to become working models of the self, from which children hold an inner picture of themselves: their self-image, self-esteem and sense of worth. These may be positive or negative, depending on the nature and quality of a child's past and present internal and external experience (Bowlby 1979: 118). They lead to a range of expectations being established and a particular outlook on life and in terms of the future.

Bowlby's work (1980) revealed that infants formed different kinds of attachments, influenced by the behaviour of the parents/carers, as well as the situation and social context. He identified three stages of reaction to separation from an attachment figure. These include:

- *Protest* At this stage, children demonstrate clear signs of being tearful, upset and agitated, sometimes calling for the attachment figure or searching for them.
- *Despair* When the protest fails to bring the attachment figure back, children enter a period of despair, characterized by withdrawn behaviour, tearfulness, refusing to eat, bed-wetting and soiling.
- *Detachment* At this stage children become detached, appearing to have adapted to the situation and to be disinterested in the attachment figure. They have learnt to fend for themselves and may use thumb-sucking, rocking or masturbation in an effort to comfort themselves.

Alongside Bowlby, others studied infant–parent relationships, including James Robertson and Mary Ainsworth, and developed new theories based on their observations and classifications. For example, the research of Ainsworth *et al.* (1978) led to the development of a different attachment classification system: secure attachment; insecure attachment: avoidant; and insecure attachment: resistant. To this, Main (1995) added a fourth category known as insecure: disorganized attachment. (For a more detailed description of these different categories of attachment and their impact on psychosocial development, see Howe 1998: 177–80; Howe *et al.* 1999).

Over the years, the work of Bowlby and others has been important within social work in order to make links between children's emotional development and behaviour and the quality of their relationships with their parent(s), and other attachment figures. As a result, attachment theory has been used extensively, in day care settings, in residential establishments and fostering, and as part of child protection assessments (DoH 1988). It has been particularly useful in mapping continuities and discontinuities in care and the degree to which a lack of permanence or consistency continues to have an impact on children's emotional development and on their capacity to relate to themselves, to others and to their wider environment in ways that are positive and open up new opportunities.

Winnicott's writing on dependence and points of failure

Winnicott was a paediatrician and psychoanalyst, whose work had a significant influence on social work and teaching, as well as medicine, in the 1950s and 1960s. Winnicott wrote extensively but this section will focus on his writings on the journey we must all make from dependence to independence, and finally towards interdependence. It will also focus on a brief account of Winnicott's writings on the points of failure.

The journey towards independence begins with the almost absolute dependence of the new-born baby, whose needs must be responded to and adapted to almost totally in order to enable physical and emotional growth to take place. This leads to the possibility of moving towards a state of relative dependence, where the mother or carer introduces less adaptation in order to ensure that the child can begin to look outward to have their needs met, to look to themselves and their wider social environment. This time of great exploration is marked by infants and toddlers being able to leave the security of their parents/carers and to venture further afield in search of new experiences. If all goes well at this stage, a movement towards independence begins to develop, marked by a desire on the part of the child to find ways to do without actual care and to undertake more things for themselves (Winnicott 1990: 84). This stage should not be confused with premature self-sufficiency, which occurs when individuals are failed and forced into a false independence before they have the emotional resources or maturity to really manage for themselves (Winnicott 1986: 21). This kind of failure can result in the development of a 'false self', designed to protect the individual's 'true self's core' from the impact of further failures, trauma or 'impingement' (Winnicott 1975: 291–2).

In relation to the movement in and out of dependent states, the concept of interdependence is important because it describes the capacity of the individual to give and to receive from others without undue anxiety. From this, individuals are able to engage in a more reciprocal relationship with others and to relate to their wider environment and to society. Indeed, human beings rely on one another for the whole of their lives. For this reason, Winnicott regarded independence more as an illusory ideal than a realizable, or even desirable goal: 'Independence is never absolute. The healthy individual does not become isolated, but becomes related to the environment in such a way that the individual and the environment can be said to be interdependent' (Winnicott 1990: 84). This involves being able to seek help and the company of others without feeling compromised or depleted by the experience. The fact that for some service users this is not a possibility helps in part to explain why they do not take up services that are offered. This journey can be represented diagramatically (Figure 2.2).

Points of failure/failure situations

Neglect in infancy can result in 'delays and distortions' in development. One way to attempt to understand when and where the developmental process has become delayed or stuck could be to look at how past failures are continuing to have an impact. 'Failure situations' or 'points of failure' (Winnicott 1975: 281) describe experiences of being disappointed, 'let-down' or failed by others in crucial ways. These unthinkable memories and failures remain 'frozen' but they are waiting for a safe and reliable situation where they can be 'unfrozen'. The most severe and enduring failures often occur in childhood and the involuntary revival of these memories can catapult service users into a different, often earlier time-zone and 'space'. From this place it can be difficult to distinguish between past and present, primarily because unresolved and painful feelings of the past are experienced in the present, often becoming merged with present-day events. For example, the ending of a significant relationship can revive unresolved feelings of grief from the past about the death of a loved one or the loss of an earlier relationship, no matter how long ago this occurred. Whatever triggers a return to these points of failure, and this may never be fully known, the fact that they have come back into prominence – into our memory or half-awareness – is significant on two accounts:

- these feelings take up emotional energy and reserves in ways that exhaust service users and threaten their capacity to cope; and
- they provide an opportunity to recover from earlier failures and for the developmental process to start up again where this has become stuck.

This perspective sees all behaviour as providing important clues. For example, repeating harmful or self-destructive behaviour can be seen quite simply as a manifestation of distress, which it clearly is. However, it can also be seen as a return to previous traumas or points of failure in a service user's attempt to become free of their constraining impact. The energy that is taken up trying not to feel the pain of these earlier experiences – to forget, to control

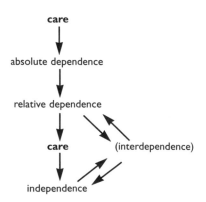

Figure 2.2   Winnicott's stages of dependence.

or to repress difficult feelings or failures – can be freed up and used creatively in other areas of our lives.

Too often, these points of failure are left unhealed or unresolved, which means that the developmental process can become locked or 'frozen' at these points. As a result, certain aspects of an individual's emotional development can become stuck. An example of this uneven development can be seen when an individual communicates a balanced perspective until we touch upon a painful, unresolved issue when suddenly the dialogue takes a different, less rational tone. Sometimes it can feel as if the individual has gone back to a younger age. For those areas where growth has become stuck, it can be difficult for people to work through these painful experiences without help because they may be unaware of them; that is, they are unconscious.

Alongside these aspects of developmental delay or 'stuckness' exist pain-free areas; that is, areas where an individual has not been hurt or where there has been the opportunity to resolve painful issues that they may have experienced. In these areas of resilience and strength there remains the possibility to grow, to change and to embrace the challenges that life brings. Experiences of success and achievement can expand an individual's emotional reserves. These resilient aspects of the personality can help compensate for those areas where a person feels hurt and vulnerable, perhaps by guarding or steering the individual away from the experiences, thoughts and feelings that are likely to trigger difficult emotions. But sometimes this vigilance is not possible, because the ongoing experiences of adversity are too severe and also because it takes energy to continuously protecting those parts of the personality that are vulnerable. Life has its own way of intruding into the best laid plans and deepest defences. Again, the death of a loved one is an example of an experience that is likely to 'throw' most people, but particularly those who already carry a great deal of unresolved grief and loss. (For a more detailed account of the relevance of Winnicott's writings to social work, see Applegate and Bonovitz 1995).

Other developments within psychology

The developments within psychology that are most relevant to social work practice concern those concepts that illuminate, in developmental terms, our understanding of the difficulties that some service users experience in relating to others and to their wider social environment. For some writers, this has led to an exploration of how, as human beings, we develop a sense of self, because it is through this notion of the self (sometimes referred to as individualization) that we come to know and understand ourselves and interact with others (Howe 1996). However, we can neither relate with confidence nor establish a meaningful identity with other individuals, or with our community, if we do not have a coherent sense of self. This 'social self' is developed in relation to others. This has led to an exploration of the importance of 'relatedness', which is a concept where, according to Portnoy

(1999), humanistic and psychoanalytic psychotherapy converge. The socially based nature of personality development is taken up by Howe, who states that 'The poorer the quality of people's relationship history and social environment, the less robust will be their psychological make-up and ability to deal with other people, social situations and emotional demand' (Howe 1998: 175).

These theories help us understand the difficulties that some service users experience in their relationships with other people and especially in their capacity to empathize. This is particularly important in relation to parents' capacity to empathize with their children and can be seen in situations where parents fail to react to their children's tears or pain because they cannot feel what it is like to be that child at that moment. As a result, they do not know what weight to give to pain, or how to react in ways that are comforting and reassuring. For the parent, what is often absent in this situation is any personal experience of being empathized with and comforted as a child. They do not have or cannot recall positive experiences that they can draw on and use in relation to their own children: they cannot give what they did not have themselves. The same can be said for parents who have not received good quality care and attention in childhood. This is sometimes described as parents failing to understand their children's needs but the implications are more far-reaching because an inability to empathize with children can leave children unprotected and unable to relate to others, particularly their peers, in ways that feel satisfying and mutually rewarding. This can lead to isolation and personal and social fragmentation: 'Those who are not embedded in social relationships find it more difficult to realize a coherent sense of self' (Howe 1996: 95). These social relationships are more difficult to establish where people come from 'adverse environments which lack love, mutuality and empathy' that have inhibited the 'formation of secure and confident personalities' (Howe 1998: 175).

Different theories attempt to understand these reactions, in the hope of being able to effect change. The emphasis on relationships and relatedness links to object relations theory, a British school of psychoanalysis, which takes as central the interrelatedness between people (Kohon 1988). This emphasis can be found in the work of Balint, Fairbairn, Guntrip, Klein, Winnicott and others. Similar concepts are described in the USA under different theories such as self theories or self-psychology, and can be seen in the works of Kohut (1971), Mahler et al. (1975) and Kernberg (1976; 1984). Through the work of Kohut, self theories are linked to another American psychoanalytic approach namely, ego-psychology, popularized through the work of Hartmann (1958), Parad (1958) and Kohut (1971; 1977), and the casework approach of Florence Hollis (Hollis 1964). Towards the end of the 1950s, ego-psychology had become very influential in psychoanalysis in the USA but, within social work, this approach is now less influential, except in relation to crisis intervention (Parad and Parad 1990). (For a more detailed summary of different psychoanalytic theories in relation to self and others, see Brearley 1991.)

Feminist writings on psychology, psychoanalysis and feminist therapy

One of the most important developments in relation to psychology, particularly psychoanalysis, can be found in feminist writings on these themes, both in the USA and in the UK. The focus of feminist writings has been twofold: firstly, to challenge male dominated and sexist assumptions about women's lives and emotional development that reinforce inequality; and, secondly, to create a new and different women-centred theory and practice, loosely labelled 'feminist therapy' (Mitchell 1974, 1984; Chodorow 1978; 1989, 1994, 1999; Flax 1981; 1991; 1993; Benjamin 1990, 1995; Seu and Heenan 1998).

The challenge posed by feminists, particularly in the 1970s and 1980s, to psychology, psychoanalysis and the mental health system was formidable. For psychoanalysis it focused on an attack of Freud's concept of penis envy and his revision and dismissal of women's accounts of sexual abuse. In the field of psychology, assumptions held by professionals who effectively saw women as being less well adjusted than men were also challenged (Broverman *et al.* 1970). Similar analyses were made in relation to research, particularly the assumption that girls' experience could be understood in terms of boys' experience. For example, Carol Gilligan identified a clear gender bias prevalent within certain developmental theories. A former student of Kohlberg, Gilligan challenged particularly the work of Kohlberg (1969) and Piaget (1932) because, within their research, girls were not included: 'the child' is male and 'females simply do not exist' (Gilligan 1993: 18). Gilligan goes on to state that Kohlberg's 'six stages that describe the development of moral judgment from childhood to adulthood are based empirically on a study of eighty-four boys whose development Kohlberg followed for over twenty years' (Gilligan 1993: 18). The absence of girls from the study meant that 'Prominent among those who thus appear to be deficient in moral development when measured by Kohlberg's scale are women' (Gilligan 1993: 18).

The attempt to create an alternative field of feminist theory and practice in relation to women has led to many interesting developments. For example, Gilligan's work led her to explore the ways in which women and men approach experiences differently, with men seeking to 'protect separateness' and women to 'sustain connections' (Gilligan 1993: 44–5). She explains that 'the failure to see the different reality of women's lives and to hear the differences in their voices stems in part from the assumption that there is a single mode of social experience and interpretation' (1993: 173).

Gilligan's concepts form part of the theoretical framework for the Stone Center, a feminist initiative based in Boston, Massachusetts (Jordan *et al.* 1991; Jordan 1997). The work of this centre exemplifies the quest among feminists to develop a theory and practice based on women's experiences of oppression and social inequality. This exploration draws on the work of a range of feminist writers, particularly Jean Baker Miller's classic text *Toward a New Psychology of Women* (1976) and also, among others, the work of Kohut (1971, 1977), Klein (1975), Guntrip (1977), Stern (1987) and Winnicott

(1990). The theoretical and practice perspective of the centre stresses the importance of the interconnectedness between people. This has led to a radical reappraisal of the concept of dependency as a necessary and important element in relating. It has also led to a critique of concepts such as mutuality and the central place that empathy plays in terms of establishing a sense of relatedness and connection. These concepts have led to important developments in terms of the relationship between therapist and service user, and have challenged whether the distance between the two works well for women.

Much of the development of 'feminist therapy' within the UK in the 1980s focused on the work of Luise Eichenbaum and Susie Orbach (1982, 1984), which drew on psychoanalysis, particularly object relations theory. It also focused on a broader theoretical and practice framework that could be seen in the development of women's therapy centres, particularly the work of the London Women's Therapy Centre, where feminists were exploring how to make available a range of different therapeutic approaches – gestalt, bio-energetics, psychodrama – and how to ensure they spoke to women's experiences. In addition, a whole range of different responses developed in relation to difficulties previously ignored, such as group and individual therapy for women with eating disorders, or who had been sexually abused or undergone abortions. The experiences of women from minority groups – black, lesbian, working-class – were also explored (Hibbert and van Heeswyk 1988; Ryan and Trevithick 1988; Trevithick 1988). These developments, and the awareness they stimulated in terms of women's oppression and how to address the impact of social inequalities, have been far-reaching, and continue to be so, particularly in relation to social work. (For a further account of feminist writings on these themes, see Howell and Bayes 1981; Ernst and Maguire 1987; Seu and Heenan 1998.)

Further thoughts, reservations and criticisms

So far, I have largely described the strengths of these theories. I have done so purposely because of the tendency within social work to cast aside concepts that are considered to be flawed or inadequate in one way or another: the 'theoretical stripping out' of theory from the social work curriculum (Jones 1996: 204). In doing so, my intention has been to keep alive the opportunity to explore and debate whether these theories illuminate our understanding of human beings and our current, day-to-day experiences as social work practitioners. They may not, but it seems important to arrive at this viewpoint from examining their strengths and limitations personally, rather than relying on other writers to do so on our behalf. The perspective I am taking is that no one theory can speak to all aspects of the human condition or to every situation that we face. Also, theories have to be located in their own history and the cultural influences and limitations prevalent at particular times. We may believe our current awareness to be superior, but who knows? Future generations may not be so kind.

There are other reasons for continuing to explore the value of the different theories described. First, these and other psychological theories form part of the knowledge base of other disciplines. Within a climate that emphasizes the importance of inter-agency collaboration and multi-disciplinary work, we place ourselves in a disadvantaged position if we are not familiar with theories commonly referred to in health and education settings. Second, it seems important for us to engage in a dialogue within social work about whether a 'normative' standard of human behaviour is a helpful way of understanding human beings, given the fact that generalizations of this kind can be dangerous in relation to minority groups. If, for example, we were to develop Lena Robinson's (1995) views about the limitations of psychology with regard to black people, we must be prepared to commit ourselves to developing new theories, or revising those that already exist, so that they describe black people's experiences more accurately. Third, where theories have shortcomings, some can be built on in the light of current knowledge and experience. As a profession, we have much to contribute in this area, and this is particularly true of practitioners. One area worthy of further exploration within psychology, and one to which social work has much to contribute, concerns the impact of oppression on the emotional and material life of service users and what we can do, if anything, to strengthen people living in situations of adversity.

It seems important at this point to highlight the main criticisms and reservations that have been made about some of these theories. One major problem relates to the assumptions made about how the experiences of different groups are represented in terms of 'normal' development. Robinson takes this point forward in relation to the assumptions made about black people:

> A main feature of Eurocentric psychology is the assumption among psychologists that people are alike in all important respects. In order to explain 'universal human phenomena', white psychologists established a normative standard of behaviour against which all other cultural groups were to be measured. What appeared as normal or abnormal was always in comparison to how closely a specific thought or behaviour corresponded to that of white people. Hence, normality is established on a model of the middle-class, Caucasian male of European descent. The more one approximates this model in appearance, values and behaviour, the more 'normal' one is considered to be.
>
> (Robinson 1995: 12)

In the case of women and black people, and in relation to all minority groups, the problem in establishing norms based on the values and assumptions of a dominant group is that they reinforce *their* reality *as reality,* leaving those at odds with this reality to be seen as deviant or deficient. Robinson goes on to describe three models that have been used to describe human development. These include:

- *the inferiority model*, which maintains that black people are 'intellectually, physically and mentally inferior to whites – due to genetic heredity' (Robinson 1995: 13)
- *the deficient (deprivations) model*, which states that black people are deficient in terms of intelligence, cognition and family structure, 'due to lack of proper environmental stimulation, racism, and oppressive conditions' (Robinson 1995: 13)
- *the multi-cultural model*, which differentiates between the difference and deficiency by acknowledging the strengths and limitations that all cultural groups possess. Like Gilligan's work, it emphasizes the importance of minority groups defining themselves.

The conclusion that Robinson draws is that 'social work policies and practices are fundamentally Eurocentric' (1995: 3), based on middle-class values and made up of 'mostly white middle-class people who are very much removed from the black population' (Robinson 1995: 4). This view does not accord with my experience of social workers but I would agree that 'traditional principles and theories in psychology have not had sufficient explanatory power to account for the behaviour of black people in Britain' (Robinson 1995: 5). This criticism could be extended to include other minority groups because none of the theories described in this chapter explore their relevance in relation to differences of class, race, gender, age, disability, sexual orientation, culture and creed. But perhaps this omission can be turned into an opportunity for others to pursue these lines of enquiry.

Conclusion

Understanding human beings is not easy because we are complex and diverse and so too is the social world to which we belong. Yet there is something deeply satisfying about finding some kind of order in the midst of chaos and confusion, when a sense of meaning emerges from situations that seem to deny this possibility or when, sometimes against great odds, there are positive changes. These experiences highlight the importance of the reciprocal nature of our relationship with service users, and how much we learn and gain from being given the opportunity to understand another human being. It leads to a certain kind of personal understanding, sometimes at a deeper level than is normally possible. Without this opportunity to learn, we cannot extend our knowledge and understanding of the human experience, particularly our understanding of the unique experiences that individual service users bring. Nor can we develop the skills needed to address more complex problems and this, in turn, can affect our confidence.

Uncertainty is endemic to social work and it is unlikely that we will ever be able to differentiate with confidence the areas of human behaviour that are knowable and those that are not. It is for these reasons that it is important to commit ourselves to exploring a range of explanations, positions and theoretical underpinnings in order for us to gain a greater understanding 'of the physical, intellectual, psychological, emotional, spiritual, sexual and social development of children and adults, and of their behaviour, in the context of a multi-racial and diverse society' (CCETSW 1995a: 21).

3 THE IMPORTANCE OF COMMUNICATION, LISTENING AND ASSESSMENT SKILLS

I begin this chapter with a brief analysis of the types of problems that social work is asked to deal with on a regular basis and what this means in terms of the 'role and purpose of social work' (Dominelli 1998: 3). I go on to look at the importance of verbal and non-verbal forms of communication, listening, observation and decision-making skills (interviewing skills belong to this 'family' of core skills but are covered separately in Chapter 4). In the final section I analyse the important role assessment plays within social work and how different emphases and approaches influence the assessment process.

Common problems

From the difficulties inherent in living, problems emerge. Some problems experienced by service users occur with worrying regularity. In order to understand the nature of these problems, some writers have attempted to categorize them. For example, Reid's (1978) influential categorization identifies eight 'unsatisfied wants'. These include:

- Interpersonal conflict
- Dissatisfaction in social relations
- Problems with formal organizations
- Difficulties in role performance
- Problems of social transition
- Reactive emotional distress

- Inadequate resources
- Psychological role and behavioural problems not identified elsewhere

(Reid 1978)

Reid's categories remain important because they describe problems that lie behind most referrals to social services (Coulshed and Orme 1998: 118). Watzlawick *et al.* (1974) analyse the nature of these problems differently. Although the words 'problem' and 'difficulty' are often used interchangeably, Watzlawick *et al.* use 'difficulties' to refer to everyday, undesirable or unbidden events that can be resolved through common-sense solutions. 'Difficulties' can also describe dilemmas that have 'no known solution and which – at least for the time being – must simply be lived with' or accommodated in some way (Watzlawick *et al.* 1974: 39). The idiosyncratic and irritating behaviour of some family members is an example of a difficulty that must be endured and tolerated.

'Problems', on the other hand, are situations, thoughts, feelings or experiences that are too troublesome, perplexing, distressing and complex to be dealt with, solve or overcome. Often several difficulties occur together, sometimes resulting in a transition from difficulties to problems. Within this conceptual framework, people with problems seek help (or are offered help) because they cannot keep going, or are unable to move the situation forward, without help. Sometimes, difficulties have become problems, or problems made worse, by the fact that unhelpful solutions have been tried, leaving people feeling demoralized and defeated. Watzlawick *et al.* (1974: 39) identify three unhelpful problem-solving actions likely to produce negative results:

- 'A solution is attempted by denying that a problem is a problem; *action is necessary, but is not taken.*'
- 'Change is attempted regarding a difficulty which for all practical purposes is unchangeable (e.g. the generation gap, or a certain percentage of incurable alcoholics) or nonexistent; *action is taken when it should not be.*'
- Action being taken which does not address the problem at the correct level. For example, this may be manifest by our asking service users to tackle certain problems for which they are ill-prepared – because they are too frightened or lack appropriate skills or confidence. Watzlawick *et al.* describe this as action '*taken at the wrong level.*'

Interestingly, Sheldon takes a similar view in his differentiation between help and support. Before deciding what form our help should take, we need to analyse whether we can be of help at all: some service users 'are beyond therapeutic help as are some medical patients, and so care and support are the best we can offer, whilst others are not, but will become so if we do not intervene' (Sheldon 1995: 125).

Solutions and services

What help is offered will depend on a range of factors, such as where the referral stands in terms of eligibility, statutory or legal obligations, the availability of staff and resources, the priority in relation to other cases and so forth. Cheetham *et al.* identify the diverse tasks and goals as:

> attempting to help vulnerable individuals to improve their quality of life or social functioning; to maintain these at an acceptable level or to arrest deterioration; to influencing systems within and outside social work, sometimes by playing a gatekeeping role; to performing some kind of controlling function, by rationing access to scarce resources, by trying to change deviant behaviour in the interests of 'society' or of deviant individuals themselves, or by using compulsory powers of removal from home.
>
> (Cheetham *et al.* 1992: 13)

In order to understand that diversity, different writers have attempted to analyse the different ways that social work responds to the human dilemmas presented. They include, for example, Dominelli's therapeutic helping, maintenance and emancipatory approaches (1998: 3–4); Payne's reflective-therapeutic views, socialist-collectivist views and individual-reformist views (1997: 4); Davies's maintenance mechanic (1981: 137) and Howe's concepts of care, control and cure (1994: 518). Another way to understand how we respond to problems and difficulties would be to analyse these in terms of the shift that has occurred within social work from:

- doing things *to* service users
- doing things *for* service users
- doing things *with* service users.

A more recent development could be described in terms of doing nothing for service users, or leaving-well-alone. This disguised form of non-help – communicated in the language of 'help yourself', 'heal-thyself', 'get on with it' – is sometimes argued for on the grounds of 'empowering' service users. However, abandoning service users in this way has to be challenged because it can turn difficulties into problems, and lead to further hardship and suffering, particularly in relation to people who are vulnerable (Pringle and Thompson 1999).

Work with service users involves both task and process elements and may include:

> assessment; providing information, advice, and sometimes counselling designed to alter behaviour or attitudes or to increase understanding; arranging service provision or arguing for it with other agencies; providing personal care in residential and day care settings; offering general support to clients and their carers; mobilizing community resources.
>
> (Cheetham *et al.* 1992: 13)

The assumption that our work will have a positive impact can neither be taken for granted nor easily evidenced (Fischer 1973; 19: MacDonald *et al.* 1992; Myers and Thyer 1997), leaving some commentators to advocate practice approaches and interventions likely to produce 'small successes' rather than 'large failures' (Doel 1998: 197).

Communication skills

Good communication skills, particularly listening and interviewing skills, are essential within social work. They require that we can combine being both sensitive and purposeful (Boswell 1997: 352) with being able to acknowledge the uncertainty that is inherent in looking across into another person's world. To understand another person, and their world of meaning, we need to start by acknowledging our ignorance of that person and their social world. We also need to learn to ask good questions, in ways likely to provide information that is both relevant and sufficiently detailed, and to watch for clues. Interestingly, according to one piece of research, 50 per cent of people seeking help do not return for a second interview (Marziali 1988). We know little about why people do not return but the reason(s) may not always be negative. More follow-up studies are needed in this area.

As human beings, we are always communicating something, although this may not be in words. For this reason, communication lies at the heart of social work. The young person who is disruptive in school, the person addicted to alcohol or drugs, the mother too depressed to get out of bed, the person whose strategy for getting what s/he wants is to steal, to lie or to cheat and the old person too fiercely independent to seek help when needed are all communicating something about how they feel about themselves, their lives and the hardships and adversity they have experienced, and may still be experiencing. For this reason, learning to understand what people are communicating, and to put our own thoughts and feelings into words, is a crucial skill within social work.

These skills involve being able to communicate across a wide spectrum, from those located at the 'higher end' of the professional ladder, such as magistrates, doctors, consultants, solicitors or Assistant Directors or Directors, to people who are struggling to survive at a different, often 'lower end' of the social ladder. My guess is that most social workers feel more comfortable talking to service users than people in senior positions. Our own reactions can be a valuable reminder of how intimidated some service users feel in relation to us, but it is important that our own lack of confidence does not disadvantage service users in situations where they need someone to represent or defend them.

Language

There is an ongoing struggle within social work about which words or what language to use to describe certain categories of people or situations. The hope is that by changing the words we use there will be some fundamental shift in the nature of the oppression that certain groups experience. A new word can give us hope, and help us to identify one another, but it cannot guarantee equality or justice. This can only be achieved through our commitment to social justice and by being honest with ourselves, and others, about the real differences that exist and the difficulties inherent in trying to establish more equitable social and professional relationships. An example of the confusion caused through differences in language is demonstrated very clearly in *Getting the Message Across* (Social Services Inspectorate 1991), where one member of the project group circulated a questionnaire to 100 service users listing a range of words frequently used within social work. Others from the project consulted service users with a variety of special needs. The following shows how certain terms were understood by these service users.

Some examples of what users thought the words meant are:

- *voluntary agencies* – people with no experience, volunteers
- *maintain* – mixed up with maintenance – money paid for children in divorce settlements
- *sensitive* – tender and sore
- *encompass* – a way of finding direction
- *agencies* – second-hand clothes shops
- *common* – cheap and nasty (it is not advisable to talk about 'common' values)
- *eligibility* – a good marriage catch
- *allocation process* – being offered re-housing
- *function* – wedding (party), funeral
- *format* – what you wipe your feet on at the front door
- *gender* – most did not know this word
- *criteria* – most did not know this word
- *equitable manner* – most did not know this term
- *networks* – no-one knew this word
- *advocacy* – some users thought this word meant that if they did not agree with the assessment they would have to got to court. They wondered who would pay the bill.

(Social Services Inspectorate 1991: 20)

For these reasons, the Social Services Inspectorate recommends that agencies should develop a local glossary of terms likely to be misunderstood and to involve service users in this task. For example, the term 'common purpose' used within this book – as well as other terms – may need to be clarified in this way.

Non-verbal forms of communication

The importance of non-verbal forms of communication, sometimes described in terms of body language, should never be taken for granted. For example, in the classic study by Birdwhistell (1970), it is estimated that in a typical encounter involving two people, the actual spoken or verbal content is likely to carry only one-third of the social meaning in any given event, whereas the non-verbal forms convey roughly two-thirds of the meaning. In addition, it is estimated that more weight is given to non-verbal forms of communication, particularly when there is a conflict between verbal and non-verbal forms, because the assumed meaning, once picked up, cannot easily be accessed or refuted (Mehrabian 1972). The ambiguity of our non-verbal communication in relation to interviewing is highlighted by Kadushin:

> Five thousand distinctly different hand gestures have been identified and one thousand different steady body postures. A precise observation of nonverbal behaviour is important. It is only a first step, however. The interviewer still has to infer some valid meaning from the data. Accurate observation is a necessary but insufficient requisite for understanding the psychological relevance of the gesture.
>
> (Kadushin 1990: 295)

The analysis of what is being communicated non-verbally is a complex undertaking and one prone to 'common-sense' interpretations that may not be accurate. For example, I once worked in a residential situation where the self-injuring behaviour of a young woman, Anna, was described by a staff member as 'attention-seeking'. Another understood the same behaviour to be an indicator that Anna was feeling 'safe'. One had a negative understanding, the other a positive, but I felt both to be wrong. Anna's own understanding, which had not been sought, was that she had 'had enough', having been let down by her parents and foster-carers. She had every reason to be distressed but this information was not sought and, as a result, her behaviour was not understood. This example illustrates a tendency within social work to attribute the behaviour of service users to personality characteristics rather than outside forces, while they themselves are likely to cite external causes and situational variables as responsible for many of their problems and choices. In all communication, but particularly non-verbal forms, there can be a miscommunication between the message sent and the message received. This is more likely to happen when we are operating from a set of assumptions. We see and hear through our histories and this can have advantages and disadvantages. Our best safeguard is to check our perceptions directly with the person in question but this too may fail if the person is not able – for whatever reason – to reveal his or her true thoughts and feelings.

Lishman (1994: 20) divides non-verbal communication into two broad areas: proxemics (distance and physical closeness) and kinesics (movements, gestures, expressions). For Kadushin (1990: 268–99), non-verbal communication includes the following:

- chronomics (time keeping, such as the likelihood of people being too early or too late; preparedness)
- smell (emotional states communicated through subtle changes in body odour)
- touch (handshaking, hugs. These tend to be defined according to the situation and cultural norms.)
- artificial communication (the language of the physical setting, such as how the home is arranged and personal presentation, such as personal dress, choice of clothes)
- paralinguistics (cues that depend on hearing and how words are said in terms of their tone, pitch, volume, speed, emphasis, intonation, articulation and intensity)
- proxemics (communication through space and distance; the distance people need in order to feel comfortable)
- body language kinesics (visual communication through the face, eyes, hands and arms, feet and legs)

Lishman also includes the importance of 'symbolic communication': 'punctuality, reliability and attention to detail can be symbolic of the worker's care, concern and competence' (1994: 18). For example, I would describe returning telephone calls to service users, foster carers and other professionals as professional 'symbolic communication', which communicates that we are disciplined and rigorous in our professional approach. It communicates that other people, and their communications, are important. How we dress can be significant: 'The way we dress communicates symbolically something of ourselves, and will have symbolic meaning for clients (and colleagues) depending on age, culture, class and context' (Lishman 1994: 18). I recall a social worker being bewildered by a service user who complained when he had arrived to introduce himself wearing dirty jeans and a combat jacket.

Observation

Our understanding of non-verbal forms of communication are usually gathered through our observations. These help us to understand and to formulate hypotheses about what is actually happening and why, and to check out the reliability of our perceptions against those of other people and any information available. Observation skills can be used quite generally or as a specific intervention. Inviting another colleague to sit in on a particular meeting or interview in order to gain a different perspective would be an example of using observation as an intervention. Whether used as a general or specific tool, to understand both the content and process of a particular interaction, observations are 'of particular relevance when the interest lies in the nature of the interaction between individuals or the styles of intervention adopted by social workers' (Cheetham et al. 1992: 44). In addition, our capacity for self-observation, although always somewhat limited, provides us with an opportunity to analyse our own role and impact (Sheldon 1995: 132–3).

If an observer is to be invited to 'sit-in', it is important to explain the purpose of the observation and to seek the permission of the service user before the session, so that they have the chance to refuse without feeling 'put on the spot'. This is important for the person being observed, because it can be quite unnerving to be watched by another human being, particularly when the observation is in silence and undertaken by a professional. As human beings, we all have parts of our personality that we do not want to be seen. Also, being observed can give rise to a range of worries and fantasies about the observer, particularly what the observer is thinking: some people interpret silence as someone being critical. Again, these concerns need to be addressed. Where part of the process involves giving feedback, unless the purpose is to be more confrontational, it can help to be more descriptive than interpretative in the observations offered, thereby allowing the individual to form their own conclusions and inferences. Finally, it is worth remembering that when observing a session in silence, particularly when it involves the disclosure of abuse, the observer can sometimes leave the session feeling distressed if they have been exposed to feelings in an unguarded way. These difficulties need to be explored beforehand and discussed in supervision so that the benefits of direct observation are not lost.

Listening skills

Listening skills are essential in a whole range of different situations – when listening to colleagues, attending meetings, engaging in inter-agency collaboration – in fact, in all situations where communication is a central theme. There are several reasons why, as people and as professionals, we listen to others:

- to acquire information;
- to empathize;
- to discriminate;
- to evaluate;
- to appreciate;
- to derive other benefits (for example, it can be time-consuming to ask a person to repeat what they have said because we failed to listen carefully);

(adapted from Smith 1986: 252–5)

Different authors stress different aspects of the listening process. For Egan, active listening is about the other person being 'present psychologically, socially, and emotionally' (1990: 111). Thus, *active listening* describes a special and demanding alertness on the part of the listener (Lishman 1994: 63), where the aim is to listen closely to the details of what is being conveyed and to ensure that the patient is aware that this is happening. *Credulous listening* is about believing what is being communicated (Feltham and Dryden 1993: 105). This description aptly fits much of social work where, in the face of evidence to the contrary, we might doubt the evidence before we would doubt the individual. While this might be the correct initial approach to follow, we must always be open to reviewing our judgements in the light of new information. *Non-selective listening,* sometimes called non-directive listening or evenly suspended attention, is where listening occurs at several levels: to what people say, how they say it; at what point they say certain things, whether certain themes recur and also to what people do not say. This is sometimes described as 'listening with the third ear'. This form of listening allows us to be sensitive to the wider social and cultural context from which an individual speaks. The following is a list of the twenty basic skills involved in listening:

- being as open, intuitive, empathetic and self-aware as possible
- maintaining good eye contact
- having an open and attentive body orientation and posture
- paying attention to non-verbal forms of communication and their meaning
- allowing for and using silence as a form of communication
- taking up an appropriate physical distance
- picking up and following cues
- being aware of our own distracting mannerisms and behaviour
- avoiding making vague, unclear and ambiguous comments
- being aware of the importance of people finding their own words in their own time
- remembering the importance of the setting and the general physical environment
- minimizing the possibility of interruptions and distractions
- being sensitive to the overall mood of the interview, including what is not being communicated
- listening for the emotional content of the interview and adapting questions as appropriate
- checking out and seeking feedback wherever possible and appropriate
- being aware of the importance of timing, particularly where strong feelings are involved
- remembering the importance of tone, particularly in relation to sensitive or painful issues
- avoiding the dangers of preconceptions, stereotyping or labelling, or making premature judgements or evaluations
- remembering to refer to theories that are illuminating and helpful and also, where appropriate, to explain, in an accessible language, theories that may aid understanding
- being as natural, spontaneous and relaxed as possible.

By adopting a non-selective or non-directive approach when listening to others, the intention is often to try to minimize our own personal bias and stereotypical assumptions. It also helps us to follow the speaker's lead. The importance of creating a safe environment, free from distractions, when listening to others has to be stressed. Listening provides a creative opportunity to demonstrate our commitment and care; it is an essentially respectful undertaking, particularly if done with generosity. When listening in silence, this commitment, warmth and concern must be conveyed through our body language which, if done well, may speak so clearly that the individual never realizes that we have said nothing in words.

Most people think that listening is an easy activity. As a result, for many it is considered an innate skill that comes naturally and, therefore, needs no training. This is not the case. The essence of good listening is learning about how to reach the emotions and thoughts of others – this is not a skill that can easily be taught. The misconception that listening is easy can be based on a confusion between listening and hearing. We may hear what is being said, but this may be a passive activity, whereas listening requires a more active involvement. Kadushin differentiates between the two by describing hearing as a physiological act, the appreciation of sound, whereas listening is seen as a cerebral act, that of understanding (Kadushin 1990: 244). It is estimated that something like 45 per cent or more of our waking lives is spent listening. However, where listening performs part of our professional role this figure is higher. Smith (1986: 261–2) divides poor listeners into three categories:

- *pretend listeners* – are 'not actually listening at all but only pretending to'. They have learnt to respond in appropriate places, thereby giving the impression of listening.
- *limiting listeners* – practice 'a type of partial listening where the listener consciously determines that he will attend only certain portions of the speaker's remarks', often those aspects considered more interesting.
- *self-centred listeners* – 'are concerned only with themselves and pay little or no attention to others'.

(Smith 1986: 261–2)

There are times, particularly when we are tired or preoccupied, when we are all prone to being poor listeners. However, a more serious situation occurs when we become locked in the habit of failing to listen carefully because these patterns are difficult to shift.

Organizing and planning skills

It is estimated that as practitioners we spend approximately one-third of our working week in direct work with service users, although some would put the figure lower. This means that roughly two-thirds of our time is spent dealing with 'indirect' tasks, such as liaising with other agencies, mobilizing resources, attending meetings and training, and so forth. The multiple roles we perform, amid competing pressures, call for sound organization and planning skills if we are to be efficient and effective in our work. Too often, we are not: 'But busy doing what? For to be busy is also often to be too busy to think and at times of confusion this state has advantages' (England 1986: 2).

By establishing good organizational and administrative systems we are in a position to ensure that we make the best use of whatever time and resources we have available to us. This involves devising a personalized administrative system for planning, organizing, monitoring and reviewing our work to ensure that we are keeping to agreed programmes, action plans, targets, aims and objectives and that these are consistent with the expectations of our agency in terms of its policy, practices and administrative structures. The emphasis is on an administrative system that aids practice, but this requires discipline. It also requires that the demands of the agency in terms of form-filling and other administration do not detract from practice. The disruptions caused by constant agency reorganization are a case in point.

For example, it would be helpful for practitioners to be given feedback about data collected. However, I know of situations where the data collected has not been looked at but instead left to gather dust: practitioners know this is the case and feel rightly demoralized and reluctant to engage in further form filling exercises. Some of these tensions could be avoided if agencies, senior management, managers and practitioners could establish clear priorities and expectations, so that feedback can be built in and work planned and organized accordingly (Howe 1997: 172). Otherwise, we run the risk of our work being dictated to by the urgency of the latest 'crisis' or being allowed to drift in an 'anything goes' attitude (Payne 1997: 55). The importance of planning and preparation in relation to interviewing is looked at again in Chapter 4.

Forming decisions and making judgements

Central to the assessment and decision-making process is forming judgements. However, forming judgements is sometimes confused with being judgemental: that is, with being critical or oppressive, or holding prejudicial or stereotypical views:

> Social workers are regularly exhorted to retain an open mind about their judgements. Indeed, judgmentalism has become a dirty word in social practice to such an extent that we sometimes find practitioners tolerating harmful circumstances for some family members in their efforts to avoid appearing judgmental . . . There is a very important distinction, however, between 'making a judgement and 'being judgmental'. Social workers must face the challenge and responsibility of the former in order to be helpful; they must avoid the prejudice, closed-mindedness and blaming implicit in the latter. The avoidance of making a moral judgement remains in itself a moral judgement.
>
> (Milner and O'Byrne 1998: 165)

This concern about being judgemental has, according to Lloyd and Taylor, led to practitioners failing to explore key areas of enquiry and 'to operate in a narrow, blinkered way and at a very superficial level' (1995: 706). In relation to child protection, part of the problem is that 'Our understanding of human nature in general and of child abusers in particular mean that we are always making decisions based on imperfect knowledge' (Munro 1996: 793–4). Nevertheless, the findings of the child abuse enquiries indicated that a 'closer study of these reports shows how resistant social workers are to changing their minds and how powerful an influence this has on the conduct of a case' (Munro 1996: 794). For these reasons, it is important to highlight the importance of being able to form independent, balanced, courageous and sometimes critical judgements, based on critical thinking and the 'best evidence' available to us at that time.

The purpose of assessment

Most service users seek our help in relation to themselves, others, their current living situation or wider social network, for three main reasons:

- to help and support individuals to *maintain* the quality of life they currently have and to avoid a deterioration;
- to help and support individuals to introduce *limited changes* (first-order change, where the system itself remains unchanged);
- to help and support individuals to introduce more *radical change(s)* (second-order change where changes occur to the system itself).

For a fuller account of first- and second-order change, see Watzlawick *et al.* 1974: 10–12. It is sometimes assumed that 'involuntary clients' who come within our remit unwillingly are always resistant to change. This may not be the case. Important breakthroughs can occur with individuals who are involuntary or who demonstrate the greatest resistance, but we are unlikely to be successful in initiating change if we lack optimism and a sense of hope (Trotter 1999: 116).

There has always been an acknowledgement of the essential role of assessment within social work. However, its significance took on a new meaning in the 1980s and 1990s following several public inquiries into the deaths of children known to social services. Other negative media coverage in relation to people discharged from psychiatric hospitals also called into question our role and capacity to make professional judgements. This new emphasis on the importance of assessment, particularly where risk is involved, was incorporated into three major new pieces of legislation that appeared in the 1990s, each stressing different elements within the assessment process. For example, the Children Act 1989 (implemented in 1991) emphasized partnerships with parents; the National Health Service and Community Care Act 1990 stressed the importance of inter-agency collaboration and multi-disciplinary assessment processes, and the Criminal Justice Act 1991 shifted the role of assessment towards a more punishment- and surveillance-oriented approach in relation to offenders. In addition, assessment formed an important feature of the new guidelines for the Diploma in Social Work introduced by the Central Council for Education and Training is Social Work (CCETSW) in *Paper 30* and later publications (1991, 1995b, 1996).

UNIVERSITY OF HERTFORDSHIRE LRC

Yet, while government bodies have been keen to promote general principles in relation to improving assessments, (seen in the consultation draft *Framework for Assessment of Children in Need and their Families* (DoH 1999), written to update the previous assessment guideline commonly known as the Orange Book), it is still true now that there remains 'no single overarching framework' in relation to how assessment should be approached (Milner and O'Byrne 1998: 20). The reluctance to lay down a single format is understandable given the wide range of assessment tasks that social work encompasses and the fact that too rigid a format could result in practitioners missing or ignoring vital information for which there is no heading. On the other hand, having a standard format in certain aspects of the work could help achieve greater uniformity and clearer standards across different local authorities.

The fact that assessments serve different purposes means that they can encompass different social work approaches and perspectives, give weight to certain factors or problems more than others, and propose different solutions (Milner and O'Byrne 1998). One of the clearest general definitions of assessment is provided by Coulshed and Orme:

> Assessment is an ongoing process, in which the client participates, whose purpose is to understand people in relation to their environment; it is a basis for planning what needs to be done to maintain, improve or bring about change in the person, the environment or both.
>
> (Coulshed and Orme 1998: 21)

This definition emphasizes general principles in the collaborative nature of the relationship between practitioners and service users and the importance of incorporating social and environmental factors within the assessment process. Other definitions are based on a particular practice approach. For example, following a cognitive-behavioural approach to assessment, Sheldon focuses on a more here-and-now approach by attempting to identify the factors that influence problems. These include three elements: 'cognitive patterns, emotional accomplishments and behaviour itself' (1995: 158). This practice approach stresses the importance of attitudes and observable behaviour ('in excess, in deficit, inappropriate in relation to time and place') and being able to assess changes based on before and after comparisons of events, behaviours or difficulties (Sheldon 1995: 111–13).

Other assessments analyse problems presented differently. For example, some assessments attempt to assess service users' coping capacities (England 1986: 14; Perlman 1986: 261; Howe 1998: 181) and how these can be strengthened in order to help people through difficult times. The part that protective factors play in helping individuals, including children, to deal with adversity is important (Boushel 1994: 173–90). Other approaches are interested in people's coping capacity but may describe this in different terms. For example, task-centred approaches attempt to assess what service users can achieve in terms of specific tasks designed to meet agreed objectives (Marsh 1997: 196). This may involve attempting to identify what problem-solving activities have already been tried, and to what effect, in order to avoid situations likely to produce negative results (Watzlawick *et al.* 1974: 39). The focus may also be one that acknowledges the particular strengths and motivation that service users bring to the encounter (Miller and Rollnick 1991). Where an approach includes, or incorporates, an anti-discriminatory/anti-oppressive perspective (Doel 1998: 198), more weight is likely to be given within the assessment process to the positive and negative influence of social or environmental factors (Thompson 1997: 244; Dominelli 1998: 5) and the dangers of our adopting 'discriminatory assumptions and oppressive practices' (Thompson 1997: 244). All practice approaches and perspectives, in their different ways, emphasize the importance of practitioners being warm, genuine, respectful and caring in their contact with service users (Cheetham *et al.* 1992: 51).

Some writers describe the assessment task as a one-off event, whereas for others it is an ongoing process. Nevertheless, most acknowledge the importance of monitoring and responding to new developments. Although the emphasis on working in partnership with service users as part of the assessment process is important, it is not always clear how this can be made a positive experience when working with 'involuntary clients' (e.g. offenders) or people who cannot see the benefits of participation.

Practice emphasis

The range of activities involved in assessment includes practitioners and service users being part of a process that involves being able to:

- describe
- explain
- predict
- evaluate
- prescribe

(Coulshed and Orme 1998: 22)

A controversial issue in assessment is the extent to which service users can and should be central to the decision-making process from the outset. A second tension relates to the extent to which we need to understand a particular problem – particularly its cause(s) – for us to work effectively with others to help bring about change. These decisions are even more difficult where problems are complex, multi-dimensional, severe and enduring.

In relation to the past, Sheldon regards with suspicion the 'search for long-lost causes', except in the case of major trauma, for the following reasons:

(a) there is no guarantee that they will ever be found;
(b) because the exercise is costly in time and resources;
(c) when views as to the original causes of problems *can* be elicited they are not always agreed upon by the protagonists, nor are they necessarily valid;

(d) dwelling on the history of problems can sometimes serve to intensify bad feelings and can distract from the necessity of doing something positive in the here and now.

(Sheldon 1995: 112–13)

This last point is important, particularly when the dialogue about the past has been initiated by the practitioner, perhaps because we cannot see how to address the problems presented. Sometimes service users want to explore past events, and it can be unhelpful and over-prescriptive to steer them away from their natural inclination. Also, some approaches use a service user's self-selected 'story-telling' as a particular intervention and approach to assessment. For example, a psychoanalytic/psychosocial approach tends to use this form of narrative, but others have also found it a helpful way to understand how service users see their lives and the difficulties they have encountered. 'People live stories, and in the telling of them reaffirm them, modify them, and create new ones' (Clandinin and Connelly 1994: 415). What is attractive about this intervention is its 'client-centredness' and the fact that people often greatly appreciate the opportunity to describe themselves in this unhurried way. However, it is a time-consuming activity and needs to be well thought out if we are to take full advantage of the opportunity it provides to work closely with service users.

Needs-led versus resource-led assessments

So far, the focus has been on 'needs-led' assessments. Others are 'resource-led', and is used within agencies to establish eligibility for particular services or resources. A tension exists where demand for resources exceeds supply. The question of who gains access to resources and what happens to those who fail to qualify – perhaps because they do not know how to use the 'system' to their advantage, or because they have been designated ineligible – is a crucially important issue (Jordan 1990: 87) and an ongoing concern for practitioners and policy makers committed to creating a more equitable allocation of resources. For our purposes, the degree to which an assessment is needs-led or service-led will affect the range of information sought and the overall focus of the assessment. This can be seen in the different assessment formats identified by Lloyd and Taylor (1995: 700), which include:

- third party assessments (for example, pre-sentencing reports; case conference reports; social history assessment);
- investigative assessments (for example, risk assessments in relation to child protection and mental health);
- eligibility/needs assessments (for example, in relation to community care and children in need);
- suitability assessments (for example, in relation to prospective child-minders, foster carers, adoptive parents);
- multi-disciplinary assessments (for example, in relation to hospital discharge, statementing in education).

Finally, it is worth noting that there are different ways to undertake an assessment. These include:

- *practitioners working alone*, which is the most common format;
- *joint assessment*, which mainly refers to two practitioners working together. This is particularly valuable where the situation is fraught or the problems are complex;
- *group or team assessment*, where everyone who has had contact with the family or group contributes what they have experienced or perceived; and
- *multi-disciplinary assessment*, which involves professionals from different disciplines working together, sharing their knowledge and expertise in ways that effectively meet the different needs of service users. This way of working is central in community care.

Multi-disciplinary and inter-agency work has many advantages but it also has serious disadvantages, particularly where the theory and practice model and value base differ markedly (Bywaters 1986) and differences in status limit the contributions of some professionals. Tensions that emerge in relation to professional roles, boundaries and practice autonomy need to be addressed if a sound collaborative framework is to be established (Lloyd and Taylor 1995: 701). This involves finding a balance between conflicting demands because time spent communicating with other professionals is likely to lead to less time being available for direct contact with service users. A final danger in relation to multi-professional collaboration relates to the assumption that the bigger and more varied the group making decisions, the better the decision making. Compliant decision making or groupthink, sometimes influenced by a dominant individual or representative of a profession, can lead to assumptions not being questioned and, ultimately, the wrong decisions being made (Milner and O'Byrne 1998: 174). This danger has already been noted in relation to child protection case conferences and is likely to emerge in other settings given the government's commitment to inter-professional collaboration (Bywaters 1999).

These tensions become heightened where the system for controlling the intake and allocation of work is inadequate. This can lead to agencies becoming defensive and adopting a range of different strategies 'whereby they keep a low profile in their communities; they draw back from them, dilute the standard of the services, set up queues, use deterrents such as leaving telephones and offices unmanned, give a more privileged service to certain service user groups (such as children) or spend time fighting invisible enemies' (Coulshed 1990: 70). One way to ensure that service users can access services easily would be for organizations to accept responsibility for introducing a system for monitoring referrals and prioritizing cases and access to resources. This can ease the 'irreconcilable demands' made on social workers in relation to the number of cases that can be worked with effectively at any one time (Macdonald 1990a: 541).

In relation to assessment, the expectation that practitioners are able to work from a range of different practice orientations, approaches and perspectives and a sound knowledge base, is important. However, this involves moving away from choosing practice approaches that suit our personal preferences and styles, and instead choosing ways of working that best meet the needs of service users, or the particular problem presented. This requires that we are more rigorous and creative in the way we approach our work and the relationship between theory, practice and research. This subject is likely to remain important and part of the ongoing debate about how we can work more effectively, efficiently and collaboratively in relation to the range of problems for which our help is sought. Research findings that indicate the effectiveness of particular practice approaches and interventions are particularly important for practitioners struggling to find the best and most effective course of action.

Evaluating outcomes

A differentiation needs to be made between:

- evidencing our own practice effectiveness; and
- evaluating the overall success of a piece of work in terms of the final outcome or result.

The reason for this is that it is possible to be successful in terms of the interventions and skills used in a particular situation, and yet to find that the overall final outcome is negative.

Thus, an evaluation 'goes beyond the identification of effectiveness . . . [and] may conclude that an intervention has been successful in terms of the objectives, but argue that these are either trivial, inappropriate or misconceived. To evaluate social work, therefore, involves assessing it within the broader context' (Cheetham *et al.* 1992: 10). Cheetham *et al.* identify two broad outcome categories:

- outcomes of a particular service (service-based outcomes) that is, 'the nature, extent and quality of what is provided';
- outcomes for service users (client-based outcomes) that is, 'the effects of a particular provision on its recipients'.

(Cheetham *et al.* 1992: 63)

As with measures of effectiveness, evaluations have to be related to context and the many variables that influence a particular outcome or result. Some variables are predictable and need to be acknowledged in the objectives and outcome statements agreed. Information that has been systematically gathered and analysed as part of the ongoing system for monitoring developments should help to indicate how well the work is progressing and what decisions need to be taken.

Another differentiation within the evaluative process involves distinguishing between the task and the process. There is a danger that the task and process elements of our work may be placed in competition with one another or made to appear mutually exclusive, rather than being viewed as an integral part of the whole. For example, Howe emphasizes the importance of process: 'it is not the specific technique that is important but the manner in which it is done and the way it is experienced' (Howe 1993: 3). However, external constraints and poor agency policies and procedures can mar our progress, and these factors need to be taken into account, particularly where the work involves an 'outcomes approach', that is, an approach that works backwards from an outcome statement. For example, if an outcome statement, agreed by all parties, is for a child to be rehabilitated with his/her family, it is hopefully incumbent on the agency – social services – to provide the necessary resources to ensure this outcome is possible. Otherwise, as practitioners we can easily be left with tasks or outcomes that are impossible to implement.

There are several ways to evaluate: through our own perceptions and through asking for feedback from service users, colleagues, supervisors, other professionals or individuals involved in a particular piece of work. We can also seek evidence from external events. For example, if we have helped a service user to complete a benefit form, the success of this intervention should be evidenced in the benefit being received. This information can be gathered from a variety of sources: direct observation, feedback from service users and others, information from other agencies, such as hospital or education records, or feedback from colleagues and other professionals. However, this raises the issue of service user confidentiality. It also raises serious questions about the validity of evidence gathered.

Supporters of evidence based practice in social work, many of whom are strongly committed to cognitive-behavioural approaches, argue that the best way to evidence effectiveness is by using random-controlled trials (RCT), which involve large numbers of people being 'randomly allocated to groups only one of which receives the help under scrutiny'. Evaluations 'provide the only sure-footed way of piecing together a picture of what works' (Macdonald and Macdonald 1995: 49). However, the idea of withholding a service from one group of service users raises important ethical issues. Other concerns about this approach focus on whether it is amenable to all aspects of practice and whether the emphasis on outcomes detracts from exploring quality issues in relation to process considerations (Adams 1998: 179).

User feedback

In recent years, there has been a commitment to eliciting feedback on how service users experienced the services provided. However, many authors encourage caution about using service user feedback or evaluations as the only or main indicator of practice success, without considering the context within which the evaluation takes place (Cheetham et al. 1992: 53; MacDonald et al. 1992: 631; Fuller and Petch 1995: 41). Nevertheless, all would also argue the importance of our 'seeking and actively responding to [service users'] perceptions and evaluations' (Lishman 1994: 4) because failure to do so can easily lead to the mistaken view that our beliefs and assumptions are shared by service users, when clearly they are not (MacDonald *et al.* 1992: 624). We cannot hope for positive outcomes if we side-step individuals, whether service users or other significant individuals, who play a key role (such as parents suspected of abuse), no matter how difficult or stressful their inclusion might be (Thoburn *et al.* 1995). Successfully creating partnerships with individuals who are resistant and hostile may be one of the most important objectives we can set, and one that can sometimes have enormous benefits in terms of moving a situation forward. For example, research undertaken by O'Hare (1991) suggests that the difference between voluntary and involuntary service users in terms of willingness to change is not as marked as often assumed. These changes were measured using the stages of change scale drawn up by Prochaska and DiClemente (1984) which identifies six stages of change: precontemplation; contemplation; preparation; action; maintenance and termination (Trotter 1999: 39).

Conclusion

In this chapter I link the effectiveness of different courses of action, tasks, activities, interventions and skills to the outcomes that can be achieved, informed by a sound knowledge base and practice experience. Drawing up action plans, or similar working agreements, can help to keep our work focused. However, for any endeavour to be successful involves developing administrative, organizational and record-keeping systems, as well as the ability to engage, communicate and negotiate with a range of different people, including family members, neighbours, friends and other professionals. In all aspects of our work there is always more to learn, particularly about creating partnerships with parents for whom the idea of collaboration based on a common purpose may have little meaning. We are all confined by what is possible and achievable within the resources of finance, staff and time available, but these limitations are made more restrictive when we fail to explore fully the opportunities and possibilities that exist. More than ever, the part we play in helping to bring about lasting positive change is located within a collaborative framework. This has clear advantages but it can also be difficult to implement. The challenge lies in our being able to form a partnership with service users and others, so that together we can successfully address the dilemmas for which our help is sought.

4 BASIC INTERVIEWING SKILLS

In this chapter I translate into practice some of the key points made earlier in the text. I describe 20 skills and show how our theoretical knowledge can be put into words to aid our communication with others. This includes being able to communicate our understanding, and the meaning given to experiences, and being able to respond in ways that foster greater understanding and the opportunity for people to move their lives forward. For CCETSW, these attributes and qualities are implied in all 26 competences but are particularly central to those that require social workers to be able to: communicate and engage; promote and enable; assess and plan; intervene and provide services (CCETSW 1995a). Moreover, our communication and interviewing skills extend beyond our direct contact with service users and include being able to communicate with other professionals, family members, neighbours and the general public. Within social work, interviewing plays a vitally important role: 'Although social work involves a great deal more than interviewing, social workers spend more time in interviewing than in any other single activity. It is the most important, most frequently employed, social work skill' (Kadushin 1990: 3).

One way to see an interview is as a 'conversation with a purpose'; that is, it is designed to meet a 'specific and usually predetermined purpose' (Barker 1995: 195). For this reason good planning and preparation are the hallmarks of a successful interview: 'failing to plan is planning to fail'. The purpose of many interviews is laid down by the type of task they are designed to address. For example, the primary purpose of some interviews may be to give or gain information or to ascertain whether the particular help being sought falls within the remit of social services. This may be the primary task of the initial (screening) interview or assessment. In recent years there have been important developments in relation to information gathering and giving described under the heading 'information technology', which could have 'radical implications, opportunities and risks for social work' (Shaw 1996: 5). For further information on this theme, see Shaw (1996).

This information gathering and giving is central to the assessment and decision-making process and can be roughly divided into more formal interviews, such as child protection 'investigations', mental health or community care assessments, and those less formal interviews more common to everyday problems presented (Doel 1994: 26). Skills have to be developed in both areas because the two can overlap and the balance shift between one and another. Also, the demands made on practitioners can change because interviewing is sensitive to and influenced by developments within social work. For example, in relation to children and families, since the 1990s, there has been a shift away from an emphasis on investigation and surveillance, prevalent from the mid-1970s, towards attempting to include and involve parents and children in the problem-solving and change process (Waterhouse and McGhee 1998: 273). This links the interviewing skills to concepts of 'partnership' and 'empowerment' because the interview may be the medium through which important connections and relationships are developed.

One way to see the task of gathering information is as a sort of detective – a Sherlock Holmes or Miss Marple – where our purpose is to find out as much as possible in ways that open up the possibility for an honest and respectful dialogue and 'partnership' to be created. This process can touch on the lives of a wide cross-section of people – service users, their families, friends and neighbours (Lishman 1994: 71) – yet it is sometimes worrying to see how narrowly we cast our net when exploring the problems placed before us. For example, absent fathers tend to be ignored (Munro 1998: 93), and so too are other family members deemed to be hostile to social work or to the particular service user in question. We can learn a great deal from people who have an axe to grind, although it is important to be careful about how, if at all, this information can be used. Although it is quite natural to want to avoid people who may prove 'difficult', this selecting out of key individuals can seriously limit our understanding and the options available. It is a shortcoming that should reveal itself in supervision.

For example, I once worked with a 6-year-old girl, Alice, who was allocated to me at the point where she needed to be found a new placement while the adoption process was in motion. Alice had been made the subject of a care order due to her father's cruelty. Tragically, this had resulted in her being brain-damaged but, because of her trauma, it was not clear to what extent. Almost by accident I found an old reference to her paternal grandparents in her case file, dating back several years. We had no address but the case notes stated that Alice's grandfather worked for the local gas board. With this information, through a range of informal networks, I was eventually able to track down the grandparents whereabouts. They had lost contact with their son because of his threatening behaviour towards them and, as a result, had also lost contact with Alice (in fact, their son was by then in prison). They did not know of her abuse or that she was now in care but they were pleased to hear of Alice and delighted at the prospect of seeing her again. To cut a very long story short, Alice's grandparents eventually adopted her. She now attends a special school and, as can sometimes happen, she appears to be less permanently disabled than originally thought (Sinason 1988). Her grandparents love her enormously and I believe that for the first time in her life she knows what it means to live in a peaceful, secure and permanent environment. Not all children are so fortunate and it may be quite rare for us to bring about this kind of change because too much is working against us. Nevertheless, most social workers can describe situations where they felt truly helpful and, amid the doom and gloom of everyday practice, it is important to remember that positive outcomes are sometimes possible, but may call for us to be imaginative and determined and to cast our nets wide.

Transferability of skills

One of my main purposes in this and the following chapters is to give a name to the range of skills used within social work. It is difficult to transfer skills if they do not have a name. However, once a skill has been named, it can prove difficult to describe its key features because words alone cannot convey all that is being communicated. For example, good communication skills also involve our use of tone, timing, body language and choosing words that can convey our care and concern, knowledge and experience. Clearly, it is not possible to include these elements in the examples provided and, because of this, there are times when some case examples described in this chapter come across as clumsy or simplistic. This is due, in part, to my desire to avoid adopting more specialist terms common within social work, instead using more direct and accessible language, drawn from my own experience as a practitioner and from encounters that actually occurred. In a book of this kind it seems fitting to give examples whenever possible in order to bring to life the skills being described. This makes it possible to analyse the quality of our communication and whether we have been able to 'get through'.

Our poor ability to explain the reasons for our involvement or why we have chosen a particular course of action has been criticized in public inquiries (DHSS 1982; Hill 1990; Gough 1993) and continues to be a source of concern (Munro 1996, 1998). Without this clarity of purpose – the language to describe what we are doing and why – and the skills to help service users to be clear about their needs, we cannot properly evaluate or research the appropriateness of specific interventions in terms of what is being communicated, both verbally and non-verbally. Nor can we evaluate how effective we and others have been in our efforts to bringing about desired and agreed outcomes.

We know a skill has been acquired when it is enduring, when it is reliable even under difficult, if not impossible, circumstances. I am reminded of this fact regularly when I ask students to role-play an interview. Some students respond by claiming that they can normally conduct a good interview but not when they are being observed by me or other students. My reply is to remind students gently that, firstly, we have no evidence of competence if we cannot allow our work to be observed and, secondly, being put off-stride in this way can be an indicator that our skills are not yet fully acquired because they are not reliable, resilient and enduring under pressure. Although the development and perfection of skills is a lifelong learning process, once we have acquired certain skills, they are available to be transferred across different service user groups and adapted to fit different settings and circumstances. To do this well involves linking theory to practice, particularly our understanding of human behaviour and the uniqueness of every human being and experience (Parsloe 1988: 8). It also involves using the findings of research to influence practice. For example, the importance of our being reliable and consistent in our contact with service users cannot be stressed enough. Punctuality is particularly important (Lishman 1994: 18–19). So too is the importance of returning phone calls at the first opportunity. These skills may seem trivial but they communicate a great deal. Failing to attend to these details can severely limit our ability to establish a good 'working alliance'.

The skills covered in this chapter include:

- engaging with the task and purpose of the interview
  - planning and preparing for the interview
  - creating a rapport and establishing a relationship
  - welcoming skills
  - empathy and sympathy
  - the role of self-knowledge and intuition
- questioning
  - open questions
  - closed questions
  - 'what' questions
  - circular questions
- confirming what has been said and heard
  - paraphrasing
  - clarifying
  - summarizing
  - giving and receiving feedback
- sticking to the point and probing deeper
  - sticking to the point and purpose of the interview
  - prompting
  - probing
  - allowing and using silences
  - using self-disclosure
- endings: disengaging and termination skills
  - ending an interview
  - closing the case and ending the relationship.

Engaging with the task and purpose of the interview

Engaging skills have, as their starting point, the importance of taking seriously the weight given to problems by service users, but doing so within a context where there is a critical awareness of information that appears to be inconsistent or incomplete or to have been omitted. This process also entails social workers being explicit about what we are doing and why (Munro 1998: 89). Our willingness as practitioners to engage with the difficulties people are experiencing can be one way that we communicate the values we hold, such as a belief and confidence in people's ability to change their lives, the importance of self-determination and people's right to be given help in times of hardship. Our success in this communication can be seen when individuals leave the interview with an increased sense of self-confidence, self-respect and energy because they feel that they have been heard, and that the meaning they give to their experiences has been understood. People who feel positive about themselves and their capacity to influence others, including their ability to influence us, are more likely to be successful in changing their lives. However, it is important not to overemphasize the degree of influence that we and service users can exercise (Dominelli 1998: 9). Limitations are particularly difficult to overcome in relation to structural inequalities, such as the hardships and oppression encountered among people who are poor (O'Sullivan 1999: 16). For O'Hagan, this means that 'in social work, the task of communicating and engaging is often more complex and hazardous than it is in everyday life' (1996: 4–5).

Planning and preparing for the interview

Before beginning an interview it is important to think carefully about its purpose and what we hope to achieve in the time allotted. Good planning and preparation are most important, and the interview should be considered within its widest context, which involves taking into account the particular needs and/or expectations of:

- the individual or group of people seeking our help
- other people involved with this individual or group of people (e.g. neighbours and other family members)
- ourselves as practitioners, in terms of our personal and professional expectations
- agency policy, procedures, practice, resources and requirements of us, as employees or representatives of the agency
- other professionals connected to this individual or group of individuals.

There are essentially two ways of preparing ourselves for this task. Both cover many of the same issues but in different ways. One could be called a *reflective* approach, where information is gathered up in a less systematic but more empathic and intuitive way. This is my preferred approach, and involves using our empathic skills to 'enter imaginatively into the inner life of someone else' (Kadushin 1990: 51) through the thoughts and feelings, fears, expectations and fantasies of the person attending the interview, and the reality of their situation in terms of their home life, financial situation, journey to the locality office, and so on. If, for example, we imagine that the service user might feel nervous, what evidence would we look for to confirm or deny this hypothesis: at what point will we combine 'intuition and analysis' (O'Sullivan 1999: 89). If confirmed, what can we put in place to help this individual to feel at ease?

Another way of preparing for an interview involves using a *checklist*, made up of a list of the tasks or issues that need to be considered (see Appendix 6 for a description of an interview preparation checklist). Both a reflective and checklist approach require that we familiarize ourselves with the case notes and update our knowledge in terms of recent events, particularly in relation to others involved in the case. It is important to note that in relation to the 45 public inquiries into child abuse cases between 1973 and 1994, it has been concluded that the family's past history was a major area of omission: 'eight reports noted that social workers failed to read their own files and so overlooked important facts such as previous child abuse' (Munro 1998: 91). Finally, it is essential for us to make a note of our own thoughts and feelings, particularly whether we are harbouring negative stereotypical attitudes or beliefs about the individual in question. For any interview or interaction to be successful, service users and others involved in the work need to feel that, as professionals and as people, we are competent and caring human beings, capable of understanding their concerns and worries, both from a general and specific standpoint. Here it is worth remembering that some service users approach their contact with professionals harbouring a range of fears that include worries that they may be blamed, criticized or turned away. For these reasons, it is important to be aware of these concerns and how they can be addressed (Lishman 1994: 17).

These considerations help to give the interview some structure and establish a clear role in terms of the boundaries of the task, time and territory but, once having scanned these factors, it is then important to concentrate on being as open, relaxed and natural as possible in order to ensure that a rapport can be created and a relationship established with the person seeking our help. Every individual is unique and every interaction different and these facts must be conveyed in our planning and preparation. Otherwise the interview runs the risk of being perceived as a cold, uncaring, impersonal experience, which hinders the possibility or quality of future contact. Being able to respond with flexibility and adaptability to an individual's needs is also a sign of a successful interview, although agency policies and constraints may limit the options available to us, particularly in relation to the availability of services.

The difference between service user's expectations and what is possible in terms of agency policy and resources is an ongoing tension within social work and the interview is often the setting where these tensions are aired. Careful planning and preparation can be one way to open up new possibilities. For example, Braye and Preston-Shoot make the point that social workers could make greater use of legislation and policy guidance to ensure that service users' needs are met and their voices heard in the unsympathetic climate of 'top-down hierarchical bureaucracy' (1995: 109). A similar point is made in relation to the list of services available under the Children Act 1989 designed to support families: 'Surveys (Aldgate *et al.* 1994) have shown considerable discrepancy in the way in which these provisions have been implemented. Some authorities have adopted a minimalist approach, whilst others provide a much wider range of services' (Thoburn 1997: 292). These points stress that interview planning and preparation involve more than focusing on ourselves, but need to be extended to include drawing on information from a wide range of sources, particularly using our knowledge of the law and government guidance to push for more and better services.

Interviews in different settings

From time to time our work involves undertaking interviews in other settings, sometimes called 'secondary settings' (Lishman 1994: 141), which can include:

1 social services/probation office interviews
2 the home (including foster homes/adoption placements)
3 residential settings
4 prisons
5 schools
6 hospitals (psychiatric and general hospitals)
7 day centres
8 community centres
9 informal, transitory or detached settings (e.g. conversations in cafés, car journeys)

Every setting has its own characteristics and idiosyncrasies. A useful description of some of the above can be found in Davies (1997). These accounts include community care settings, the hospital, probation settings, the psychiatric unit, foster care and adoption settings, the community child care team, and divorce court welfare settings. Kadushin gives an interesting account of interviews that take place in the home, where service users can defend themselves through the intelligent use of 'arranged distractions':

> The interviewee can exercise a measure of self-protection by 'arranged distractions' such as a radio or TV going at full volume, a warm welcome to neighbours who drop in, or vigorous rattling of pots and dishes which are washed during the interview. Since it is the interviewee's home, she has to take the initiative in turning down the radio or TV, although the interviewer can request this. Of course the interviewer can, somewhat more subtly, gradually lower his voice until the interviewee is prompted to turn down the radio in order to hear.
>
> (Kadushin 1990: 109)

Another interesting account of more informal interview settings is provided by Davies (1981: 176–9) in his account of 'detached work'. These interviews often happen spontaneously and can take place in a range of different situations: while driving in a car, going for a walk, playing sport, washing up, fixing a bike, playing a computer game. All can provide opportunities for people to explore their thoughts and feelings in ways that do not feel too focused or overexposing. However, it is important that honest and clear professional boundaries are maintained because in more natural settings it can be easy for people to be taken off-guard to the point where they find themselves revealing more than they wish.

Creating a rapport and establishing a relationship

For any interview to be successful a rapport must be established. In relation to the social work interview, rapport is described as 'the state of harmony, compatibility and empathy that permits mutual understanding and a working relationship between the client and the social worker' (Barker 1995: 320). Sometimes the word rapport is used instead of the word relationship, or they are both used interchangeably, but they describe different experiences. To establish a relationship implies a type of contact that is ongoing, or a connection that continues over time. The best known example of a relationship is friendship. We may not see our friends often, but that may not diminish the quality of the contact and how much we care for one another. A professional relationship is different and is sometimes described as a 'working alliance' between two or more people.

To establish a rapport implies a more spontaneous interaction, based on mutual understanding. Taken from the French, it implies that a 'close or sympathetic' (Haynes and Holmes 1994: 275) connection has been made, and may best be used to describe the quality of a particular interaction at a particular point in time. As such, it is possible to establish a good rapport quite quickly with a complete stranger, as if by chance. 'Hitting it off' or 'clicking' with someone in this way, which is often intuitive, can be the basis from which a relationship can begin. On the other hand, it is possible to have a good working relationship yet fail to establish a rapport or to 'hit it off' during a particular interview or encounter. For these reasons it is important that the word rapport is used rigorously to denote a genuine and meaningful point of contact and not allowed to slip into an idealized description.

Establishing a rapport involves creating a climate where the interviewee can begin to gain confidence in our personal and professional integrity. This is important because it creates the favourable conditions necessary for people to be able to discuss and reveal problems or difficulties, successes or failures, and strengths or weaknesses in ways that aid understanding and allow for a realistic plan of action to be created. However, for a rapport to be created requires that both parties are active and willing participants in this process. This may not be achievable, particularly when working with people who are mistrustful or reluctant or who have been coerced into making contact or attending certain events. For this reason, Feltham and Dryden state that 'there are limits to the therapeutic effectiveness of spontaneous and genuine rapport' (1993: 192).

The relationship

The relationship we build with service users is central to the social work task, and often forms part of what is being described in the term *social work process*. The following description captures the importance of the relationship we strive to create:

> While it is true that people do not come to us looking for a relationship, and while it is no substitute for practical support, nevertheless we are one of the few groups who recognize the value of relating to others in a way which recognizes their experience as fundamental to understanding and action.
>
> (Coulshed 1991: 2)

However, in my experience a confusion can exist about why relationships are important, and their purpose. Sometimes establishing a relationship is cited as the sole focus of the work or an end in itself. This can lead us nowhere in terms of the changes being sought. However, there are situations where relationship building is identified as central to the task of establishing a 'corrective relationship' or experience, designed to compensate for previous unsatisfactory or painful relationships and failures (Payne 1991: 85). But even then the ultimate aim of this work should be to restore lost confidence in order for the individual to be able to explore relationships with others, particularly their peers.

The relationship is 'the communication bridge between people' (Kadushin 1990: 36). It is the boat in which we travel together towards agreed and desired destinations; a vital part of the repertoire of skills we require in order to be effective and to arrive at some agreed outcome. The quality of the interaction, the trust and understanding that are held within the relationship, act as a vital thread that opens up the possibility for defences to be lowered, for the truth to be faced, for doubts and fears to be worked through and change to be integrated and embraced in ways that are not possible without this connection to another trustworthy and reliable human being.

In terms of the importance of relationships within social work, we still know little about their specific characteristics and benefits. This is partly because every relationship is unique and made up of intangible factors that are difficult to identify (Cheetham *et al.* 1992: 12). Yet establishing sound working relationships is essential to many activities that we value, such as building partnerships, creating alliances, adopting approaches and interventions where mutuality, reciprocity and power sharing enhance the possibility of empowerment, self-determination and independence. Feminists working and writing from the Stone (Women's) Center in Boston, USA, see building relationships as central to the empowerment and growth process (Surrey 1991: 167). Drawing on the work of Miller (1976), five positive outcomes of a good relationship are identified:

- a greater sense of zest and vitality
- a sense of empowerment and ability to act
- an enlarged picture of oneself and others

- a heightened sense of self-worth (i.e. greater confidence and competence)
- a growing desire for more rather than less connection and contact with others.

(Jordan 1991: 95)

This description serves as a reminder of the immediate sense of well-being and heightened feelings of self-worth that a good relationship can foster. For example, I recall working with a woman, Sally, with a long history of depression. For much of her life, she had lived with her ageing mother on a council estate, with very little contact with family or friends. This was partly because her mother still carried a profound sense of shame about Sally being illegitimate. From this lonely childhood, Sally had little opportunity to learn important social skills. As a result, she developed a strange mode of communication, which led to further social exclusion. It became clear that a major focus of our work involved helping Sally to establish relationships with others. Her relationship with her mother provided a sound foundation from which to build a relationship with people involved in the project, including other women suffering from depression. In order to track Sally's progress, we paid close attention to changes in her outlook, both in relation to herself and in terms of how she saw the possibilities and opportunities available to her within her social sphere. These changes formed part of our discussions with Sally. This involved using Jordan's (1991) account of the 'relational model', which stresses the importance of using the professional relationships we created as a way to help Sally 'achieve and maintain a sense of contact and connection' (Jordan 1991: 283–9) with others. It involved 'normalizing' reactions, thoughts and feelings, which Sally tended to exaggerate because of her lack of experience of social settings and being with other people.

The skills involved in creating a rapport and successful relationships overlap. In relation to those central to forming a relationship, these include (Kadushin 1990: 39–57):

- demonstrating a concern for the issue of service user self-determination
- showing an interest, conveying warmth, generating an atmosphere of trust
- demonstrating a respect for the service user's individuality
- conveying an acceptance of the individual
- demonstrating an empathic understanding
- conveying a sense of genuineness and authenticity
- showing the professional ability to decide which information needs to be kept confidential and which does not

Welcoming skills

One way to establish a rapport is to ensure that the welcome people receive is warm and respectful. This helps to allay some of the fears and uncertainties that may exist. For service users, these anxieties may be due to the difficulties inherent in asking for help or because they have never asked for help before.

Or it may be their first experience of social services, the probation service or a voluntary agency. As a result, service users may have little idea of what to expect or what help can be offered and this can be worrying. Others may be wary because they have had contact with social services, the probation service or similar agencies in the past and these experiences have left them feeling negative about the prospect of future contact. Whatever the concerns, to provide a warm welcome on all occasions can be one way to ensure that a good rapport and 'working alliance' can be established.

Shaking hands

Although shaking hands is becoming less popular, in some circles it is still used as a formal gesture. Moreover, in professional settings the encounter or meeting may begin with people shaking hands as they are introduced. This makes it genuinely important that we know how to shake hands in a way that conveys that we are not reluctant to make contact in this way. Some people place great store on how people shake hands.

In relation to service users, the picture is more complex and subject to wide variations according to individual preference and cultural influences. For example, women tend to shake hands less than men and children almost never offer their hand unless they do so for fun. Generally, men tend to be more at ease and practised in this type of physical contact but even among men there are wide variations according to class, race and age.

Deciding whether or not to shake hands can be a test of our intuitive skills because we are often asked to gauge what is needed on little evidence. Clearly, no one should ever be coerced into shaking hands. However, if a service user comes across as relatively relaxed and able to manage this more formal contact, my preference is to shake hands because it marks a clear beginning and end to the encounter. I also find it helpful to have the opportunity to 'touch' a person physically and to gain some impression, however tentative, about where they are coming from, although I would exercise great caution before drawing any conclusions from a handshake. Shaking hands also creates the need to say a few warm words of welcome or farewell. This too can be quite revealing. Whatever our personal preference in relation to handshaking, the point to stress is that it is important to think about how to welcome or bid farewell to people we encounter. However, it may not always be possible to end on a positive note.

Other forms of physical contact

A question that constantly arises is whether or not it is appropriate for service users, or others being interviewed, to be touched during the course of an interview. As a general rule, this is not wise, although there are some exceptions to this rule. For example, if someone is crying it can feel inhuman and unprofessional not to offer some physical contact; perhaps tap the shoulder, touch their hand or offer a cup of tea. However, a word of caution is needed because what we consider comforting may not be the same for all people. Some people who have been abused find any kind of physical contact difficult: being touched, including being hugged, can feel like a violation or run the risk of awakening earlier abusive memories. Similarly, to touch individuals when they are crying can make some people feel guilty or inhibited about express-ing emotions in this way, and may have the effect of closing them down. They may worry that they have 'upset' us; here it is important to offer reassurance that this is not the case.

These complexities are difficult to unravel and call for us to be intuitive. They highlight the importance of self-knowledge and the distinction that needs to be drawn between our personal reactions and our professional responses as a person-in-role. One of the most useful things we can do is to try to 'be with' the feelings being expressed and to provide comfort in ways that feel appropriate. Another is to encourage the expression of emotion by talking to the individual who is upset. A soft, gentle voice offering realistic reassurance can feel like a blanket, wrapping itself around someone to keep them safe. However, the ability to soothe in this way cannot be learned because it must come from a different, more sensitive and intuitive part of our personality, but it is all the more important for this reason.

Informal opening conversations ('social chat')

Another way of providing a relaxed welcome might involve starting up an informal conversation. This frequently involves talking about uncontroversial subjects, such as the weather or the journey. Again, our intuitive skills are needed to gauge how long a discussion of this kind should last. To be too brief can leave people feeling hurried and rail-roaded. On the other hand, it can create unnecessary anxiety if these informal conversations are dragged out longer than necessary. This kind of conversation, sometimes called a 'social chat', should not be trivialized because it allows people to gain an impression of us before the interview begins. As practitioners, it gives us the opportunity to create a climate that makes it possible for people to ask for help or to dis-cuss difficult subjects. For some individuals, initial impressions are important and are formed within the first few moments of contact; hence the phrase 'you only get one chance to make a good first impression'.

Service users can feel welcomed and respected by the kind of reception they experience when first walking into an agency (Lishman 1994: 17). Some of this reception is communicated by the receptionist, who can do a great deal to create a caring environment. Over the years, I have seen some highly skilled and sensitive work undertaken by receptionists in these situations, sometimes on the telephone and sometimes in person. Another way to think about the reception a service user might receive relates to the actual physical decor of the reception area in relation to whether:

- it is too formal or informal
- it is comfortable, tidy and well decorated
- it has an appropriate range of seating (comfortable seats, including seating appropriate for older people, chairs and a desk if needed)
- it is private and confidential

- interruptions and disruptions can be avoided
- it reflects the multiracial, multicultural, age and gender composition of people seeking a social work/probation service
- it is wheelchair and pram accessible
- it provides enough sufficiently current and interesting magazines to help pass the time away if service users have to wait to be seen.

It is important to see ourselves as partly responsible for the kind of reception and welcome that service users receive, and to ensure that, as far as possible, this is a warm and welcoming experience.

Empathy and sympathy

Empathy

Creating good working relationships involves being able to empathize with others. For Egan, the effective use of empathy is dependent on the 'skill of the helper and the state of the client' (1990: 135). It describes an attempt to put ourselves in another person's place, in the hope that we can feel and understand another person's emotions, thoughts, actions and motives. Empathy involves trying to understand, as carefully and as sensitively as possible, the nature of another person's experience, their own unique point of view, and what meaning this carries for that individual. It goes beyond sympathy (passive understanding) in conveying a willingness to 'enter imaginatively into the inner life of someone else' (Kadushin 1990: 51).

Shulman (1984) divides the skills involved in empathy into three sections:

- *reaching for feelings*, which involves 'stepping into the client's shoes' (Shulman 1984: 67), thereby coming as close as is humanly possible to another person's experience;
- *displaying understanding of client's feelings*, which entails suspending disbelief or similar reactions and instead 'indicating through words, gestures, expression, physical posture, or touch the worker's comprehension of the expressed affect' (Shulman 1984: 68); and
- *putting the client's feelings into words*, which is particularly important when clients are unable to articulate certain feelings, because they do not fully understand the emotion or because 'the client might not be sure it is all right to have such a feeling or to share it with the worker' (Shulman 1984: 69).

Being empathic is not a request for practitioners to be perfect or mechanical in our responses, but to present ourselves as real human beings, reliable and consistent in our contact with service users, capable of conveying 'interest, warmth, trust, respect' (Kadushin 1990: 44). At times it can be difficult to differentiate empathy from those attributes that are about being concerned professionals, which Egan addresses by differentiating between empathy as 'a way of being and empathy as a communication process or skill' (Egan 1990: 123).

Some authors describe 'an empathy which goes beyond placing oneself in another's shoes by daring to put these on and wear them for a while' (Dominelli 1998: 10). This begs the question about whether it is actually possible to experience another person's reality in this way, which it clearly is not. To do so runs the risk of our intruding uninvited into another person's world. For this reason, Rogers (1957: 4) is correct in stressing the importance of our exercising great caution about where we tread, always taking our lead from service users and not from our own desires, however caring and honourable.

The ability to be empathic is one of the most important skills used when interviewing and is central to client-centred approaches. It involves attempting to understand thoughts, feelings and experiences from another person's point of view in order to understand how they might be feeling. It can be difficult to put into words a sensitive and accurate understanding of another's experience. Our own subjective experience is a useful starting point. However, in some ways, our attempts to understand the meaning others give to their experiences will always be elusive, although our failures may be forgiven and bridged by our willingness to try to understand. For this reason, such a crossing over of meaning and understanding can have a profound impact and one that may be remembered for a lifetime. As stated earlier, the importance of being understood by another human being is enormously important, not least because it can lead to self-understanding. Self-understanding can last a lifetime; longer than our professional involvement, which may be fleeting. Nevertheless, our role in this process of self-discovery may be deeply significant.

The actual words used to convey empathy need to be easily understood and consistent with the mode of communication with which the individual is familiar. For this reason it is important to avoid seeing empathy as an opportunity to indulge in philosophical ramblings or personal statements about the meaning of life or how much we admire the individual in question. Empathy is based on self-knowledge and self-reflection and an ability to reach into and to communicate that knowledge, in words and/or body language. One way to see this two-way communication is as a conversation using two mirrors, where the reflection of another person is always seen alongside our own reflection. Sympathy, on the other hand, is more about looking solely at the mirrored reflection of another person.

Example: Empathic response

Service user: My husband died last year. It's been hard without him.
Practitioner: You sounded very sad when you said that. How have things been since he died?

Asking a general question, such as 'How have things been?', is sometimes preferable to asking a more specific question, such as 'Are you still finding it difficult to adjust to life without your husband?' General questions allow the individual to self-select the issues and concerns they choose to include in the word 'things'. However, closed questions are often preferable if someone is distressed.

Service user: I had to take to the streets when I left care because there was nowhere else to go.
Practitioner: I think that this is one of the worst experiences that we can have as human beings – to feel that we have no home, nowhere to go. How did you manage to survive?

Sympathy

Sympathy is about being moved by another human being. It is sometimes described as feeling *for* another person (passive) as opposed to empathy, which is described as feeling *with* another person (active) (Shulman 1984: 64). In some social work texts, this emotion is seen as inferior to empathy because it is sometimes viewed as a form of pity and/or as implying an unquestioning acceptance of an individual's experience (Egan 1990: 139). However, sympathy can be, and often is, a genuine, human response to another person's experience of hardship or suffering. We cannot be empathic all the time. That would be exhausting and fail to do justice to the unique features of this emotion. But we can allow ourselves to feel sympathy with the plight of others. It is, therefore, a particularly important skill when we meet someone for the first time, where the need to convey a sense of concern, warmth, interest, care and compassion is paramount.

Example: Sympathetic response
Service user: My husband died last year.
Practitioner: I am very sorry to hear that. How are you managing?

Service user: I had to take to the streets when I left care because there was nowhere else to go.
Practitioner: It must have been a hard time for you.

The role of self-knowledge and intuition

The use of self-knowledge or self-awareness in professional practice involves the conscious employment of social work skills, knowledge, values and personal experience in ways that are illuminating to the work at hand. Shulman describes this self-knowledge as follows:

> The capacity to be in touch with the service user's feelings is related to the worker's ability to acknowledge his or her own. Before a worker can understand the power of emotions in the life of the client, it is necessary to discover its importance in the worker's own experience.
>
> (Shulman 1984: 64–5)

It implies the ability to be open and available, to become involved but not merged with service users and to be sensitive and intuitive about the verbal and non-verbal communication taking place. It is about allowing ourselves to be affected by the experiences and hardships that people face in ways that 'move us'. In the case of injustice, it can encourage a healthy sense of outrage, which can act as an impetus and driving force in our efforts to help bring about change. However, it is important that this impetus does not slip into a need to 'rescue' people (Karpman 1968), perhaps by taking on too much responsibility or promising more than we can deliver. One example of the professional use of self can be seen in the appropriate and judicial use of self-disclosure. Another can be seen in the way we create and maintain professional boundaries. In personal terms, it is where we take up an appropriate position of separateness while also maintaining a clear connection to service users, so that we are not too distant or inflexible on the one hand, nor too merged or inappropriately accommodating on the other.

Self-knowledge is not easy to acquire but is central to good practice, including anti-oppressive approaches, because the 'importance of knowing oneself in order to engage effectively with others who are different is . . . essential to carrying out anti-oppressive practice but immensely difficult to do' (Dominelli 1998: 10). We may only begin to know the limits of our self-awareness when presented with problems that trigger reactions inappropriate to the situation. For example, we may feel we have come to terms with childhood experiences of rejection until we encounter a service user who is deeply rejecting of us, and we find ourselves shaken unexpectedly by our reactions. Once we realize our vulnerability, we have a professional responsibility to attend to these unresolved emotions so that we can continue with the work at hand. Our personal commitment to sort out and work through these personal dilemmas can be an invaluable source of knowledge in helping others in similar situations to work through similar feelings. Unless we do this, we are forever vulnerable to falling into pockets of distress or anxieties 'that lead to inattention, poor listening and inappropriate responses and actions' (Lishman: 1994: 60).

Intuition

Linked to the professional 'use of self' is intuition. England strongly emphasizes the importance of intuition, imagination and experience as central components to good practice but within a framework where these attributes can be evidenced and measured: 'the practice of social work must be evaluated . . . and . . . subject to a description and analysis which can determine quality' (England 1986: 139). Other more recent publications also stress the importance of intuition (O'Sullivan 1999: 87; Seden 1999: 128, 133), but with well founded reservations. Hypotheses or actions based on 'intuitive reasoning' or 'intuitive judgements', should always be rigorously tested against other sources of information available (Munro 1996: 795). We still know so little about how to bring about positive change and the part played by intuition within this process. Where theories and methods are cited, 'we can find numerous conflicting or complementary theories, many of which are highly speculative and little researched (Munro 1998: 96). Further research is needed on the place of intuition within social work: ' "Hard" knowledge such as facts are pertinent, but so too are thoughts and feelings and the worker's own clarified intuition' (Coulshed 1991: 24).

The use of intuition relates to our being able to read non-verbal forms of communication accurately. It is a 'knowledge or perception not gained by reason and intelligence' (Hanks 1979) and links to Schön's concept of *tacit recognitions* (1991: 50), where we are involved in making sense of communications that come in the form of thoughts, hunches, instinctive reactions, impressions, associations, insights, impulses and guesswork. For example, in the Jasmine Beckford inquiry practitioners had formed 'hunches' but felt unable to act on them (London Borough of Brent 1985). There are times when it is only a 'hunch' that tells us that something is wrong or that alerts us to the possibility that a dangerous situation is developing. It is from this place that the impetus to gather evidence or 'hard facts' emerges, but until our intuition can be clarified in this way, our ideas must continue to be considered as hypotheses (tentative propositions) or as possible indicators (a sign, warning or a pointer to a particular direction, event or outcome).

Case example: Bee

For example, as a fieldworker I once worked with a group of 8–10-year-old girls, all of whom were experiencing difficulties likely to result in their being brought into care. One member of the group, Bee, displayed particularly disturbing behaviour. She seemed oblivious to the social conventions in relation to when and where to touch other members of the group and bewildered or unaffected by the hostility her behaviour provoked in the other girls. This provocative behaviour felt out of keeping with the fact that, in most encounters involving adults, Bee demonstrated a worrying level of compliance and desire to please. It was as if she was trying to read our minds. This situation was made more complex because Bee had been assessed as having learning difficulties and it was not always clear she had understood what was being communicated.

One night, I was asked to drop Bee off at home because her social worker was unwell. As we drove nearer to her house, Bee appeared to become more agitated and quite bizarre in her behaviour. Her father was waiting for us at the door, arms folded. We arrived late and as I moved to get out of the car to offer my apologies, Bee began to panic. She hurriedly gathered her belongings together, insisting that I drive off. I did as she asked but on my way home, I felt deeply confused and concerned about Bee's behaviour. I felt frightened and felt that I had picked up this fear from Bee. The following day I mentioned this to her social worker who reassured me that Bee was 'always like that', that the behaviour I had witnessed was quite 'normal for Bee'. Apparently, her father had a profound mistrust and dislike of social workers and the agreement was that Bee could attend the group on the proviso that this did not involve having contact with social services or the group leaders.

Bee never found her way to the group again. Over the weeks and months that followed, I continued to feel concerned and encountered the same reassurance from her social worker that she was fine. Several months passed until it came to light that Bee's 16-year-old sister was expecting a baby by her father and a careful investigation of this situation led to questions being raised about Bee's relationship with her father. It transpired that she had been the victim of physical and sexual abuse not only by her father but by other men invited into the home. The father was eventually sent to prison and Bee and her sister received into care. This experience again reminded me how difficult it can be to differentiate between learning difficulties and the effect of sexual abuse on children. In order to survive, and to keep alive any good feelings in relation to parents who abuse, some children have learned to develop behaviours needed to protect themselves: they 'have to smile or become stupid or blind to what is happening' (Sinason 1988: 99). This case example reminds me also of the importance of revising our judgements and decisions in the light of new events, and of seeing this as a sign of strength not weakness (Munro 1996: 799)

Questioning

Asking a range of different questions is central to interviewing. Different authors highlight the qualities that practitioners need to demonstrate in order to frame questions in ways that are helpful, illuminating and empathic (Lishman 1994: 24–5; Seden 1999: 30; Nelson-Jones 2000: 183). Most stress that *before asking a question we must be interested in the answer*. This goes back to the point made earlier, that most people intuitively know whether they are being listened to and whether their thoughts and feelings are being given the importance they deserve. It is important to note that questions can be used as a way of stimulating self-reflection – as a way of returning people to their own thoughts and their own knowledge base – because it is here that the kernel of self-determination and empowerment is located.

On the other hand, Kadushin describes five forms of unhelpful questions (1990: 191–200):

- leading or suggestive forms of questions
- too many 'yes'/'no' questions
- garbled or unclear questions
- double or multiple questions
- too many 'why' questions.

It can be very easy to think that as practitioners we know how to ask questions but the above dangers need to be considered seriously, particularly the point about avoiding leading questions or 'putting words into other people's mouths' (Seden 1999: 31). Most of us come to the task of interviewing with fixed patterns of behaviour of which we are largely unaware. Some of these behaviours may be facilitating, but others may be off-putting or unhelpful. Hence the value of watching ourselves on video. For example, how well do you think you can tolerate silences? Many practitioners think they can manage silences without difficulty until presented with a situation where they are required to remain silent or to work with someone who is silent. Here the compulsion to speak is almost unbearable and can lead to all kinds of strange questions being asked simply in order to break the intense discomfort that silence can engender.

Open questions

These are designed to give freedom of choice, enabling service users to express their thoughts and feelings in their own words and in their own time; to choose or to ignore certain concerns. However, it is important to set aside sufficient time for this kind of exploration.

It is suggested that open-ended questions should form a major part of an initial interview or first encounter. However, these can feel threatening or overwhelming for service users who are not used to formulating their thoughts and feelings into such an open space. Some individuals try to address their confusion and anxiety by trying to guess the response we are looking for. This kind of mind-reading can seriously detract from the purpose of the interview unless it is addressed. Other people find difficulty answering open questions because they do not yet have words with which to explain what has happened to them.

Some fear is due to a worry about coming across as 'stupid', or of being judged. It may be possible to overcome any difficulties by addressing them directly or by stressing what we are hoping to achieve and how this will benefit the individual concerned. It may help to ask a range of open and closed questions. These different approaches require that we are flexible and able to change the form or content of the interview in ways that enable people to tell their stories and to gather their thoughts and feelings with greater freedom. When people remain agitated and defensive the only option may be to stop the interview or to spend time explaining in greater detail why it is important for us to ask these questions. At this point, and at other points in this and other interviews, it is important to inform people of their rights and of agency policy in relation to information that is recorded about them or other members of their family.

Example: Open questions for initial interview or assessment
Practitioner: How can I be of help?

Practitioner: I've got some information about what happened [shows charge sheet] but I want you to tell me what happened – in your own words.

Example: Life-story work
Practitioner: One way for me to get to know you would be for you to say something about yourself. How does that sound? [Nod]. Where would you like to begin?

For an informative description of life-story work with children, including the use of play, life-story books and Fahlberg's (1991) ecomap, see Brandon *et al.* (1998: 18; 154–62). Garbarino *et al.* (1992) provide a helpful account of how to elicit and evaluate information from children.

Closed questions

Closed questions can often be answered 'yes' or 'no', or with other responses that only require a few words, such as asking a person's name, address, age and so on. This form of questioning is useful when trying to elicit factual or detailed information, particularly when time is limited. It can also be used to keep the interview focused, to open up new areas, to change the direction of the interview, to draw the interview away from or towards sensitive or emotional topics, to slow an interview down and to allow missing details to be covered. However, this does place more responsibility on the interviewer, who must both choose and formulate relevant questions and listen carefully to the answers so that questions follow on naturally. This can require a great deal of concentration and is one reason why interviewing can be so tiring. On the other hand, closed questions can foreclose exploration. For example, doctors seeking to diagnose a patient quickly are more likely to ask closed questions (Corney 1991: 5).

Closed questions can be particularly valuable when working with people who do not have a great deal of confidence, perhaps because they feel reticent or mistrustful or find it difficult to formulate their thoughts and feelings. People involved in accidents or who have been traumatized in other ways may find themselves uncharacteristically unable to answer open questions, but able to manage closed questions relatively well. People vary, and all situations are different, so it is important that we are able to adapt.

The main disadvantage when using closed questions is that they may steer the interview in the wrong direction by being too focused. This can lead to a sense of frustration on the part of the interviewee, who can easily feel that their experiences are being disregarded, or categorized and squeezed into little boxes. Here, it can be helpful to spend time before and after the interview talking about the difficulties involved in having to answer questions in this way and reaffirming why it was important. It is sometimes assumed that open questions are more in keeping with anti-discriminatory/anti-oppressive practice than closed questions. This implies that all people are the same and that all interviews can be conducted in the same way. This is clearly not the case.

For some people, 'why' questions can be experienced as accusatory or authoritarian (Seden 1999: 31). Thoughtful wording, accompanied by careful tone and timing, can ensure that this danger is avoided. In most circumstances it is unhelpful to ask combined questions but where a great deal of factual information is being sought, to avoid the interview feeling like an interrogation, combined questions may be necessary. For example, rather than ask 'Are you on medication?', which, if affirmed, will require a second question ('What are you taking?'), it may be better to ask a combined question: 'If you're on medication, can you tell me what you are taking?'

Example: Gathering basic information
(Choice of words, tone and timing are important.)
Practitioner:　Okay. Can I have your name and address, please?

Service user: Yes. Michael Smith, 37 Baron Street, Newtown.
Practitioner: Thanks. What's your date of birth, Michael?
Service user: Fourth of September 1983.
Practitioner: So you're sixteen?
Service user: Yes.

Example: **Clarifying the reason for the referral**
Practitioner: I see from the letter from your doctor that she thinks you need a
                   social worker to help you to sort out some problems you're
                   having at home. Is that how you see the situation?
Service user: No. I didn't know that my doctor had written. I came because I
                   got a letter from you asking to see me.
Practitioner: Okay. I think it would help to go back and start at the beginning
                   so that I can understand why your doctor has referred you to us.
                   Is that okay?
Service user: Yes.
Practitioner: When did you last see your doctor?
Service user: Last week.
Practitioner: What was that for, Mrs Day? ['What' question]

'What' questions

This form of questioning is particularly popular in family therapy and in certain types of brief therapy. Its main advantage is that it is quite unspecific in terms of what constitutes the 'what' implied in the question, thereby leaving the interviewee free to define for themselves the issues or concerns that they wish to focus on. Another advantage is that its emphasis is on the present rather than the past, but with an opportunity for additional questions to be asked relating to the past, if that is considered necessary (Lishman 1994: 77).

Sometimes there is insufficient time, and it is not always useful, to explore the past or the cause of a problem, because this may not help us to formulate what the current impact of the problem is and how it might be rectified or solved (Watzlawick *et al.* 1974: 84). Indeed, an exploration of the past can be a way of avoiding what is actually happening in the present. However, some 'why' questions can come across as accusatory or blaming, although this difficulty can be overcome when a sensitive and caring tone of voice is used.

'What' questions are immensely adaptable, particularly when attempting to explore wider issues and the part that other individuals or factors play in the perpetuation of the problem encountered. This emphasis is consistent with a systemic perspective that stresses that no one person is solely responsible for a problem or a difficulty that exists, although as human beings we are all responsible for our actions. For example, 'what' questions can be asked in most situations: 'what is going on?'; 'what plays a part in perpetuating this problem?'; 'what part does this problem, individual or family play in relation to the whole (system, family, community etc.)?'; 'what needs to happen to bring about change or a solution to this problem?'; 'what is needed to keep the momentum for change alive?'; and 'what would tell us that the intervention, approach or work has been effective?'

Examples: Initial interview

Practitioner: What's happening – as you see it – Mr Black?

Practitioner: What do you think will happen if we leave things as they are?

Practitioner: What can I say or do to make a difference?

Asking a purposely vague question, such as 'What is happening?' allows the individual to decide what they see to be 'happening'. This can include anything and take us to some unexpected places. This in turn can enable us to judge whether different parties see the situation in the same way and, if not, to explore what these differences are and, if important to the task, how they can be bridged and a common purpose agreed.

Circular questions

Another helpful intervention, frequently used in family therapy, is circular questioning. This is an important form of questioning but it is also the most complex and is rarely described in social work texts. For this reason, I shall go into some detail about it here.

The purpose of circular questioning is to gather information using a format that highlights differences and how individuals relate to one another or to a particular problem. This involves asking each member of the family (or group of people) in turn to comment on the behaviour, event or problem of other members of the family in ways that reveal the 'circular causality'; that is, the recurring and circular way that certain behaviours impact and affect different family members. For example, a child sulks when chastised. The father reacts by shouting at the child, which results in the child becoming more withdrawn and the mother shouting at the father, which the father blames on the child, who withdraws further, and so forth.

The range of questions that can be asked is vast, and subjects of them may include absent or deceased family members, but this form of questioning must always be linked to a hypothesis (Burnham 1986: 110). The term 'hypothesis' has a broader application (see pages 16–17), but in this context is used to mean 'a supposition or conjecture, constructed from information available about a particular family, which serves as a starting point for investigation. It is not meant to be "true" but simply "useful", neither more nor less so than other hypotheses' (Preston-Shoot and Agass 1990: 55).

The fact that all family members can be included in this form of questioning helps to validate their presence and importance within the family system. Drawing attention to the ways in which they perceive certain behaviours or events can allow new information to be brought into the system. This in itself can help bring about change, particularly when behaviours can be seen in their complexity and a 'positive connotation' found. 'Positive connotation' and reframing are similar except that reframing is directed more towards individual change, whereas 'positive connotation' has a broader impact because it has the potential to change the meaning different family members attach to certain behaviours or events and how they relate to one another. For people locked in negative or rigidly held perspectives, this creates the opportunity for these defensive patterns and behaviours to be changed, so that new ways of addressing problems can be sought. This avoids doing more of the same: situations where 'attempts to solve problems become part of the problem' (Preston-Shoot and Agass 1990: 55).

As practitioners, the advantage of this form of questioning is that it helps to avoid 'taking sides' or seeing different family members in terms of 'good' and 'bad' characteristics. Another advantage lies in the way that this intervention can actively engage different family members:

> It is extremely advantageous with families who are initially reluctant to answer direct questions about relationships. It only needs one family member to 'drop their guard' and reveal an important piece of information for a cumulative effect to develop; soon everyone is willing to talk. Those family members who do not respond verbally cannot help but betray their non-verbal message since it is impossible not to communicate on this level.
>
> (Burnham 1986: 110–11)

It is important to note the non-verbal communication. However, within different 'schools' of family therapy, and others outside, this intervention has been criticized by those who think it inappropriate for one family member to speak for another or for someone who is not present: 'Family members should speak for themselves. They should tell their own story . . . [and] . . . should not tell what other members think or feel. Two members should not discuss a third who is present without his [sic] participation' (Minuchin 1979: 16). Similarly, interventions of this kind can be experienced as oppressive for family members who have been at the receiving end of negative comments about their behaviour. For these individuals, to be asked to listen to more hurtful or insulting remarks may be unbearable. In these situations, much depends on the skill of the social worker in providing reassurance that this intervention is about changing family perceptions and repairing self-esteem, and not merely a re-enactment of the past.

Several types of questions, the most common being 'mind-reading questions', involve an investigation of the 'triadic' (group of three) relationship between people, where each participant is asked to state what he or she thinks and feels about a relationship between two people from the perspective of a third person. This reveals the extent to which different family members are aware of each other's thoughts and feelings and where they disagree.

Example: Circular question

This case example relates to Jane, aged 26, who has a history of depression, sometimes resulting in hospitalization. In the past, family conflict has played a major part in Jane's admission to hospital. Jane is thought to be severely depressed and the purpose of the interview is to try to see if there is a link between family conflict and her emotional state. The use of circular questions needs to be introduced carefully and sensitively, giving a clear explanation of what the interview involves and the value of this kind of questioning. For brevity, it is assumed that this explanation has taken place and met with the family's agreement.

Practitioner: [To Jane's sister] Sarah, what does your father do when Jane becomes withdrawn and depressed?

Sarah: [A hesitant, worried response] He tells her to pull herself together – that there are people in the world much worse off than Jane and that she should stop feeling sorry for herself.

Practitioner: Sarah, what does your mother do when Jane becomes depressed and withdrawn?

Sarah: [Looking defeated] She tries to make it all right for Jane – by doing things for her. She makes a fuss of her. I feel left out. She cries a lot when Dad is shouting at Jane.

Practitioner: What does Sarah do when Jane becomes withdrawn and depressed?

Mrs Wilson: [Looking angry] She starts playing up. She's always been jealous of Jane.

Sarah: [Shouting] No I don't. That's not fair. You always take Jane's side. What about me?

Practitioner: [Speaking slowly and kindly but with authority, showing a clear determination to take hold of the direction of the interview] Okay, I know these questions are difficult but it's important that you stick to the rules and let one another have their say. This session must not be allowed to turn into another row – that will get us nowhere. To avoid this, you must stick to answering the questions and stop arguing. That's only fair and what we agreed. Okay? [Looking at everyone present but getting no response] . . . [Pause] Do you agree? [The practitioner waits until all communicate their agreement] Okay. Let's keep going. Mr Wilson, what does Sarah do when Jane becomes withdrawn and depressed?

Mr Wilson: [Looking bored and frustrated] I don't know what she does. Ask her. Nothing. I don't think she does anything.

Practitioner: I know these questions can be boring and frustrating, Mr Wilson, but it is important that we try to keep with the task. What does Sarah do when Jane becomes withdrawn and depressed?

This interview went on to assess and rank the different problems identified in order of priority. Although the original concern focused on Jane's depression and likely admission to hospital as the primary problem, further information revealed the importance of working on family dynamics, particularly Jane's guilt in relation to Sarah, Sarah's jealousy of Jane and Mr and Mrs Wilson's ambivalence about their marriage and how they 'use' their daughters to communicate their unhappiness.

Other forms of circular questions include 'before and after' questions, which focus on changes that have taken place in relation to a particular event, and 'comparison' or 'ranking' questions, which seek to identify different reactions among family members to a particular issue or event. For a further account of different circular questions see Burnham (1986).

Confirming what has been said and heard

These interventions are designed to ensure that we have understood the content and meaning of what has been communicated so far. This is sometimes referred to as 'tracking'; that is, the 'skill of listening intently and empathetically to the moment-to-moment explorations of the client, with an ability to reflect back and/or to summarize what is said' (Feltham and Dryden 1993: 195). It combines creative listening with responding to and reflecting back what is being communicated (Seden 1999: 29).

The skills include paraphrasing, clarifying, summarizing and giving and receiving feedback. Each offers a different way to ensure that we have understood what is being communicated and provide an opportunity to demonstrate that understanding in words. This allows for misinformation to be corrected and for knowledge and expertise to be returned to the individual concerned. Putting our observations into words also allows the individual to hear their own comments and statements but in a different way. This can be both illuminating and thought-provoking, sometimes enabling new and different options to be explored. When feeding back in this way, it can be easy to slip into jargon: 'what I hear is' or 'I want to share with you what I hear'. Some people find this kind of language off-putting, which makes it important to choose words that are in everyday use and easy to understand (Social Services Inspectorate 1991: 20).

Paraphrasing

In paraphrasing, the essence of the person's statement is restated, although not exactly as an echo. It is a selective restatement of the main ideas with words resembling those used by the individual, but that are not the same: 'para' means 'alongside'. Its main purpose is to ensure that we have grasped the sense and meaning of what is being communicated. Sometimes the only sure way to know this is for us to put in words our own thoughts and impressions. In doing so practitioners:

> demonstrate they have heard the client, they offer their understanding of what they have heard (to be confirmed or otherwise), and their use of paraphrase casts a slightly different light on the original statements, allowing the client to hear their own statements in a way which itself can powerfully move her (or him) into new personal perspectives.
>
> (Feltham and Dryden 1993: 130)

Paraphrasing is not the same as imitation, repetition or mimicking, which can be experienced as humiliating and should be avoided. We seldom have permission to be familiar in this way although sometimes this permission is assumed if the service user is young or 'unequal' in other ways: this is inappropriate. Paraphrasing carries other dangers. Restating points already covered can make some people feel that their own words are not adequate or clear. This can elicit the response 'What was wrong with the way I said it?' Some people come from a history of being taunted for their style of speaking or choice of words. This is particularly true of ethnic minority groups and young people, who may find paraphrasing offensive or undermining. Where this is the case, paraphrasing should not be used unless it is to enable service users to recover from the inhibitions they feel about their capacity to communicate (Seden 1999: 50). Another danger with paraphrasing is that it can be used to change the meaning of what was said into something different. This kind of trickery can be deeply alarming because it 'sets people up' by making it seem they said something that they did not say. Nevertheless, despite these dangers, the ability to relate accurately or restate another person's words is an important skill and the basis of good report writing.

Example: Putting what has been said into your own words

Practitioner: Let me put what you have said into my own words so that it is clear that I've understood you properly. Please interrupt me if I get anything wrong. You want John to live at home but only if he behaves himself properly. You are prepared to put up with his laziness, late nights and loud music but you draw the line when he smokes or truants from school . . .

Service user: [Interrupting] I don't like the fact that he smokes but I can't stop him. What I won't have is John smoking in the house in front of the other kids. That's different.

Practitioner: Right. So the line you draw is that for John to live at home he has to agree not to smoke in the house and he has to go to school. Is that right?

Service user: Yes.

Clarifying

Clarifying is primarily used to sort out confusions and to ensure the listener has an accurate grasp of what is being conveyed. It is also used to put words to thoughts and feelings in a language that can be easily and clearly understood but without falsifying and changing the original meaning. More generally, clarifying can help the individual to identify, confirm and rank the problems that are currently most troubling. This is particularly useful where individuals have many problems and need to focus on those that could have the greatest impact on them. Clarifying can also be used to extend an individual's knowledge base or deepen their understanding of themselves and others they are close to. It differs from paraphrasing because, when clarifying, we frequently choose the same words used by the individual whereas, when paraphrasing, the emphasis is on putting some of the points covered into our own words. A further and different role that clarifying can play is in relation to checking out assumptions and expectations that may be present, on the part of either the interviewee or interviewer (Lishman 1994: 14). This allows for differences to be addressed and, it is hoped, worked through.

Like many of the skills described in this chapter, clarifying can have advantages beyond the technique itself. It can reveal that we are listening carefully and giving importance to what is being said. This can be a particularly important and validating experience for people who have rarely had their thoughts and feelings confirmed in this way. However, clarifying what has been said can interrupt the flow of the interview and, like paraphrasing, can make some people feel ill at ease because it can feel like a veiled criticism or imply that they are communicating poorly. If these concerns emerge, they need to be addressed before the interview can proceed further.

Example: Identifying and confirming events

Practitioner: Let me see if I have this right. Tell me if anything's wrong. You went into the Women's Refuge with your children in May 1998, where you stayed for six months? When your husband tracked you down there, you then went to your sister's in Nottingham where you were for three months until your husband followed you there. Then you returned to the refuge, where the workers there helped you to take out an injunction. Is that right?

Service user: Yes.

Example: Ranking problems/crisis work

Practitioner: We've covered a lot of different things – your worries about your husband, the school, neighbours and debts – but from what you've said, and correct me if I am wrong, the problem that seems to worry you the most is the fact that you've got no money and a lot of debts – debts that you can't pay. [Pause] Is that right?

Service user: Yes. I'm up to my neck in debts and I can't bear it – I can't cope [begins to cry]. I owe money all over the place – to my neighbours, at the local shop. I can't go out 'cause I'm frightened I'll bump into my neighbours. I daren't go to the door in case it's someone looking for money. I nearly didn't answer the door to you because I thought you were the bailiffs. I've taken to stuffing any bills that come through my door behind the settee – it sounds crazy but I just can't bear to see them.

Practitioner: It's not crazy but that's a terrible way to have to live. What can I do to help?

Service user: Don't know. I feel I've run out of ways to keep going – there's no let-up.

Practitioner: [When it is absolutely clear that this person cannot move the situation forward without urgent help and where it is known that there is no specialist help easily available, such as debt counselling or welfare rights advice] How would it feel if you came

	back next week and I go through all the bills that are stuffed behind the settee. I'll add up what you owe and then we can have a look at which are the most pressing and then we can sit down together to see what can be done. How does that sound?
Service user:	It would feel such a relief to hand over the problem to someone – anyone.
Practitioner:	Okay. In the meantime, try not to worry. Why not go and see your neighbours and tell them what's happened so that they know that you are trying to pay them back. Did you used to see quite a bit of them in the past?
Service user:	Yes. We got on well – always have.
Practitioner:	The way things are right now, they miss out twice. They don't see their money and they don't see you – maybe they miss you? Why not make contact – invite them in for a cup of tea?

There are several points to note in relation to this example. First, it is often preferable to refer financial problems of this kind to a debt counsellor, welfare rights advice centre or the Citizen's Advice Bureau. However, given the level of anxiety and strain that this service user is experiencing, I would only consider a referral to another agency if I knew for certain that the referral would be picked up quickly. This involves telephoning the appropriate agency to see whether they could see the service user in question and when. It is worth noting that some firms and utilities, such as gas and electric companies and water boards will, under special circumstances, consider spreading payments over a longer period or on occasion consider waiving debts.

Second, when we know that someone is frightened to answer the door, perhaps because they are hiding from debtors, it is important to state the day and time we will be returning and to keep to this rigorously. I recall working with a young mother, Ali, who refused to answer the door to anyone. This raised alarm bells among professionals, and resulted in regular visits being made to her house, but in vain. Then, one day, quite by chance, I managed to meet Ali on her doorstep and to gain access. I assumed she had left her two small children alone but I was wrong: her boyfriend, Tony, was with them. I was also wrong in assuming that her children were not well cared for. The story that unfolded was that she was frightened to answer the door because Tony was absent without leave from the army and the couple were terrified that he might be caught. The more professionals called to the door, the more frightened they became. I was later able to do some good work with this family who lived in council housing that was appalling and dangerous to their health. They were eventually rehoused in a different area of the city and, I believe, settled down well.

Summarizing

Summarizing can be useful in a number of ways. First, we can begin a new session by drawing together and summarizing points covered in earlier sessions.

Second, it can provide an accurate and succinct partial or detailed breakdown of what has been covered so far. This allows us to gather together the disparate strands and central themes of what has been covered and to check out that the understanding we have is the same as that of the individual being interviewed. Again, this can help service users to clarify their own thoughts and perceptions, and sometimes lead them to look at the issue from a slightly different angle. 'Often, when scattered elements are brought together, the service user sees the "bigger picture" more clearly. Thus, summarizing can lead to new perspectives or alternate frames of reference' (Egan 1990: 258). Third, a well timed, brief and accurate summary can be particularly useful when the discussion has started to drift or the session to lose direction. It can be used to draw one line of enquiry to a close so that a new one can be opened. Finally, summarizing is used to draw the session to a satisfactory end. Within this process, summarizing what has been covered can highlight issues that have not been explored and provide a useful opportunity to plan future sessions.

Example: **Summarizing issues still to be covered in relation to a young person being prepared for independent living**

Practitioner: Let's look at what we've discussed so far. You've talked about your experiences of being in care, your foster parents, how you got on at school. Is there anything I've left out? [Service user shakes head] What we still need to look at with the time we've got left is where you plan to live when you leave care. Is that okay? [Service user nods] Where would you like to start – what ideas have you already had?

Example: **Final summary of the points covered in an initial interview**

Practitioner: I think that's all we can cover today. What we have looked at is your childhood, your history of going in and out of hospital, your current living situation and how you are coping right now. We can talk more when we meet again next week. Does that sound all right?

Service user: Yes, that's fine.

Giving and receiving feedback

Giving and receiving feedback, both negative and positive, has advantages for both practitioners and service users. Firstly, clear and honest feedback can have a practical application as a way of ensuring that a particular course of action is 'on course' in terms of achieving agreed objectives. Secondly, feedback can be used as a way of noting the emotional content of the communication, 'reflecting feelings entails responding to clients' music and not just to their words' (Nelson-Jones 2000: 130). This can help service users to learn more about themselves – how they come across – which can be important in ensuring the success of a particular endeavour. For example, where someone is approaching a particular task with a sense of defeat or pessimism, feeding back these impressions may be essential to avoid the task being sabotaged and effort being in vain.

In practice, giving and receiving feedback is a difficult undertaking because it requires being able to deal with the feelings that this brings up in ourselves and others. Some service users find any form of feedback, positive or negative, difficult and upsetting. People who have been hurt in the past by negative feedback can easily become worried that they are going to be 'got at' again. To allay these concerns, at the outset it can help to stress that the 'purpose of feedback is not to pass judgement on the performance of clients but rather to provide guidance, support, and challenge' (Egan 1990: 389). Egan goes on to describe three purposes of feedback:

- *confirmatory* when it lets clients know when they are on course, that is, moving successfully through the steps of an action program toward a goal;
- *corrective* when it provides clients with information they need to get back on course if they have strayed;
- *motivating* when it points out the consequences of both adequate and inadequate program implementation and includes suggestions for improving performance.

(Egan 1990: 389)

Positive feedback can also create problems, particularly where people have been tantalized and lured into painful or humiliating experiences through the use of kindness and flattery. For example, I once worked with a young woman who had been sexually abused. She associated any compliments or words of appreciation as an attack because before abusing her her uncle would 'woo' her with flattering comments. Her response to kindness was to ask, quite spontaneously, 'What do you want?' or 'What's the payback?'

Given the way that some people have been hurt in the area of giving and receiving, before giving feedback it is vital to think about how they might react and to adjust our comments accordingly. Although it is always important to be honest and truthful (Clark 2000: 51), the balance between being honest and being facilitative can be a difficult one to find. When faced with this tension, it can help to remember that some things can be left for another time and that feedback is more likely to be taken on board if it is brief and to the point, and if it focuses on behaviour as opposed to statements about the individual (descriptive rather than interpretative). It also helps to give sufficient time and opportunity for service users to comment and to invite disagreement, reminding them that our views can be wrong and are not 'gospel'. To encourage self-evaluation and self-reflection can be far more valuable in terms of facilitating change than feeding back our perceptions.

So far, the focus has been on our giving feedback to service users. However, many of the same points apply to practitioners receiving feedback, because we too can feel apprehensive and behave defensively, particularly if we think the feedback we are about to be given is negative or critical. In terms of quality assurance, service user feedback is becoming increasingly important and, as expectations rise, complaints and complaints procedures are likely to become important (Adams 1998: 115). As practitioners accountable to our agency and to maintaining professional standards we can find negative feedback worrying. For this reason, it is always helpful to raise these concerns in supervision.

Sticking to the point and probing deeper

The following skills describe some of the ways that we can keep to the point and purpose of the interview. This may be necessary to fulfil a specific purpose, such as to acquire information for assessment purposes, or to ensure that we have explored the issues to be discussed, some of which may be difficult to talk about. A common problem is when the interview is allowed to drift and people are left to ramble across topics that are not relevant. This purposelessness is a problem within social work that extends beyond the interview setting. For example, we know that some children 'drift' into care and, once there, plans are not always properly executed. This is evidenced in the poor educational achievement among children 'looked after' (Aldgate 1997: 145).

There are times when this 'drifting' is important and has to be allowed to happen. It can be a form of story-telling but even in this context, the 'story' is likely to need some direction if the account raises more questions than answers. Sometimes interviews being left without a clear structure, content or purpose may be justified on the grounds that it is in keeping with service user self-determination and a client-centred approach or consistent with an anti-discriminatory perspective. None of these justifies an interview being left to drift but this issue raises the important question: whose responsibility should it be to ensure that the agreed purpose of the interview has been kept to? The presumption is that this responsibility lies with the practitioner, as the person employed to fulfil certain tasks and to ensure that interventions are effective in reaching specific outcomes (Clark 2000: 56).

Sticking to the point and purpose of the interview

The ability to ask questions that change the pace or direction of an interview, or that probe deeper, is an important skill, particularly when interviewing people who are reticent, confused, anxious or unable to give a clear picture of what they want and why. Some responses may stem from a deliberate desire to mislead but most occur because, as human beings, it is natural for us to feel guarded to some extent about what we are prepared to reveal about ourselves, particularly to strangers. In fact, I am often surprised and sometimes quite troubled by how much service users are prepared to reveal, sometimes to complete strangers.

It can be difficult for some people to broach certain issues and, where this is the case, we need to be able to offer reassurance that these subjects can be discussed, and discussed in ways that are not without clear boundaries. However, this reassurance will feel hollow if we ourselves do not possess the ability to address difficult topics. This is an example of the importance of self-knowledge. We must be able to deal with fraught situations in a professional manner, either because we have 'sorted out' and 'worked through' sensitive issues or because we have learned the capacity to manage these in ways that do not interfere with the quality of our work and our rapport with service users. Avoidance can be as much a defence for practitioners as it can be for service users. For example, it can be an abdication of responsibility for practitioners to adopt 'a non-questioning, non-directive style', where information is gathered in a piecemeal manner and based on service users being left to 'identify and address their problems themselves' (Munro 1998: 99).

Our attempts to stick to the point or purpose of an interview can be experienced as either helpful or coercive, depending on the individual and our skills in drawing people away from issues that are less relevant. The skill here is to be able to return to the purpose without disturbing the rapport and trust that has been established. There are several reasons why we might want to intervene in this way:

- the discussion has become over focused on one issue at the expense of others;
- the content has been exhausted and the communication is becoming repetitive;
- the discussion has moved on to peripheral issues or irrelevancies;
- it has moved away from difficult issues and needs to be brought back; or
- the discussion has become emotionally charged and a sense of calm and balance needs to be introduced.

Example: **Sticking to the point by focusing on issues not fully covered**

Practitioner: I now have a good picture of your mother's health problems so I wonder if we could leave this issue here, so that you can say some more about the housing problems you mentioned?

Practitioner: If I can return to something you mentioned in passing, can you say more about your children's contact with their father? How often do they see him?

Example: **Steering the interview away from an upsetting issue**

Practitioner: I can see how upset you are about being separated from your daughter – let's hope that this need not be for long . . . Since this is a difficult situation for you, perhaps we should leave this discussion about her foster home for now, so that you have the chance to take it all in and to feel less upset. What do you normally do to help to calm you when you feel upset in this way?

Service user: I usually have a cup of tea and a cigarette – that's what helps.

Practitioner: Well, I can offer you a cup of tea – and am happy to go and make this for you – but I'm afraid you'll have to go outside if you want a cigarette but that's okay. I can bring your tea to you outside. What do you want to do? Do you want to go outside and have a cigarette and cup of tea? Can we talk again when you've had a break?

It is helpful to speak slowly and distinctly when addressing someone who is visibly upset because the capacity to take in information when we are emotionally distressed is often severely limited. When speaking slowly in this way, it is important not to use a tone that is patronizing. In my experience, people tend to remember the tone we use more than anything else.

Prompting

Prompting is used to encourage the person being interviewed to begin speaking or to continue. It can take many forms such as inviting further comment through direct suggestion, by providing a link between one statement and another in order to encourage further dialogue or by helping the individual to return to unfinished sentences or comments. The need to prompt can sometimes be reduced by our making it clear why we need certain information. If a person's reticence is due to anxiety about what the information will be used for, it helps to address this concern by stating openly where information is recorded, who has access to it, where it will be kept and how service users can access their records (see Chapter 7 on recording skills).

When prompting, there is a temptation to finish off another person's sentence. This should be avoided at all cost because it is important that people find their own words to describe their thoughts and feelings. Like paraphrasing and other skills described earlier, prompting someone to continue speaking can be experienced as encouraging or coercing. Timing, sensitivity, a kind tone and caring approach are crucial in helping people to differentiate between the two.

Example: Inviting further comment
Practitioner: Earlier, you said that prison 'was hell' but then moved on to talk about problems finding work. How do you know what prison is like?

Example: Unfinished comment
Practitioner: That's twice you've started to say something about having no money but stopped. It's always hard to talk about money issues – particularly when there isn't enough to go round – but what do you mean when you say you have no money?
Service user: Don't get me wrong – I'm not saying I am bad with money. I make sure the kids always have enough to eat but they have to do without other things like new shoes, school trips, you know . . . that kind of thing.

Example: Linking

Practitioner: If I can go back to something you mentioned earlier, you said that Peter doesn't get on with your new partner. Later, you also said that Peter now wants to live with his father. Is there a link between these two comments?

Service user: [Silence] I don't know what you mean – what you're getting at?

Practitioner: I am trying to find out whether Peter wants to leave because he is unhappy about your new partner – perhaps he feels put out. You lived alone together for a long time, didn't you?

Service user: He probably is – but so what. What can I do about that?

Practitioner: Well, it depends on whether you feel you can do something about it – and what Peter really wants . . .

Probing

Probing is used to elicit more detailed or specific information and can be a useful intervention when trying to gather information from individuals who are prone to adopt more misleading patterns of communication. It is a skill central to risk assessments. Probing can take the form of questions, statements or interjections (Egan 1990: 141) and can be an invaluable skill in providing information that helps to make sense of people's experience or to provide a fuller picture of the total situation. Egan describes this as the 'magic bit of information' that helps to make sense of what has happened so far: 'prompts and probes are the salt and pepper of communication in the helping process' (Egan 1990: 147). However, probing must be undertaken skilfully so that the person in question does not become more defensive and guarded. To avoid meandering into areas that are private and personal, it helps for probing questions to be linked to a hypothesis or line of enquiry and, if possible, to explain why certain questions are being asked.

Example: Asking more in-depth questions

Practitioner: You seem to know your way round this office. Have you been here before?

Service user: What makes you say that?

Practitioner: You seemed to know where the interview room was without my having to lead you. Have you been here before?

Service user: Yes.

Practitioner: When?

Service user: About three years ago.

Practitioner: What brought you here then?

Service user: Just a little misunderstanding. [Changing the subject] Are you going to help me with my benefit problem or not?

Practitioner: Yes, in a minute. What was that misunderstanding?

Service user: My daughter hurt herself.

Practitioner: Hurt herself in what way?

Service user: She slipped and fell down the stairs.

Practitioner: Why did that involve this office?
Service user: I can't remember – it was so long ago and all a misunderstanding. Can we talk about my benefit?
Practitioner: Let's start at the beginning, Mrs Wood. Tell me what happened from the beginning so that we can move on to look at your benefit problem. Where do you want to start?

Example: **Making a statement to encourage a response**
Practitioner: You appear to be troubled about the contract we have just agreed.
Service user: Yes, I never realized that I would be expected to do so much myself. I thought you'd do it all for me and I don't know whether I am up to it.
Practitioner: Okay. Maybe I'm expecting too much of you but I'm trying to find the right balance. It's important that you play your part because otherwise, you won't feel that any headway we make was because of you. Let's take a step back, shall we? What is it that bothers you the most about the things you have to do?

Example: **Picking up an interjection**
Service user: When I left your office last week I felt a bit upset about what we had talked about.
Practitioner: A bit upset?
Service user: Well, very upset really.
Practitioner: What upset you? Can you remember?
Service user: I hate it when you're late. When you leave me sitting in that horrible waiting room with those useless old magazines. I hate it.
Practitioner: I'm sorry. That's my mistake and something that should not have happened. I'll do all I can to make sure it doesn't happen again and I'm sorry it upset you. [Pause] It's good you're able to tell me – is there anything else that I do, or don't do, that bothers you?

Allowing and using silence

Silence can generate difficult feelings both for service users and practitioners, so much so that it is not always easy to know who is feeling the most uncomfortable. This section explores some of the assumptions that are made about silence and how we can best work with this 'period filled with nonspeech, in which both the interviewer and interviewee participate' (Kadushin 1990: 253).

The assumption is that talking is better than not talking and that nothing is being communicated when silence prevails. That is not the case, because words can be used to create or kill real dialogue, to conceal rather than to reveal. Other assumptions include the view that silences should always be broken; the interview is not successful if there is too much silence; it is mainly inexperienced practitioners who feel uncomfortable with silences; silences indicate poor communication skills or are a sign of failure on the part of the practitioner to engage with the interviewee. In addition, silence within English culture can easily be confused with a lack of politeness, incivility or poor social skills. Silence can also be used as a sign of rejection or disapproval. Although there will be times when these assumptions ring true, they may also be far from accurate.

For these reasons it is important to attempt to identify what is being communicated through silences – how silence is being used. This in turn helps us to understand how long we should allow the silence to run for. What might be called 'creative silences' describe a period of non-speech that is communicating something meaningful and important about the individual and his or her situation. Creative silences indicate that the individual is happily preoccupied with his or her own thoughts and feelings. This stands in contrast to a more 'troubled' form of silence that indicates a feeling of anxiety, embarrassment or confusion on the part of the interviewee, or a withholding or punishing withdrawal. Troubled silences can also reveal that the individual is too upset or too fearful to speak, perhaps because they feel overwhelmed or feel that they need to protect themselves or others.

Several points need to be emphasized. Firstly, it takes two to create a silence in an interview: the service user and the interviewer. If a service user is silent, we need not be – unless we decide to be so. Secondly, we often do not know for certain what is being communicated through the use of silence – and this includes our own silence – and whether it is a 'productive silence' or not. One way to overcome this difficulty would be to ask the person in question what their silence means but, of course, we may not get a response! In relation to our own silence, it can help to think about what we are communicating in our silence, and what our silence means to us. Thirdly, it is crucial to remember that the briefest silence can appear to be a long time. This very quickly comes to light if we have the opportunity to do a time-check. One 'trick' I use cautiously – as a 'last straw' – when trying to communicate with children and adolescents who are determined to remain silent involves planting a deliberate error in my soliloquy. The one most likely to produce a response is when I purposely describe them to be younger than they actually are (see example). Once a silence has been broken, it may be wise not to try to analyse immediately what the silence meant. For some service users, this can feel that they have lost control or that they are being manipulated. This is particularly important to remember when working with children and adolescents.

The ability to be calm, silent and still in an interview is an important skill and one that every competent interviewer needs to acquire. One way to see a pause is as a brief silence – a resting place – that allows time to gather thoughts and feelings. However, like silences, we can find long pauses difficult to bear. Where a person is known to have a pattern of being silent, it can help to sit facing a clock, so that we can check the time without interfering with the flow of the interview. This allows for silence to be measured against reality, rather than our own internal clock, which tends to tick very slowly in an interview where silence is present (see Kadushin 1990: 252–60).

Example: **Speaking into the silence of a young person determined not to speak**

Practitioner: Well, you're a very silent 12-year-old . . .

Service user: I'm not 12, I am 13! So there!

Practitioner: Sorry – my mistake. So you're 13 – not 12?

Service user: Yeah. Do I look like a 12-year-old? [said with contempt]

Practitioner: No, you don't. When's your birthday, Jake?

Service user: In December.

Example: **Speaking into the silence**

Practitioner: You have been silent for some time now Jenny. I wonder why you don't want to talk today?

Service user: [Silence]

Practitioner: [Pause] I wonder if you are afraid that I might be angry because you didn't manage to turn up last week?

Service user: [Silence]

Practitioner: [Pause] I'm sure that you came all this way for a reason . . . but at this point in time, it's not easy for me to see what help I can be . . . why you feel you cannot speak. Has something happened?

Service user: [Silence]

Practitioner: [Pause] Are you angry with me?

Service user: [Silence]

Practitioner: [Pause] Maybe it's best if I don't ask you any more questions. Maybe I should fill this silence with my words and tell you what I think has been happening – and you can tell me if I'm right or wrong. My guess is that last week, you couldn't come to see me because you were grounded again. I think you had another row with your mother – maybe you both said some tough things – and she said you had to stay in your room until you apologized. Apologies are difficult for you and this meant you missed seeing me. I'll bet that since the row, you've felt very confused and hurt. Maybe you've said to yourself that it's better not to talk at all since talking gets you into trouble. Instead, you're left talking to yourself but the problem is that it's very hard for any of us to sort things out without talking. I think you have found talking helpful in the past and it can help you now. I am here to help you.

Service user: [Silence]

Practitioner: My guess is that you are talking but you are not talking out loud. I think that you are talking to yourself. Am I right? I wonder if you can bring yourself to tell me what is going on in your head – what you are saying to yourself so that you don't feel so alone with these feelings? These feelings can be so . . .

Service user: [Interrupting] Oh, I can't stand it when you go on and on. How come you know all this?

Practitioner: Because it's happened before and I remember things that happen to you.

Using self-disclosure

Self-disclosure highlights the importance of our being able to draw on our own personal knowledge and history to gauge what course of action is appropriate and necessary in order to be effective in a particular situation or encounter (Lishman 1994: 145). However, this self-knowledge and 'professional use of self' is taken one step further because self-disclosure relates to revealing present or past personal information about ourselves. *The general rule is that self-disclosure should not occur unless it is in the interest of the individual seeking help.* For example, it can be invaluable for people who feel isolated and alone in their suffering, or who worry about revealing themselves in any way, for us to reveal that it is all right to be *known* in certain ways. This can help to break down feelings of shame, guilt or self-blame – the feelings that say 'I'm not like other people', when in fact, many reactions that some people experience as 'odd' or 'strange' are common to much of the human race. This can bring an enormous sense of relief. For example, if we have been bereaved it can help to disclose how we overcame our feelings of devastation and grief at the death of someone we loved.

Sharing thoughts and feelings through self-disclosure can help service users to see us as 'ordinary human beings' as well as professional workers. Similarly, it can help us feel more empathic and in touch with what is being said and felt. However, self-disclosure must be handled sensitively because it carries many dangers. For example, I recall an incident where a social worker shared his history of sexual abuse with a service user. He did so for many reasons but none related to the best interest of the service user, who was left feeling bewildered, confused and powerless to help. This is an extreme but true example and one that highlights how inappropriate it can be for us to share our personal or professional problems or history in this way. Or again, it is important to avoid using certain phrases that are not accurate, such as 'I know what it's like' or 'I know what you're going through.' We can have some idea of what it is like, but all human beings are unique, which means we cannot know from our own experience what another person's experience is actually like. For this reason, it is often better to be quite vague and to keep our comments to a minimum, unless there are good reasons to do otherwise.

Example: Self-disclosing past experiences (truanting)

Practitioner: I never used to like going to school so I know a bit about what it's like to have to go somewhere that you don't enjoy. In my case, I managed to keep going because I found a teacher who I could really talk to. Is there any teacher, or pupil (student) that you like or get on with quite well?

Service user: There's a few people I like the look of but I don't come across them.

Practitioner: Well, maybe it's our task to ensure that you do come across them. How does that sound?

Service user: Dunno . . .

Example: Self-disclosing past experiences (depression)

Practitioner: I have had bouts of depression in the past and so I have some idea about how you're feeling but people experience depression in very different ways. Can you describe what this depression is like for you and when it started?

Service user: Do you still suffer from depression?

Practitioner: No, I'm fine now. It may be important to say that depression can and does lift. What we have to look at is what will help you to overcome this depression.

Some practitioners would not feel comfortable disclosing personal information of this kind and that is a valid position. There are no hard-and-fast rules. However, it is important to use self-disclosure thoughtfully. If there is any indication that it may not be received well, I would avoid self-disclosure.

Endings: disengaging and termination skills

According to Kadushin, 'preparation for termination [of the interview] begins at the very beginning of the interview' (Kadushin 1990: 206). This perspective encourages us to think of our contact with people as complete experiences: as encounters that have a beginning, middle and end, all of which should be considered at the planning and preparation stage of the work we are about to undertake. For example, work that has a focus and purpose should mean that we are able to identify how long the work will run and what outcome we are seeking when we reach the end.

One reason why significance is given to endings is because they provide an opportunity to do a great deal of important work. For service users who have experienced painful, abrupt and sometimes traumatizing endings in the past, experiencing a good ending can provide the chance to begin to sort out and work though any issues that inhibit them from moving forward. Some of these painful experiences may be due to unresolved grief at the premature death of someone close to them. Other experiences may be due to social workers and other significant figures leaving them without saying a proper good-bye. Children 'looked after' describe poignant experiences of feeling abandoned and their trust betrayed by social workers who never came to say good-bye, or who came only once, thereby giving them virtually no time to prepare for the fact that they may never see this important individual again.

For example, I once worked with Diane, who felt she had a special relationship with a particular health visitor: she felt understood and accepted by this individual in ways that were important. However, one day the health visitor did not turn up as agreed. In fact, she never turned up again. The reasons for her departure were never revealed to Diane but this experience continued to haunt her. It acted as a barrier when Diane encountered other professionals, despite the years that had elapsed, so much so that at the beginning of my work with Diane, the focus had to change (but not the overall purpose) in order to address the grief and anger that she felt about being abandoned in this way. Perhaps something untoward happened to this health visitor. We will never know. What we do know is that it is likely that Diane could have adjusted to her health visitor's untimely departure had she been offered some kind of explanation – something that said to Diane that she was important. This example shows how crucial it is that we do not forget or underestimate our importance to the service users we come into contact with.

To provide a good ending allows the opportunity for individuals to work through what it feels like to be left or to be left behind. It also provides an opportunity for people to experience what a good, well thought-out ending should involve. For example, a good ending can allow the understanding, knowledge or wisdom gained to be reviewed and consolidated in ways that can be built on and used in the future. However, some individuals find endings very hard, perhaps because they come from a history of being 'let down' and failed. As a result, changes of any kind, but particularly endings, can feel very final and devastating. For this reason, it is essential to remember that endings can give rise to a whole range of unexpected emotions. These include feelings of bewilderment, helplessness, fear and a terrifying sense of aloneness, abandonment and rejection. These reactions can happen, perhaps less intensely, when we go away on holiday or are absent for other reasons, but may remain hidden because it can be difficult for service users to reveal how much they have come to rely on us. For these reasons it is important that we do not underestimate our significance, nor the impact that an ending can bring about.

Ending an interview

Interviews have enormous variations and so too do their endings. Where a clear time boundary has been stated at the beginning with regular but unobtrusive time checks and reminders, one can assume that most people will feel ready to end the interview. However, despite these boundaries and safeguards, it can be hard for some service users to 'let go' and to move on. Some desperately try to get all they can out of the interview – right up to the end. As a result, the interview can end up being drawn to a close in a way that feels rushed, with insufficient time to review what has been covered or to work through any feelings triggered by our departure.

One way that people reveal a difficulty working within boundaries can be encountered in the form of 'doorknob revelations'. These occur where significant or painful information is revealed at the end of the interview, as we are about to leave. As a practitioner, these revelations put us in a difficult 'no-win' situation. To extend the time boundary could mean we have lost control of it, and could also make us late for other appointments, but to be too rigid could involve missing an opportunity to understand the service user better. Also, on occasion it can be very important to show that we are willing to change the time boundary – to be flexible and to adapt – in order to meet the needs being expressed. Whether we decide to respond or not, the request and our response should be reviewed and considered in terms of the overall purpose that has already been agreed. There are no easy solutions to these difficulties except to provide an opportunity early in the interview for service users to talk about what it feels like when the end of an interview is in sight.

Example: An uncomplicated ending of an interview

Practitioner: Okay. We've got ten minutes left and I wonder how you would like to use the rest of the time we have?

Service user: Can we talk about what will happen when my husband comes out of prison?

Example: A difficult ending of an interview ('doorknob revelations')

Practitioner: It's 10.20 which means we have 10 minutes left. I wonder if we could use the time remaining to look at what we've talked about and then to decide what we plan to cover when we meet again next week. How does that sound to you?

Service user: Okay but there's something I want to tell you before you go. You know I said my mother died of cancer when I was 7. Well that wasn't right. My aunt told me last year that she killed herself. That's why I went to live with my aunt – there was no one else to take care of me. [She begins to cry]

Practitioner: I'm sorry. [Pause] I did not realize that your mother died in that way. That's very upsetting for you to hear. You said your aunt told you this last year. What prompted her to tell you then, Sarah? [This ill-timed question is ignored]

Service user: [Sarah begins to sob]

Practitioner: It's okay . . . Keep going. It must have been a real shock to you to hear this. [Pause] I'm glad you've found a way to tell me.

Service user: [Still sobbing deeply]

Practitioner: [After a reasonable time has elapsed and Sarah's sobbing has begun to be less intense] I can see that you're very upset and I feel for you but I'm afraid I have to go in a minute because I have to be elsewhere.

Service user: [No reply]

Practitioner: Sarah, is there anyone you would like me to contact who could come over now to be with you?

Service user: [No reply]

Practitioner: [Pause] Sarah, would it help if I asked your aunt to come across? How does that sound?

Service user: No. I don't want my aunt. I'm dead angry with her for not telling me sooner.

Practitioner: Okay. I understand. But who can I ask instead? Who would be better?

Service user: Peter, my boyfriend.

Practitioner: Okay. Can I have Peter's phone number so that I can contact him? [After contacting Peter] Before I go, let me get my diary and we'll make another time to meet before next week.

It is important to note that the sense of time we feel when someone is crying is very similar to the time we feel when people are silent. It can seem that the individual has been silent or tearful for longer than they have in reality. Unless deeply distressed, most people tend not to cry for long periods but this does not make the experience of crying any easier to bear for everyone concerned. It is important to check how people are feeling after a prolonged tearful experience. Some may feel physically sick or have a headache. Others may appear bewildered, as if in an altered state. Where this is the case, it is important to ensure the individual arrives home safely.

Closing the case and ending the relationship

Closing a case appropriately where we are ending the prospect of future contact can be one of the most difficult yet important skills to acquire (Kadushin 1990: 206–17). It is made more difficult to achieve when, through lack of resources, other forms of help are not forthcoming. This is particularly troubling when working with people who do not have the emotional, practical or material resources needed to manage without support of a particular kind. These concerns are very real. Sometimes this can lead to a situation where we continue to work with service users longer than is appropriate. We may be justifying these in sophisticated ways but, nevertheless, extending our involvement longer than appropriate can create a situation where our work becomes purposeless and devoid of direction. It can also result in an unhealthy dependency being created, based as much on our own concerns as those of the service user. This is not the hallmark of a competent practitioner. Focused, thoughtful and sensitive supervision can be enormously helpful in addressing these difficulties.

Under ideal circumstances, cases should be terminated at a point that has been mutually agreed: when goals have been reached or the time allocated for the work has come to an end and the service user feels ready to end the contact. Well planned endings often involve a tapering down of services, for example extending the length of time between appointments. This then also allows for the progress to be properly evaluated against agreed goals, aims and objectives. This may include identifying how to build on what has already been learned and achieved, perhaps by referring the individual to other appropriate agencies, as well as providing the opportunity to work through difficulties, such as those triggered by separation and loss. It also allows the service user the chance to look ahead, and to propose appropriate courses of action, including where to find additional help if this is needed.

One of the most valuable skills in relation to endings involves encouraging people to bring other people into their lives to replace us, by helping them to turn to others who can provide the care, concern, guidance and support that they need. However, for a range of different and complex reasons, in practice many endings are not mutually agreed nor carefully planned and prepared. As a result, they do not leave either party with a sense that there has been a satisfactory completion of an important and valuable piece of work. Closing cases at an inappropriate point does little to enhance the reputation of social work. However, where resources are limited, cases may have to be closed in less than ideal circumstances. Other agencies may request our continued involvement but do so without taking into account the fact that resources allocated to one case necessarily involve those resources being unavailable elsewhere. This highlights the complexities involved in social work and the difficult decisions we have to make. It can leave us in a 'no-win' situation and vulnerable to attack, which in turn can affect our judgement about whether or not to close a case.

Example: **Preparing for the contact and relationship to end**

Practitioner: Greg, You may recall that our agreement was to work together for six months. You may also remember that three months into our work, when we'd reached the half-way point, we agreed to review our progress. We now have eight weeks remaining, which means that we will meet eight more times before we stop meeting. Endings can be difficult but they can be made easier by talking things through and by looking at what it will be like when we stop seeing one another. What comes to your mind when I say that our work will be ending in eight weeks' time?

Service user: I don't think I'd realized that we only have eight weeks left. I have been thinking in terms of months and two months seems a long way off. But eight weeks, or eight more meetings, seems like no time at all. I am already feeling that I would find it difficult to manage without your help.

Practitioner: It's good that you're in touch with how you're feeling. Let's look at this a little more. What do you think you will miss most about not seeing me?

Service user: Having someone to talk to. I know lots of people but it's hard to talk. You let me say whatever comes into my head and you never tell me off or say that I am wrong or stupid or tell me to shut up.

Practitioner: That's right. Part of our agreement was to work together to help you to trust your thinking. When you're not scared or worried about being criticized, you think very well. You know what you want even if you don't always know how to get it. The question we must now think about is who would be the best person for you to turn to when our work and relationship comes to an end?

Service user: No one.

Practitioner: Let's try that question again. We need to be sure that there definitely isn't someone out there before we look at the possibility of finding new friends and relationships. Of all the people you know, who is the easiest person for you to talk to?

Service user: My friend John.

Practitioner: Right. What is it about John that makes it easy for you to talk to him?
Service user: He never puts me down. My parents put me down all the time but John doesn't.
Practitioner: So, what John and I have in common is that we don't criticize you or put you down?
Service user: Yes.
Practitioner: Who else do you know who doesn't put you down?
Service user: No one.
Practitioner: Let me put this another way. Who do you know who doesn't like being put down?
Service user: My sister. She hates being put down and my parents have done that to her a lot.
Practitioner: Good. Now you are able to name two people who you think might be good to talk to about things that are important to you when our work comes to an end: John and your sister. You have also been able to say why these people might be good to talk to – because they are less likely to put you down or to criticize you. What you have said is very important. Over the next eight weeks, I want to suggest that one of our tasks will be to spend some time trying to help you to strengthen your links with John and your sister – and any other relationships that come to mind that may be valuable to you – so that when the time comes for us to end our work together, you have other people to turn to.

If Greg's contact with John and his sister does not work out well, it may be worth considering meeting them. The purpose of this meeting would be to try to sort out and work through issues that inhibit Greg forming a relationship with them. It is likely that difficulties encountered here happen in other situations.

Conclusion: interviews as 'positive experiences'

It is likely that many of the 20 interventions described in this chapter already form part of the skills repertoire of most social workers. In addition, the task of interviewing can be thought of as an intervention in its own right because of the opportunity it provides to gain a greater understanding of people and their situations. This in itself can bring about change. For these reasons, interviewing skills are as important to experienced practitioners as newly qualified staff because they help to ensure that our work has a structure and purpose, with clear objectives located within a meaningful value base. They are also crucial when we encounter difficult or chaotic situations or complex and intractable problems. For example, as an experienced practitioner I still find myself needing to draw on interviewing techniques when I encounter situations that I find overwhelming or frightening, or when I am tired and lacking in concentration at the end of a difficult day. They act as a safeguard – as a compass when I find myself lost in the wilderness of my own preoccupations and fears. The following two chapters continue this theme and explore interventions that can be used to help people to move their lives forward and to bring about change.

5 PROVIDING HELP, DIRECTION AND GUIDANCE

Unlike in Chapter 4, the interventions I describe in the first part of this chapter describe reactions that are not solely the domain of professionals: family, friends, neighbours, concerned individuals or strangers can be skilled in helping a human being who needs help. As practitioners, our role and responsibilities result in different expectations. Accountability is different. The second part covers skills that are more specialist. The following skills are described:

- giving advice
- providing information
- providing explanations
- offering encouragement and validation
- providing reassurance
- using persuasion and being directive
- providing practical and material assistance
- providing support
- providing care
- modelling and social skills training
- reframing
- offering interpretations
- adaptations
- counselling skills
- containing anxiety

Providing help

CCETSW uses the word 'help' throughout *Quality Assurance*; for example, 'helping children and adults to change'. When defining social work, the requirement is that social workers will provide 'appropriate levels' of support and care (CCETSW 1995a: 16). In addressing this requirement, CCETSW recognizes the skills involved in trying to decide what kind of help may be needed and how to offer this in ways that are personally and culturally acceptable to the individual. These skills are at the heart of social work but difficult to acquire. Nevertheless, according to England, 'good social workers *know*, through their experience, the value of their helping work with clients. That value cannot be abandoned' (England 1986: 4, original emphasis).

It is the uncertain nature of the value of helping – what it means to give and to receive help – that must be unravelled, clarified and articulated so that the essential part that help plays in sustaining and creating positive change can be identified and utilized to the fullest. To fail to enter into this dialogue about the value of helping leaves us caught in an ambivalence – trapped between those who desire to care for vulnerable people within a 'caring society', and those who despise and attack vulnerability and who demean those who care for vulnerable people. Without this clarification, we are open to being stereotyped as ineffective 'do-gooders', where our work and the help we offer is characterized as ineffective, coercive and controlling, and beyond scrutiny and evaluation (England 1986: 5).

To begin to unravel what is included in the term 'help' is difficult because there is no uniformity across social work and, as a result, being helpful can involve a range of different interventions. In an attempt to clarify the use of these terms, *practical* and *material assistance*, *support* and *care* are differentiated in this book and used to describe different activities and different skills. However, none of these interventions is mutually exclusive. For example, most problems have an emotional element. Some service users may feel ashamed or embarrassed about asking for practical assistance. In order to ensure that they can take up and utilize whatever practical help is needed, emotional support may be required (Lishman 1994: 7). The converse is not necessarily the case. Emotional support itself may be all that is required. For example, practitioners using counselling skills working with someone who has been bereaved may only work with the feelings of bereavement and loss, if practical support is being provided elsewhere.

Much of our willingness to help may be conveyed quite subtly through our behaviour. Yet, despite our best efforts, some service users may still dislike having to seek or ask for help. These negative feelings may include a concern about how they might be seen by others, or have their roots in a fierce sense of independence. The possible responses are endless and very much dependent on what it was like for the individual to have to rely on others in the past. Memories of earlier failures, disappointments or humiliating experiences can result in people feeling guarded. Some professionals respond inappropriately, by treating service users like children or as if they are stupid. Others demand compliance, insisting that service users should be grateful, cooperative and deferential. Too often, this results in people feeling robbed of their self-respect and sense of personal autonomy. It can be difficult for any individual to accept and to benefit from services when these are offered in a demeaning way. Older people are particularly susceptible to this kind of patronizing behaviour. So too are children and young people and others, such as people from minority groups, whose right to be respected does not always come automatically.

All professions are prone to treat people badly, sometimes in ways that are less obvious, such as making people wait for long periods. Citizens and patients charters are designed to address these difficulties and inequalities but have limitations because they neither guarantee people's entitlement to certain services nor the right to be treated fairly (Adams 1998: 193). While there is no room for complacency, social work is noticeable in its commitment to embrace practices that demonstrate anti-discriminatory and anti-oppressive perspectives (Thompson 1997: 241).

According to Howe, 'helping is a test of the helper as a person' (1987: 113). This statement emphasizes that much of our ability to give help appropriately relates to our own personal history of being helped and our ongoing capacity to receive help from others in our everyday lives. It reinforces the importance of self-knowledge and of our being in touch with what we feel when we are at the receiving end of help and the anxieties felt from being beholden to or having to depend on others. Howe's statement also emphasizes the importance of creating and sustaining a more equal, mutual and reciprocal relationship when working alongside or in partnership with service users. For example, I once worked with a social worker who had a remarkable capacity for being able to empathize accurately with service users and to translate that understanding into appropriate and creative forms of help. However, his ability to communicate that understanding was on the whole quite poor. After a time, and some serious misunderstandings, it came to light that the reason for this difficulty lay in the fact that this worker was brought up in a mixed race, immigrant family where the language used took the form of commands: 'do this/do that'. Questions or requests were not the kind of phrases commonly used. Although his language had changed over the years, the legacy of this early form of communication remained, particularly when he felt under attack or nervous. This example highlights how our early experiences can affect our capacity to provide help, both negatively and positively.

Providing help also offers an opportunity to give more than practical services. It allows us to stretch the experience across other needs. For example, in setting up a nursery place for a child, we could use this opportunity to pass over a sense of enthusiasm for the possibilities this opens up for the mother or father, as well as for the child. We could use it as an opportunity to explore what direction this parent might want for their life and for their child. Clearly, encouraging someone to pursue their hopes and desires in this way has to be tempered by the reality of the situation. Yet too much realism can be a reflection of our own depressed outlook, and dampen enthusiasm and the opportunity to herald something new and exciting.

Taking hold of opportunities and stretching them in this way can demand a great deal from us and, inevitably, we cannot always put forward our *best selves* because there will be times when we do not feel able to respond in this way, when we find ourselves guarding resources as if they are our personal possessions or when we feel too put-upon, depleted and empty to be able to give at all, let alone to give generously. Service users may pick up on this fact, and in such a situation it may be wise for us to acknowledge our weariness and temporarily bow out as gracefully as possible, in the hope that we can return soon with renewed energy. This may be preferable to our struggling to give from a depleted part of ourselves. If persistent, difficulties of this kind can mark the beginning of burn-out: that is, a situation where we feel dis-illusioned, undervalued and exhausted by expectations and demands that feel overwhelming and impossible to process (Feltham and Dryden 1993: 23; Payne 1997: 23).

Giving advice

Advice and guidance are sometimes used interchangeably because both involve recommending something or directing an individual towards one or several courses of action. In a professional context, both can carry the expec-tation that our views are backed by knowledge and/or experience. However, guidance tends to sound less prescriptive (vocational or career guidance agen-cies) whereas the word advice tends to have a more definite flavour.

Advice is often sought either to help identify the problem clearly or to help identify possible solutions, but should be offered with the greatest care because we can be inaccurate or simply wrong in the advice we offer. Offering advice inappropriately can also reinforce a sense of personal inadequacy or be experienced as intrusive (Feltham and Dryden 1993: 7). For these reasons, it is important to be judicious and thoughtful about the kind of advice we give, perhaps only offering advice when asked and with the proviso that we may be wrong. These safeguards help to ensure that any advice given is sensitive to an individual's personal situation and expectations, including their cultural and social context.

In recent years some social workers have felt reluctant to give advice. It can be seen as 'imposing our values and morals on our clients' (Lishman 1994: 83); as contradicting the principle of client self-determination (Biestek 1961); as failing to acknowledge the importance of service users taking on the role of 'experts' in relation to their own lives; as patronizing and disempowering; or as discouraging self-sufficiency and personal autonomy by creating an unhealthy dependency. As a result, offering advice can generate anxiety among practitioners, in case we give the 'wrong' advice and are held account-able. One way to manage these anxieties is to be honest and open about what we do and do not know, and to avoid bluffing or hedging our responses. How-ever, certain areas of knowledge are required of us and are essential to the social work task, which means that in certain situations we have a responsi-bility to offer advice and to provide advice that should include, as a minimum, 'detailed, accurate and up-to-date knowledge about the law, welfare rights and local community facilities' (Davies 1981: 52). This links to the point made earlier about the importance of social workers developing a sound knowledge base.

It is interesting to note that service users do not always share our reservations about being given advice (Lishman 1994: 8–9). As with the offer of explanations, advice can be particularly important for people who feel bewildered and confused or who need to base their decision on our opinions. For example, offering advice for people who have been recently bereaved can help to structure what they have to do and in what order. For this reason it is important for service users to decide for themselves whether or not they want to hear advice that is on offer, rather than us deciding for them. Most service users weigh up the advice they are given quite carefully and will tend to ignore advice that seems inappropriate. However, the timing of advice giving is important. As a general rule, it should only be offered when other possibilities have been exhausted and the decision-making and problem-solving processes have broken down. It is important that advice is not 'thrown in' at the end of the session, as a parting shot, because this does not give the individual the opportunity to take new information on board and to work through whatever thoughts and feelings have emerged.

Providing information

Recent years have seen the development of specialized information services and centres, such as those in relation to housing, welfare rights, legal rights and those providing information on local resources, such as self-help groups and social networks (Lishman 1994: 78). This development has left some social workers unsure about whether it is appropriate to offer certain kinds of practical help, such as welfare rights checks, where specialist expertise may be more accurate and up-to-date. Nevertheless, even if we do not undertake welfare rights checks ourselves, it is essential that we know where these more specialist advice centres are and the nature of their referral criteria.

In more general terms, providing information can be central to problem-solving and the decision-making process. For this reason, it is important that any information offered is accurate. Updating the information we have on local resources can be a time-consuming task, particularly without proper organizational structures to feed in new information and developments. However, for service users to act on information later found to be wrong can result in a serious loss of trust and confidence in the competence of social work as a profession.

Where the task involves referring people on to other agencies or organizations, it helps to check the accuracy of the information to hand, perhaps by telephoning the agency before referring people on, having ensured first that we have the service user's permission to do so. It is alarming how many service users are given incorrect information at this stage: for some, it must feel like being sent on a wild goose chase, where only the most charmed or most determined get through. Checking disabled access is particularly important.

The following points need to be stressed. Anxiety and fear can interfere with an individual's capacity to listen and to digest information, because emotional energy is being taken up attending to these anxieties. This may be conveyed by the individual appearing confused or preoccupied. Where this is the case, it can be helpful to repeat information, using a language that is simple, steady and accessible. This is particularly true when communicating bad news, such as details of an accident or illness. If this does not work and the individual still seems confused and lost, we need to consider ending the session.

Again, it is vital not to give important information right at the end of a session when concentration may have lapsed: sometimes it is essential to be present to see how well information has been processed. Where we suspect that a person might forget the details covered, a follow-up letter may prove helpful but only where we know the service user has adequate literacy skills and where receiving a letter would not be experienced as daunting.

Leaflets and other written information

The importance of providing written information in the form of leaflets and handouts is likely to depend on the situation and what knowledge the individual already has and needs. This may vary over time. For example, an asylum seeker who has recently arrived in this country is likely to need a great deal of information, which may have to be translated. This may entail explaining basic information, such as how different services and government departments operate and how to access these. For example, it can save a great deal of time and anguish if we explain the difference between social security and social services. Leaflets must be adapted where service users' capacity to understand and to take in information is limited. Special care needs to be taken in relation to differences of age, physical disability, hearing or sight impairments, emotional state, literacy and comprehension skills, and so on. There are many imaginative ways to overcome such difficulties, such as using drawings, pictures, figurines and videos (Lishman 1994: 82–3).

It can be too easy for people to be 'fobbed off' with information, as if by handing out a leaflet, we are always giving something useful, helpful and appropriate. Sadly, that may not be the case and, instead, we could be handing out worry or confusion, particularly if the leaflet is not written in a way that meets the needs of the person seeking this information. The test lies in whether they were able to use this information, and the best and easiest way to find this out is to ask for feedback. Another way would be to read the information or leaflet as if we were a stranger to the issue – a visitor from Mars – to see if it is informative. We may find, as is sometimes the case, that too much knowledge is assumed: this can raise more questions than answers.

Information giving, whether given verbally or in written form, can be seen as an opportunity to provide new meaning and understanding. As a symbolic communication, providing advice, guidance or explanations can have far-reaching consequences (Lishman 1994: 15–19). Information that is passed over well not only helps people to make an informed choice but can also give confidence in a way that encourages individuals to act independently and effectively on their own behalf in the future (Millar et al. 1992: 108). Therefore, how we communicate information can be as important as the information itself. Leaflets handed out with an attitude of indifference, or as an afterthought, are likely to be treated in the same way. For this reason, it can be helpful to bring the leaflet/information 'alive', by reading it beforehand, marking those areas considered relevant and important and by making it personal by adding the individual's name to it. These gestures are important because they reveal a commitment and thoughtfulness: they can also save valuable time.

Finally, it is important to note that under the Disabled Persons Act 1986, social work departments and voluntary agencies have a duty to provide leaflets and information in an appropriate and accessible format for people with disability, such as providing information in Braille, or via tape recordings. Equally, it is required that information is provided in the language of the people who use the service. This expectation also extends to information on health and welfare issues. For example, the current Attendance Allowance leaflet (DS 702) is available in several other languages: Bengali, Chinese, Greek, Gujarati, Hindi, Punjabi, Turkish, Urdu, Vietnamese and Welsh.

Providing explanations

Explaining is a core skill in social work, and important in other health and welfare settings, but it is a subject covered very little in social work texts and in communication studies research. Brown proposes two reasons for this neglect:

> First, explaining is a taken-for-granted activity; a great deal of time is spent explaining in everyday life and in various professional contexts, so it is assumed that everyone knows how to explain. Second, for some professional groups such as counsellors, therapists and social workers, explaining has associations with authority-centred approaches, with telling, instructing and didactics; hence the study of explaining is shunned.
>
> (Brown 1986: 201)

Explanations differ from advice and guidance because their purpose is not to offer direction but to illuminate, clarify, reconcile or interpret events with a view to providing greater understanding. They attempt to throw light on the cause, nature and interrelationship of different thoughts, feelings and events.

Explanations can be divided into three forms: illustrations, demonstrations and verbal explanations. Of these, the focus of this section is on verbal explanations, which can be seen in terms of three main categories, each addressing a different type of question:

- interpretative explanations – what?
- descriptive explanations – how?
- reason-giving explanations – why?

(Brown 1986: 203–4)

Some explanations may involve all three categories, in an attempt to describe the problem or situation in words that can be understood and absorbed, so that a new understanding can be reached. This endeavour is more likely to succeed if it is, firstly, sensitive to the service user's thoughts and feelings; secondly, delivered in a way that is interesting, involved, clear and well structured; and, thirdly, where the communication has been planned in a way that maximizes learning and understanding – 'a little remembered is better than a lot forgotten'.

Responsibility for an unsuccessful communication should lie with us and not be blamed, implicitly, on service users. One way to check whether a new understanding has been reached is to ask service users to recall what they have heard or to ask them to apply this understanding to specific and relevant situations in their lives. This needs to be undertaken sensitively, drawing on points made earlier in the text on the 'nature of helping', and the importance of understanding the meaning given to experiences.

Explanations as a way of addressing emotional needs

In relation to emotional needs, explanations can be profoundly important for people who are confused or who easily become confused because they have little confidence or trust in their own thinking and how to understand and link different experiences. Some of this confusion may be short-term and likely to lift relatively easily. However, for some people this state of confusion is severe and enduring, and in some cases may be the result of discontinuities and disruptions in childhood. For example, I once worked with a young woman, Jo, whose family was always moving house, possibly to avoid debts, although this was never known for sure. Her parents never appeared to offer any explanation about events, which meant that there was never any transition or bridge between one experience and another. This situation reflected a serious lack of consistency and predictability in Jo's life. This difficulty was compounded by the fact that Jo was not a 'wanted child'. She felt this acutely, and it was later confirmed by her mother, who admitted she had tried to have an abortion when she knew she was pregnant with Jo. The result of these experiences meant that Jo lived with the dread, throughout her childhood, that one day she would come home and find her family gone and her house empty; she would be left behind, with nowhere to go and no means of knowing where to find her family.

Jo found it virtually impossible to link events or to bring cause and effect together. She thought 'things just happened' for no reason, or no reason she could work out. The absence of words and explanations from her parents meant that Jo found it hard to sort out one feeling from another or to know which feelings belonged to her and which belonged to others (Howe et al. 1999: 145). This profound sense of confusion and bewilderment haunted Jo's struggle in the world and, when she left care, she eventually became rootless, living in doorways, with no sense of belonging anywhere, as if searching for something. One of her greatest joys was to have things explained to her, which she once described as 'a word lullaby', because it attempted to provide some order, certainty and predictability in a world that otherwise felt frightening and beyond comprehension.

The importance of explaining the world and what is happening, for service users who have not had this experience in childhood, needs to be emphasized. It is for this reason that story-telling (Jewett 1997: 119–23) or narrative accounts (Shaw 1996: 62–3) are important. We can recognize these gaps and confusion when, as with Jo, we encounter service users who regularly manifest a profound bewilderment, asking what appear to be naive questions but with little capacity to remember the answer. Such bewilderment can be painful and terrifying. For this reason, the ability to explain situations to service users – to help them to understand past and present events and future possibilities – in a language and tone that is accessible and kind, is one of the most important communication skills that we can develop as practitioners.

Offering encouragement and validation

Offering positive encouragement can be an important intervention within social work. However, according to Lishman, research suggests that these interventions may not be widely used by practitioners:

> There seems [to be] general hesitancy or ambivalence in social work about the value of explicitly conveying approval or positive encouragement. This may reflect in part a cultural bias against giving or accepting positive feedback, an anxiety that giving approval can be patronizing. It may also reflect underlying values and prejudices in social work.
>
> (Lishman 1994: 51)

An exception is where encouragement forms part of a particular practice approach as, for example, in Rogers's (1957) concept of *unconditional positive regard* or where, as with praise, encouragements are used as 'support interventions' (Kadushin 1990: 175) intended to ensure that certain options are explored or undertakings completed. In relation to cognitive-behavioural approaches, encouragement and validation are described in terms of *positive reinforcement* (Sheldon 1995: 63; Cigno and Bourn 1998: 18).

Encouragement can be seen in two ways: to help service users *towards* or *away from* a particular course of action, experience, thought or feeling. Both can be particularly helpful when individuals have poor self-esteem (Mruk 1999: 153), little self-confidence or limited experience, or when they feel overwhelmed and afraid of what they may encounter. Encouragement can help to smooth the journey towards these experiences or can be a low-key means of drawing service users away from certain actions or activities that may be dangerous or damaging, and/or pose a threat to themselves or to others.

Some practitioners feel reluctant to attempt to steer another person's behaviour in this way. The concern is that they could be used unethically, perhaps as a means of controlling or manipulating individuals in a particular direction: these dangers have to be guarded against. Nevertheless, some people need encouragement to keep them going and give them confidence and, although it may not always be appropriate to respond to these needs, they should not be ignored. A further difficulty is that it can be hard to know how to express our encouragement in ways that do not sound soppy or 'over-the-top'. This skill comes with practice and experience and is not always an easy balance to find.

Validation

Whereas encouragement is oriented to inspire or motivate people to think or act differently *before* an event or experience, validations tend to provide a positive appraisal *after* the event. In this sense they are a form of feedback but often have a more personal orientation because they provide an opportunity to applaud the commitment and effort put into a particular situation and to celebrate any achievements or personal learning that have been gained. Validation of this kind is important when working with people who lack confidence in themselves, perhaps in relation to their appearance or in their ability to make sound decisions and to act independently. However, care must be taken that the validations we give are honest and truthful and not exaggerated or given merely to make someone 'feel better'. Validations sound hollow or patronizing if they are not based on actual abilities or real achievements.

Providing reassurance

Offering reassurance can be an important way to ease anxiety and uncertainty – to smooth troubled waters – and to provide comfort. This can be particularly important for times when an individual has lost touch with a more balanced view of what is happening in their lives and, as a result, needs someone to assure them that, despite their worries, everything is basically in order. However, reassurance should not be offered where we are not confident that our words will come true. To be over optimistic or over reassuring when the outcome cannot be clearly predicted or controlled is to run the risk of letting people down and putting our relationship and credibility in danger. If our reassurances are later proved wrong or unfounded, this could seriously – perhaps even irreparably – undermine confidence in our judgement. It is worth remembering that people can feel reassured indirectly by the way we conduct ourselves, including the way we dress (Kadushin 1990: 275–8; Lishman 1994: 18), and by our ensuring that they are treated with respect (Clark 2000: 50).

Some people repeatedly seek reassurance yet somehow they remain agitated, as if the words of reassurance have not been meaningful – have not touched them or 'got through'. Where this is the case, repeating reassurances is unlikely to produce any reduction in the anxieties being experienced and, in fact, can be counterproductive because 'the repeated seeking of reassurance undermines the person's confidence to deal with the problem himself' [*sic*] (Trower *et al.* 1988: 110). Instead, it may help to draw attention to the fact that our words are not reassuring and to ask the individual to explore what is happening to them at this moment, in this 'here-and-now' conversation. The person needing reassurance may not be able to explain or to understand their behaviour but this line of questioning can help to break into the repetitive nature of the communication and mark the beginning of a real engagement.

In these and similar situations, it can be helpful to ask ourselves 'What is this individual trying to communicate about themselves?' or 'What or who have I become for this person?' and to feed back our thoughts and feelings. For example, it can help to ask 'What do you think I could give you that would be useful or helpful to you right now'? This helps to break into the repetitious nature of the communication and establish a more direct rapport.

Using persuasion and being directive

Persuading service users to behave differently or to see themselves in a different light can be very difficult. People can become very fixed in their ways, and although this intervention attempts to create some possibility for change, it also runs the risk of our being too coercive and influential, sometimes to the point where we persuade service users to do something they are not yet ready to do. This can foreclose exploration and restrict the opportunity for people to find their own way in relation to decisions that affect their lives. Too often the result is failure, which can have a negative impact on a person's confidence and their hopes for the future.

In any attempt to influence others, power differentials have to be taken into account. Being persuaded by someone in authority can feel like an instruction or a command – as a 'should' and an 'ought' – where the only option possible would be to comply. Failing to acknowledge inequalities of this kind can mean that we create or reinforce feelings of poor self-esteem or personal inadequacy. It is important that these feelings, and the reality of power differentials, are addressed (O'Sullivan 1999: 118; Clark 2000: 200).

In some professional circles, such as medicine or dentistry, persuasion is more highly valued than it is in social work, where it tends to be viewed with reserve and suspicion because it involves attempting to influence people. However, this can be a denial of the sometimes uncomfortable fact that, as human beings, we all try to influence one another to lesser and greater degrees, whether this is undertaken in blatant or subtle ways.

Although non-directive approaches seem to be preferred by social work practitioners, particularly those embracing a more client-centred/person-centred approach, there will always be situations that warrant our being directive. For example, there can be risks involved if we do not attempt to persuade someone away from danger, or when we do not use our knowledge and experience to direct someone towards a course of action that could be of benefit. The key is to use persuasion – as with all other directive interventions – judiciously, basing our decision making on the interest of the service user and on the best information we have about the potential advantages of a particular course of action. There are times when we need to 'respond to a client's need for structure and direction' (Lishman 1994: 116) by being more directive, but this should be undertaken as a short-term intervention.

Being directive and persuasive is more likely to be successful where we have a good relationship with the individual in question, where the person is open and responsive to our viewpoint, and where we feel we have sufficient knowledge and experience to steer people in the ways suggested. For further reading on the use of more directive interventions, cognitive-behavioural approaches provide good examples, such as those found under the heading *positive* and *negative reinforcement* (see Sheldon 1995: 63–4).

Providing practical and material assistance

One of the ways that we communicate our care, concern and commitment to others is through offering practical and material assistance. Research findings indicate that service users greatly value being given practical help, particularly when it addresses problems they are struggling to deal with themselves, such as writing letters, transportation or acting as an advocate (Mayer and Timms 1970; Fisher 1983; Lishman 1994: 8–11). Equally, being given access to resources that would otherwise be difficult to access – such as day-care provision, after-school activities, respite accommodation or laundry facilities – can greatly ease the pressures and stresses that service users experience, often on a daily basis (Dartington Social Research Unit 1995; Thoburn *et al* 1995; Thoburn 1997). In this respect, the limited financial assistance available to service users remains a serious problem, given the fact that, for many, poverty is the major issue (Clarke 1993; Jones 1997, 1998). Sainsbury *et al.* summarize the situation as follows:

> Social workers (compared with their clients) overestimated the relative helpfulness of insight work, the use of authority and giving advice, but underestimated the helpfulness experienced by clients as a result of material and financial help and negotiations with other agencies on their behalf.
>
> (Sainsbury *et al.* 1982: 19–20)

Two problems exist in relation to providing practical and material assistance. First, it is sometimes undertaken without a clear sense of purpose or strategy in terms of a particular outcome or goal: 'rushing about merely doing might say more about needing to be helpful as opposed to trying to understand the meaning of someone else's experience' (Coulshed 1991: 2). Such activity is devoid of purpose and, therefore, prone to having little real impact. For England, providing more 'active' forms of material and practical assistance should be offered in order to improve a service user's 'coping capacity', that is, they should form part of an identified strategy and always be related to the service user's 'objective resources' (England 1986: 14).

The second problem relates to the fact that the request for practical assistance may not meet a response at all. Instead, emotional support or counselling may be offered, perhaps because this accords with the orientation of the practitioner or because practical or material problems, such as those relating to social security benefits, debts, poverty, homelessness, unemployment, ill health, and so on, are not given the priority they deserve by the practitioner within the employing agency. Much of the time this shift towards counselling and away from providing practical support goes unnoticed, but can become evident when the service user's perceptions of their problems and their preferred solutions are compared to those of practitioners and this difference or discrepancy is noted.

Providing support

'Support' is one of the most imprecise words used within social work. It can mean almost anything from offering assistance, backing, sustenance, reassurance, guidance, encouragement, validation, care, concern and love (Feltham and Dryden 1993: 187). For this reason it is important that we are clear what we mean when we use the term. In this book, 'support' is used to describe *emotional support*; that is, responding to the need that we all have to be able to turn to a person, perhaps located in an agency, who can give us appropriate back-up during periods of strain, stress or crisis, so that we can continue to cope and to keep going. Talking through problems with a sympathetic listener is a common source of emotional support. This may sometimes be described as social support (Sheppard 1997), which may be preferable because the word 'emotional' may be exposing or off-putting.

Ideally, this kind of support will be met by partners, family, friends and neighbours (Thoburn 1997: 292). However, where this is not the case, individuals may need help to locate appropriate sources of support, such as a support group for parents or mental health 'survivors'. There is much evidence from mental health and child-care research that the availability of support is associated with lower levels of stress and can result in, for example, more competent parenting (Thoburn 1997: 292), and in fewer admissions to psychiatric hospitals (Sheppard 1997: 321). For some people, however, this support may not exist, or may be too difficult to access. For others, the support may be offered too late, or be inappropriate or inadequate, perhaps because their own personal resources and support systems have become seriously depleted. In such cases, service users may look to practitioners for this kind of emotional or social support. This may be difficult to provide on an ongoing basis without adequate back-up in the form of sound, structured supervision, and peer and agency support.

The point to be stressed is that where we encounter a serious breakdown in a service user's capacity to cope with everyday tensions, our responses in terms of alternative sources of support have to be both robust and reliable, if we are to avoid a further deterioration in the quality of life for that individual. This involves our being clear about what support is needed, and is being offered, for how long, by whom and for what purpose. It also involves checking that the support is being received in the way intended and that it is helpful. When carers are asked to provide this support, they too can show signs of being unable to cope with the demands placed upon them (Phillipson 1997: 161–2).

The consequences of this kind of breakdown in support networks are profound. It can lead to greater marginalization, isolation and loneliness, and further demands being made of social services to provide alternative back-up. As practitioners, this calls for us to use our skills effectively in order to be able to create or to re-establish support networks and, in the meantime, to find ways to sustain the demands placed upon us by service users who have no alternative sources of support.

Providing care

When related to social work, notions of *care* and *caring* have many meanings, such as: care orders, *care and control, in care,* Care in the Community, care assistant, carers, care packages, care planning and care management, and many more. Implicit in these different terms is an orientation to provide for the well-being of others. To *care* could be seen as allowing ourselves to be affected emotionally by another human being, while to be *caring* could involve being able to demonstrate a warmth, gentleness, kindness and concern for others (caring *about*) or providing physical help or comfort (caring *for*).

One way to view the relationship between helping and caring is to see helping as relating to the *task,* and caring to the *process* of providing for others. Cheetham, developing a point suggested by Salisbury (1987), sees *helping* as tangible and *caring* as intangible:

> Some social work is about *helping*, while some may emphasize *caring*. Helping clients seems to imply some observable difference made to their lives; and there are indeed some quite clear-cut, tangible social work tasks, for example providing information or arranging a specific service, the presence of which can be noted as one outcome of intervention. Caring, on the other hand, may involve the intangibles of a personal relationship without necessarily making an outwardly observable difference.
> (Cheetham *et al.* 1992: 12, original emphasis)

The rewards in providing help, whether as a carer or as a professional, can be many. For example, it can be deeply satisfying to know that, through our efforts, we played some part in enabling an individual to keep going, to gain more from life or to move on to new experiences. It is this mutuality and reciprocity that motivates us to want to do our best and to care for others. This mutuality is defined as 'the recognition of mutual obligations towards others, stemming from the acceptance of a common kinship, expressed in joint action, towards a more equitable sharing of resources and responsibilities' (Holman 1993: 56).

The fact that it is predominantly women who care for others, often in difficult and pressured circumstances, has been described as 'compulsory altruism' (Land and Rose 1985). The extent of the lack of understanding in relation to the emotional, physical and social cost of caring for others was starkly demonstrated by the Audit Commission report that described 'the care provided by relatives and friends as "free" ' (Audit Commission 1992: 3; Davis and Ellis 1995: 146). An important role we could play as practitioners would be to highlight these gender inequalities and to agitate for better care, practical assistance and support for those who give and for those who receive this care.

The pitfalls in caring

The ability to provide 'appropriate levels' of support and care is a requirement laid down by CCETSW (1995a: 16). However, with few guidelines, it is not always easy to know how to pitch our care and support and there are many pitfalls. For example, our attempts to be helpful can sometimes come across as and be experienced as patronizing or condescending. Much depends on our intention, choice of words, timing and tone. It also depends on the way in which we ourselves have been cared for in our lives and how comfortable we feel in the role of helper. Where people, practitioners and service users alike, have been hurt in terms of their capacity to give and to receive – to give out and to take in – the 'give and take' that is central to creating a rapport and being empathic can be difficult to achieve without understanding and patience. When these different factors fail to fit together well, we can indeed easily fall into the trap of being patronizing or condescending, and find ourselves speaking down to the person in question. When this happens, it is important that we do not become defensive or apologetic to the point where service users feel they must neglect their own issues to care for us. Instead, it is better to try to understand how our words and gestures have been experienced and learn from our errors.

People's rights to help and the way that help is offered are important issues. People who have for years prided themselves on their ability to be self-sufficient can find the offer of help offensive or intrusive. To touch on delicate subjects is a skilful endeavour. For example, I recall once suggesting to an elderly couple living in a second floor flat that they might find a second handrail helpful. Both had fallen down the stairs on a number of occasions, but not seriously. My suggestion was poorly received; in fact it was received as an insult. It took several weeks of gentle persuasion and another fall before they felt able to consider a second rail and then with the proviso that it would be removed if they 'didn't take to it'. Luckily, it was installed by two very thoughtful council workers who played their part in helping this couple to adjust to the change: they would not now be without their rail. This example shows that unless we attend to emotional issues – in this example, the importance and meaning that this couple gave to their capacity to be independent – our efforts can be sabotaged.

In relation to the wider picture within social work, a further pitfall in relation to caring for others is that, in some professional and personal contexts, caring can be used as a means of control, to engender guilt, obligation and compliance and to take away an individual's right to self-determination and autonomy. In its blatant form, this kind of 'social control' can be challenged but it can be quite subtle and, therefore, difficult to detect and to confront, particularly in relation to vulnerable groups, such as people with learning disabilities (Clark 2000: 29). The development of 'service user movements', such as those in relation to people with disability and people in receipt of psychiatric services, challenges the way that services are controlled and highlights instead the importance of 'user-led' policies and provision (Croft and Beresford 1997: 276). Similarly, concepts such as 'normalization' and 'the social role of valorization' (Wolfensberger 1984) attempt to address the way that certain groups of people are devalued by society, stressing, in the area of disability, that disabled people have the right to lead a 'valued ordinary life', based on a belief in their equality as citizens and as human beings (Ramon 1991). In relation to social work skills, we need to take account of the wider context within which our work is located because the realities of practice may require great flexibility; we may walk in the door offering one skill and leave having offered another. At one time I found myself being asked to 'sort out' the 'problem behaviour' at a particular school, only to find myself acting in the role of advocate for young people's rights. My experience is not unique.

Modelling and social skills training

According to Feltham and Dryden, modelling is 'the behavioural/social learning method of demonstrating procedures which the service user wishes or needs to adopt' (1993: 115). These behaviours or new responses can be acquired through various processes including 'observational learning, vicarious learning, modelling, or imitation' (Sheldon 1995: 81) and can be broadly divided into two categories: inadvertent and deliberate modelling.

Inadvertent modelling refers to behaviour that the service user has learned through watching others. Most behaviour is learned in this way, both good and bad, particularly from parents and, in recent years, through the mass media:

> Modelling accounts for the acquisition of a vast range of very different behaviours: skills simple and complex, from washing dishes to brain surgery, from social good manners to conducting philosophical debate; and also those kinds of behaviours we do not designate as skills, such as reacting with anxiety to thunderstorms or being brave in the face of danger. Numerous experiments have shown that skills, attitudes and emotional responses can all be acquired through modelling.
>
> (Hudson and MacDonald 1986: 41)

In the social learning approach developed by Bandura (1977), modelling is more likely to be attractive and successful where the model is seen to have some standing and where the respect given to a model is linked to a particular behaviour. Also, it is important for there to be a similarity or shared sense of identity between subject and the model, an opportunity to practise the behaviour soon after it has been modelled, and a climate where the newly acquired behaviour is reinforced by others (Hudson and MacDonald 1986: 45).

Deliberate modelling is generally employed in order to address behavioural problems, to reduce anxiety and to help re-establish or reinforce lost or suppressed behaviours (Sheldon 1995: 87). This may involve the live enactment of certain behaviours by the practitioner and, in formal modelling, include the following steps:

1 Specify the behaviour to be demonstrated and ask the observer to attend to it
2 Arrange demonstration
3 Ask the observer to imitate the behaviour immediately after the demonstration
4 Give feedback to imitate the behaviour immediately after the demonstration
5 Give further practice, and so on

(Hudson and MacDonald 1986: 141)

Modelling is particularly useful where individuals have encountered worrying situations that they feel ill equipped to manage. In relation to service users, this intervention can be important in helping to tackle daunting situations such as court appearances, social security tribunals, and school exclusion procedures, with the practitioner running through the various stages likely to be encountered.

Social skills training

Social skills training is based on the same social learning principles used in modelling. It is most often employed in helping service users overcome behaviours that render them vulnerable to being isolated or socially excluded, or to develop and extend certain skills, such as how to respect another person's sense of space and privacy or how to be more assertive. Again, this may involve direct instruction or modelling by a practitioner, video demonstrations, role-plays and homework. A danger in relation to both modelling and social skills training is that social and cultural influences and differences may be ignored in favour of the norms of the dominant culture.

Reframing

This intervention is described little in social work texts yet it is one of the most important skills that a practitioner can have. It is a major technique of neurolinguistic programming (Feltham and Dryden 1993: 158) and family therapy (Watzlawick et al. 1974; Burnham 1986). Reframing also has much in common with cognitive-behavioural approaches where the aim is to change thought processes and behaviour. Its main advantage is that it provides an opportunity to describe a situation or behaviour from a different, more hopeful and optimistic perspective. This allows service users and practitioners to revisit decisions or opinions made previously, often by people in positions of authority, and to pose a different view of 'how situations are to be understood and what knowledge is to count as relevant' (Howe 1994: 526). As a result, factors located within the 'frame' can be viewed differently. For example, people described as having 'no motivation' can, within the same 'frame', be described as not wanting what is on offer, for very good reasons: 'For many stigmatized and oppressed groups "help" has come to equal control because that has been their experience' (Sheldon 1995: 241).

Reframing involves taking the same 'facts' but placing them in a different context or 'frame'. As a result, the 'entire meaning' is changed (Watzlawick *et al.* 1974: 95). Its purpose is to 'change the meaning that an individual or family attaches to certain behaviours or interactions in such a way as to render the situation more amenable to behavioural and/or emotional change' (Burnham 1986: 147). These redefinitions can help to lift some of the 'sting' – the guilt or shame – and help to bring the behaviour within the grasp of the individual, perhaps through normalizing it. For example, reframing can be used to view a negative behaviour in a positive light or allow a less judgemental and more compassionate understanding of events. This is particularly valuable when working with people who have little confidence or self-esteem or who are racked with self-blame or guilt, such as parents experiencing difficulties with their children. Often the messages that service users give to themselves can be deeply critical, harsh and self-punishing. Reframing offers a way to replace these painful, negative *internal conversations* with words that are more understanding, optimistic and caring. It is important to stress that for reframing to be successful it must use the same concrete facts, and the alternative 'frame' should be believable and communicated in words that can be easily understood.

Reframing can sometimes be confused with making excuses but it is not the same. Making excuses involves justifying actions, thoughts and feelings or unacceptable behaviour, sometimes because we cannot deal with the conflict this arouses in us or because we feel scared to stand our ground. However, it is important to see the 'gentle art of reframing' (Watzlawick *et al.* 1974: 92–109) in its own right as an intervention that can be enormously valuable in helping people to feel less stuck, and as a way of enabling people to move forward.

Examples

Service user: I'm too lazy to get out of bed.

Practitioner: Perhaps what you describe as being lazy is a feeling that there is nothing to get up for?

Service user: I think I'm a horrible mother. I'm really tired and bad-tempered and shout at my kids all the time . . .

Practitioner: The fact that you felt able to tell me about how you are with your children shows that you want to have a better relationship with them – that you care about them. It takes courage for a parent to admit that things are going wrong – as you just did. It gives us the chance to build on the fact that you want to do something about these difficulties.

Service user: I decided yesterday not to come to see you today because I felt you would criticize me.

Practitioner: Then you were very brave to come.

Offering interpretations

Interpretations offer a new frame of reference, based on information provided by the individual but extended to include inferences derived from that information and from the practitioner's own perceptions and intuition. Three types of interpretation are common. Firstly, in the field of therapy, particularly in psychoanalytic psychotherapy, interpretations are used to bring unconscious conflicts and motives into the conscious in order to facilitate integration through acquiring insight (Rycroft 1968: 76). This 'helps clients to understand the origins of their problems, and thereby gain more control over them and more freedom to behave differently' (McLeod 1998: 38). This kind of interpretation involves psychotherapeutic training and is, therefore, beyond the practice remit of social workers. Secondly, in relation to cognitive approaches, the emphasis is on understanding how service users interpret and misinterpret events, rather than the worker formulating interpretations (Feltham and Dryden 1993: 96). Thirdly, interpretations are used to link and to connect the significance of certain thoughts, feelings or behaviours in order to draw the service user's attention to something that they appear to be unaware of (Feltham and Dryden 1993: 96). This is the form of interpretation most used in social work and the one emphasized in this section.

As social work practitioners, there is an ongoing and understandable tendency to want to 'interpret' a service user's behaviour; that is, to link one event with another. However, this presents problems because the connections we are making may be inaccurate and difficult to evidence (in terms of 'hard facts'). It is always difficult to know with any certainty whether our awareness is accurate unless the situation or relationship is uncomplicated. If it is accurate, however, it can place us in the difficult position of knowing more about an aspect of a service user's behaviour – or life – than they themselves are aware of. It can be hard to know how we can use this 'interpretation' in ways that enable service users to gain this awareness for themselves, thereby gaining advantage from this knowledge.

One of the most common examples of this dilemma relates to child sexual abuse, where it is quite common to hear disturbed or distress behaviour being 'interpreted' as a manifestation of early experiences of abuse, particularly sexual abuse. For some children, this interpretation may be true, but for others it may not. In fact, in my experience it is unlikely that severe disturbed behaviour can be linked to any one cause. This makes it important to analyse and question the assumptions that guide decision-making about when and how to offer an interpretation and to review critically evidence used to support a particular proposition. For example, it may be that not all abused children are traumatized by sexual abuse in ways that continue to have an impact on their behaviour or to limit their outlook on life (Bagley and King 1990: 220), but it is also possible that children can be traumatized by the manner in which professionals react and attempt to address their experiences of abuse. To communicate a healthy sense of outrage at the suffering children experience is appropriate and understandable but needs to be kept within professional boundaries through the process of self-reflection in order to ensure 'that our responses arise from the client's situation rather than our past or needs' (Lishman 1998: 94).

Well timed and carefully worded interpretations have particular value in helping children and adults to understand themselves better but this process can neither be rushed nor imposed from outside. Truth has to be discovered by the person in question. This can be a difficult undertaking, particularly if the truth is locked within painful memories. For this reason, it is important that careful thought is given to the possible consequences of offering people and children information or interpretations that they are not yet ready to hear and integrate. One way through these dilemmas is to frame our awareness and understanding as tentative hypotheses (Feltham and Dryden 1993: 96) and to present these in a low-key way that leaves service users free to take them up or not, depending on how they are feeling at the time. This emphasis places less importance on the content of the interpretation than on the process of trying to ensure that service users are aware of our commitment and our willingness to get alongside them in ways that facilitate greater understanding and the possibility of moving their lives forward.

Adaptations

Most practitioners have met service users who communicate a need for help but who cannot make use of the services or resources on offer, and frustrate our best efforts to get help to them. Such individuals are sometimes wrongly described as 'unmotivated'. Sheldon takes issue with this, stating that: 'Psychologically speaking, there is no such thing as an "unmotivated person" '. Instead, he suggests that the poor take up of services may be an indication 'that they have not learned to want what we would like them to want' (Sheldon 1995: 126). This may be true. However, generalizations of this kind can fail to address all that is subtle and complex about human behaviour and motivation (Coulshed 1991: 19). A different way to understand behaviour which is frustrating or 'unmotivated' would be to emphasize that some service users may want what is on offer but lack what it takes emotionally to allow their needs to be met. This may be because their history of giving and receiving does not allow this freedom.

This difficulty in accessing or utilizing services on offer frequently indicates 'failures' experienced in early childhood. Such failures are, I believe, best understood in terms of an individual's attachment history and other 'relationship based theories' (Howe et al. 1999: 30), such as those put forward by Bowlby (1979), Winnicott (1990), and later writers in this field. This difficulty is often manifest in service users being unable to adapt their behaviour or needs in ways that facilitate the helping process. For example, service users may try to control events or the relationship, perhaps by refusing to see us unless we are prepared to visit them at home. This may mean that they miss out on being able to access other services available from our agency or within their local community. However, the need to control what is happening is so powerful that some service users would rather do without than accept services that are not presented on their terms.

Sometimes this need to control is understood in terms of service users being manipulative or uninterested and this may be the case. But, in other situations, it may be a need to ensure that predictability is preserved and uncertainty kept to a minimum. Another way to analyse this behaviour would be to see it as a manifestation of service users being wounded in the area of give and take or giving and receiving. People who have been given to in ways that were cruel, humiliating, or where the 'pay back' was too great, can find it hard to take from others – it can feel like losing control or exposing themselves to danger and further pain. Giving to others may be an easier undertaking but only if fear of rejection is not paramount.

These difficulties can be compounded in adulthood when service users have been 'abandoned by other sources of potential help' (Sheldon 1995: 118) or 'let down' in their significant attachments in other important ways. Whatever the reason, to be offered something – even something good and desired – can give rise to conflicts that can result in people failing to take up what is on offer, or needing to transform it in such a way that they lose some of their original benefits. For example, they may attempt to control what can or cannot be discussed to a point where the value and benefits inherent in the practitioner–service user relationship are lost.

One way to enable service users to take up the services on offer is through *adaptation to need*, which involves setting up situations where we attempt to meet the unique needs of each individual. Many social work interventions personalize services in this way but, in the adaptation to need I am describing, this personalization is more detailed, focused and purposeful. It is based on Winnicott's work, described briefly in Chapter 2, on the importance of adaptation in early childhood development, relating to the journey from almost total dependence, to relative dependence, and independence towards interdependence (1986: 21–38; 1990: 83–92, 303). In this theory, healthy emotional development is based on the child being adapted to by his or her carers in ways that facilitate growth and the capacity to relate to self, others and their social environment. Failures in adaptation can result in infants developing a sense of self that is fragmented and unintegrated (Winnicott 1990: 56–63): this can result in a premature and isolating self-sufficiency. To use Winnicott's words, the adaptation need not be perfect but only 'good-enough'.

In terms of our work, we regularly come into contact with men, women and children who have been neglected and uncared for in childhood, whose capacity, therefore, to see their environment and other people as a resource is severely limited (Howe *et al.* 1999: 30). In this context, adaptation to need can help to make resources and services more accessible for people who struggle in this way. Examples include tasks commonly undertaken by social workers, such as providing practical help (taxis, child-care, bus fares, adjusting our work patterns). The emphasis is on our adapting to the individual, rather than expecting service users to adapt to us or to 'fit in' (Trevithick 1993, 1995,

1998). Adaptation to need is consistent with user-led perspective approaches and particularly valuable when working with minority groups, people with low self-esteem or those who feel marginalized and excluded. However, it may be a difficult intervention to implement in terms of agency policy and practice.

Counselling skills

The British Association for Counselling (BAC), the main accreditation body for counselling in the United Kingdom, describes counselling as:

> the skilled and principled use of relationships to develop self knowledge, emotional acceptance and growth, and personal resources. The overall aim is to live more fully and satisfyingly. Counselling may be concerned with addressing and resolving specific problems, making decisions, coping with crisis, working through feelings or inner conflict or improving relationships with others. The counsellor's role is to facilitate the client's work in ways that respect the client's values, personal resources and capacity for self determination.
>
> (BAC 1992)

Of the different 'schools of counselling', five are particularly influential within social work. These include:

- client-centred counselling (sometimes called person-centred or humanist counselling)
- feminist counselling
- cognitive-behavioural counselling
- psychodynamic counselling
- eclectic and integrative counselling (adhering to no one single 'school' but instead combining different approaches).

Within social work, humanist approaches have been particularly influential, specifically the work of Egan (1990), Rogers (1961) and Truax and Carkhuff (1967), mainly because they promote personal freedom and are consistent with anti-discriminatory and anti-oppressive perspectives. Brown summarizes Egan's model as having four components: 'exploration, understanding, action and evaluation' (1998: 146). Rogers' 'core conditions' include congruence, unconditional positive regard and empathy, which Carkhuff and others adapted and developed to emphasize honesty and genuineness, warmth, respect, acceptance and empathetic understanding (Payne 1997: 178).

However, the place of counselling within social work is more confused than it first appears because a differentiation is not always made between the use of counselling skills, counselling or therapy (e.g. cognitive-behavioural therapy). Epstein illustrates this point: 'the practice of enhancing clients' knowledge and skill is referred to as counselling, or it may be called therapy or casework, depending on the language habits and preferences of a particular branch of the delivery system' (Epstein 1980: 26). Or again, in the past, 'counselling' has been used interchangeably with 'casework' (Pinker 1990: 18), or any form of one-to-one work. Indeed, Parton argues that 'In effect, casework has been reconstituted as counselling and a new, diverse and fast-growing occupation has developed' (1996: 12). This shift has been aided by the development of care managers.

For England, a social worker's role becomes that of a counsellor when he [sic] 'is concerned with improving his client's capacity' (1986: 14). However, social work 'usually exceeds counselling' because it emphasizes problem solving and help that is 'concrete, specific and focused' (England 1986: 26). This distinction is important because it differentiates between counselling skills focused on addressing the emotional life of an individual and counselling skills focused on more problem-solving and practical aspects. Although counselling and social work practice may draw on the same concepts and skills, as this book confirms, and qualified social workers 'should be equipped to undertake at least the basics of counselling' (Thompson 1998: 315), their purposes may be different. For this reason it is essential to be clear in terms of our purpose, professional boundaries and the implications of our work in relation to confidentiality (Seden 1999: 15). This is particularly important when we find we have been drawn to explore emotional issues where this is not our primary role or purpose. Where we find ourselves having to deal with emotional issues on a regular basis, it may be advisable to seek additional training in counselling.

Aims of counselling

Depending on the needs of the 'client' and the different practice orientation adopted, McLeod identifies the following aims of counselling:

1 *Insight.* The acquisition of an understanding of the origins and development of emotional difficulties, leading to an increased capacity to take rational control over feelings and actions.
2 *Self-awareness.* Becoming more aware of thoughts and feelings which had been blocked off or denied, or developing a more accurate sense of how self is perceived by others.
3 *Self-acceptance.* The development of a positive attitude towards self, marked by an ability to acknowledge areas of experience which had been the subject of self-criticism and rejection.
4 *Self actualization or individuation.* Moving in the direction of fulfilling potential or achieving an integration of previously conflicting parts of self.
5 *Enlightenment.* Assisting the client to arrive at a higher state of spiritual awakening.
6 *Problem solving.* Finding a solution to a specific problem which the client had not been able to resolve alone. Acquiring a general competence in problem solving.
7 *Psychological education.* Enabling the client to acquire ideas and techniques with which to understand and control behaviour.

 8 *Acquisition of social skills.* Learning and mastering social and interpersonal skills such as maintenance of eye contact, turn-taking in conversations, assertiveness or anger control.
 9 *Cognitive change.* The modification or replacement of irrational beliefs
   or maladaptive thought patterns associated with self-destructive
   behaviour.
10 *Behaviour change.* The modification or replacement of maladaptive or
   self-destructive patterns of behaviour.
11 *Systemic change.* Introducing change into the way in which social
   systems (e.g. families) operate.
12 *Empowerment.* Working on skills, awareness and knowledge which will
   enable the client to confront social inequalities.
13 *Restitution.* Helping the client to make amends for previous destructive
   behaviour.

(McLeod 1998: 8)

These aims are illuminating because they cover many areas of interest to social
workers. Research also indicates that counselling and casework approaches are
highly rated by service users (Hardiker and Barker 1994: 34). However,
although counselling is likely to flourish in the voluntary sector, its future in
relation to statutory services remains unclear.

Containing anxiety

'Anxiety . . . is a constant feature of our work with clients' (Sheldon 1995:
108), and many of the practice approaches used within social work acknowledge this fact and the distorting and debilitating impact that anxiety can
have. The causes of anxiety are unique to each individual, and dependent on
different past and present experiences. However, one of the primary causes of
anxiety is conflict, both internal and external (Howe 1987: 71). It is helpful to
differentiate between fear and anxiety because they are different on two
accounts and require different interventions. Fear is used to describe a reaction
to present dangers, specific objects or events, where the object of the fear is
known and, therefore, can be identified and talked about. Anxiety is used to
describe a more generalized emotional state, where the sense of threat or
danger does not have an object and, therefore, cannot be identified but is
instead anticipated or imagined (Reber 1985: 271).

Common fears that service users describe include feeling ashamed about
having to seek help, frightened that their children will be removed, worried
that they will be criticized, and so forth (Lishman 1994: 8). Often, offering
reassurance can help to allay fears but the skill is not to minimize the pain or
confusion being experienced nor to be overly reassuring unless we are confident about what we are saying. Being patient, kind, caring, understanding,
non-judgemental and non-intrusive are important attributes.

Anxieties, on the other hand, are more likely to be experienced as states
of agitation, nervousness and panic, where service users find themselves

forgetting things that they would normally remember, including the reason for their anxiety. Often what happens is that fear and anxiety run together. For example, a person may be frightened to go to the housing department because they remember previous visits that were unpleasant (fear) yet also find themselves being unable to get out of the house, losing their house keys, unable to find a relevant letter, unable to remember the reason for their visit once they arrive, and so on. This kind of amnesia is very common in anxiety states and something that militates against people being able to see things through and to effect change.

In these situations, containing anxiety involves being open and receptive to the thoughts and feelings of others – becoming a 'container' – so that these can be transformed into something more manageable. This is often achieved through the process of talking to someone who has the ability to listen, to empathize, to take in and to bear the worries being expressed, and the ability to come alongside the individual in ways that communicate an understanding and give the sense that the person is not alone. The final stage of this process involves offering back the concerns to the anxious person but in a modified form, where the major anguish is acknowledged but also altered so that it no longer carries the same 'sting' or sense of agitation or anguish. In situations of mild anxiety, helping a service user to contain these feelings may not be a time-consuming activity. Often our openness, communicated by a few well thought out words or gestures, can be sufficient to help people cope with mildly difficult emotions. In more intractable anxiety states, anxieties can feel like an unbuffered oil slick that keeps on spreading, contaminating almost everything we see and do. In these situations, greater resilience is called for on our part if we are to help service users to bear these difficult feelings. One way to do this may be to 'meet' the concerns by asking service users to describe in detail the thoughts, feelings, worries that they have. In doing so, our purpose is to try to break the hold that these anxieties are having on the individual concerned.

Conclusion

As human beings we gain great relief from the knowledge that others are prepared to help bear the weight we are carrying. The above skills demonstrate the importance of being able to embrace a range of different interventions, depending on the dilemmas being presented. However, the use of these interventions also involves building on the strengths and abilities that service users bring to an encounter. These may take different forms; for example, they may involve our acknowledging the courageous and honest way that service users explore what empowerment means to them, or the way they square up to the part they played in a particular dilemma. The ability to tell ourselves that truth can be a painful experience but one that can be deeply healing and reparative. For these reasons, it is important to remember that none of the interventions described in this and other chapters can be successfully undertaken without the active cooperation of the individuals involved, because this is central to the reciprocal relationship that lies at the heart of effective and reflective practice. In the past, we have not always created this participative and collaborative framework and this has, as a result, limited our effectiveness (Everitt and Hardiker 1996; Shaw and Shaw 1997).

6 EMPOWERMENT, NEGOTIATION AND PARTNERSHIP SKILLS

Many of the skills I describe in this section relate to working with a third party. I take as my starting point the importance of acknowledging and respecting other people's points of view and the need to establish a common purpose in relation to our work. This requires a degree of 'give and take', and stresses that the ability to compromise and the capacity to be flexible are essential qualities when attempting to work alongside others. The following skills are described:

- empowerment and enabling skills
- negotiating skills
- contracting skills
- networking skills
- working in partnership
- mediation skills
- advocacy skills
- assertiveness skills
- being challenging and confrontative
- dealing with hostility, aggression and violence.

Some skills belong to the same 'family' of negotiation skills but each carry important differences. Some skills are built on other skills. For example, advocacy carries with it the ability to negotiate. Most are finely balanced between the conflicting responsibilities of care and control, yet their overall purpose is to address the concerns of those individuals who seek, or are required to have, a social work service.

Empowerment and enabling skills

Considerable controversy surrounds the concept of empowerment: what is meant by the term; whether it is possible for us to empower others and, if so, how this is achieved in terms of the skills and resources required; and whether this falls with our role and agency expectations. For some writers, to 'empower' involves practitioners having to 'reinvent their practice and their perceptions of particular problems and solutions' (Smale and Tuson 1993: 42). Other writers are more cautious. Stevenson and Parsloe use the term to denote both 'process and goal' (1993: 6), but empowerment is more commonly used to describe service users being given 'meaningful choice' and 'valuable options' (Clark 2000: 57) in order to 'gain greater control over their lives and their circumstances' (Thompson 1997: 241). For some, this process involves addressing the impact of inequalities, oppression and discrimination (O'Sullivan 1999: 27).

Interestingly, CCETSW refer to 'concepts of empowerment' in *Paper 30*, but with no definition of what empowerment means. For the most part CCETSW prefer to use the term 'enabling'. However, in most social work texts enabling is not referred to as a specific skill and, when it is, the reference tends to be quite general (Fawcett and Lewis 1996: 40; Payne 1997: 146; Seden 1999: 107). One reason for this may be that enabling is not seen to embody distinct characteristics nor, more importantly, to address the issue of power and power imbalances in ways embraced by concepts such as empowerment (Braye and Preston-Shoot 1995: 102), 'normalization' (Ramon 1991) or 'user-led' initiatives or movements (Croft and Beresford 1997). Instead, enabling could be thought of as emphasizing the importance of making something 'possible or easy' (Hanks 1979) and, like 'promoting', may be best thought of as forming a part of the empowerment process.

Braye and Preston-Shoot, drawing on user-led literature, write in detail about 'the key characteristics and qualities required' in relation to empowerment. These include:

- clarity about what involvement is being offered, and what its limits are;
- involvement from the beginning in ways which are central to agency structures and processes but which are also flexible;
- tangible goals for involvement;
- involvement by choice, not compulsion;
- involvement of black and minority perspectives;
- individual and collective perspectives;
- provision of time, information, resources and training;
- openness to advocacy;
- clear channels of representation and complaint;
- involvement of key participants, not just some;
- open agendas;
- facilitation of attendance;
- emphasis on channels, particularly when rights are at risk and the agency's perspective is backed by the statutory power to impose it.

(Braye and Preston-Shoot 1995: 118)

This account highlights important organizational and practical issues and attitudes. The use of advocacy, self-advocacy, users' rights, and the development of user-led services and agendas is obviously important to this process (Braye and Preston-Shoot 1995: 102–18), but how effective these interventions are in practice – in relation to clients' capacity to direct the course of their lives and to improve their lives and situation – is not always clear (Thompson 1998: 319). This has led to the criticism that empowerment has limited application in practice and that it is a term that 'is often invoked without being explained' (Wise 1995: 108). Part of the difficulty that the term empowerment causes relates to the context within which social work is located. As practitioners we do not have unlimited choices. We are bound by the law and agency expectations, as well as the needs of service users. Social work agencies are also constrained by legal requirements, financial limitations and the expectations of government, other professions and the public at large.

Yet, despite these constraints, the concept of empowerment is important because it attempts to identify particular purposes and how these might be achieved; namely how to help service users to take their lives forward. One account of this process is described in the work of Lorraine Gutiérrez, an African-American feminist, who identifies the changes sought through the process of empowerment as occurring 'on the individual, interpersonal, and institutional levels, where the person develops a sense of personal power, an ability to affect others, and an ability to work with others to change social institutions' (Gutiérrez 1990: 150). For Gutiérrez, empowerment provides a way to describe the transition from apathy and despair towards a sense of personal power. This involves four psychological changes:

1 Increasing self-efficacy (moving from reacting to events to taking action)
2 Developing group consciousness
3 Reducing self-blame
4 Assuming personal responsibility for change.

In this framework, to achieve this transition or change, practitioners need to be able to embrace five 'techniques' or interventions, which include providing practical assistance:

1 Accepting the client's definition of the problem
2 Identifying and building upon existing strengths
3 Engaging in a power analysis of the client's situation
4 Teaching specific skills
5 Mobilizing resources and advocating for clients.

(Gutiérrez 1990: 151–2)

This account is helpful because it identifies in greater detail the specific skills involved in empowerment. However, some writers in this field would be uncomfortable with this account because of its emphasis on the individual and on looking at psychological processes (Dominelli and McLeod 1989). It is these differences of opinion that make concepts like empowerment and partnership, 'a minefield of ethical issues and dilemmas' (Stevenson and Parsloe 1993: 15). These dilemmas are not confined to direct work with service users because the concept of empowerment can be extended to include the empowerment of social workers, groups of people, organizations and agencies (Clark 2000: 29).

Internalized oppression

It is important to recognize that it takes time to help people to empower themselves, and to find ways to move their lives forward, not least because the very nature of oppression means that, for some, the confidence and courage to explore new areas and to take risks feels beyond their reach. When we encounter this sense of impossibility, hopelessness and defeat, the notion of 'internalized oppression' can give us a way to help people to understand and to talk about how they have come to believe negative statements about themselves to the point where they believe that these negative personal characteristics are fixed and part of their personality. Negative beliefs of this kind can sometimes be shifted by tracking their origins. Many stem from hurtful comments made by parents, but in my experience an alarming number can be traced back to teachers. For some years I ran workshops for working-class women at the London Women's Therapy Centre (Trevithick 1988). Much of our work involved helping women put words to negative beliefs that they had about themselves, locating the painful experiences that surrounded this process of internalization and helping them to see how untrue, unfair and unkind many of these comments were. They served to keep these women 'in their place' and to hold them hostage to these untruths.

People who come to believe, through the process of internalized oppression, that they are worthless, 'stupid', 'no good' or that they 'don't count' find it very difficult to stand up to others, to protect themselves or their loved ones from further oppression or to take risks without help. The way that help is offered is important: compassion, concern and the fact that we 'care' are an important value perspective we bring to our work but, in my experience, we are more likely to be successful and resilient in our efforts if our approach has a theoretical underpinning. In addition to Gutiérrez's work, quoted above, I have gained a great deal from the writings of Jean Baker Miller (1973, 1976), particularly her concept of 'temporary inequality' (1976: 4–5). This describes how we can use the inequality that exists between workers and service users to name, analyse and address differences, including difficult feelings located in the present, as well as painful memories from the past. These difficulties are always present yet are rarely acknowledged when people of unequal status, authority and power encounter one another. (See Chapter 2 for a further account of Miller's work and that of the Stone Center, Boston, USA.)

Negotiating skills

Negotiating skills tend to be well covered in social work texts (Coulshed 1991: 62–5; Lishman 1994: 100; O'Sullivan 1999: 48), some concentrating on specific areas, such as negotiating the focus of the work (Trower et al. 1988:

34–6) or setting up contracts (Sheldon 1995: 185–7). The following is a summary of the main considerations and skills involved in negotiating.

Negotiation is primarily directed at achieving some form of agreement or understanding. Its importance can be seen in two ways. Firstly, in relation to direct work with service users, negotiation skills are the tools that establish the climate of shared decision making and collaboration that lies at the heart of the concept of partnership. It is through negotiation that we arrive at a common agreement across different parties in terms of how problems are understood and how these might be overcome. Negotiation skills are also important in situations of disagreement. There may be no obvious way to overcome underlying differences but, where a degree of flexibility and compromise exists, this can be a foundation on which to negotiate. One way to achieve this would be to explore with service users – and other parties involved – their perception of events, particularly how they arrived at the particular position, or belief, they are holding, and what was their starting point (Lishman 1994: 100). For Sheldon, 'beliefs are settled views of experience' (1995: 153) that we seek to preserve and have confirmed. Entering into a dialogue about how an individual arrived at a particular view or position can reveal how painful certain experiences have been and how much their stance is designed to protect them from further pain. Part of our task may involve negotiating a shift in the balance, based on an understanding, respect and acceptance of people's perception of events but not necessarily our agreement. Since our position and starting point is likely to be different, it may be essential to point this out in a sensitive way as part of the negotiation.

For example, I once worked with a family where one of their five children, Tim, was constantly being scapegoated and marginalized within the family. A common phrase his parents used was 'He's always been like that, ever since a baby. When he's being like that, we ignore him'. 'Like that' was the shorthand way the parents communicated and justified their lack of empathy and tolerance for this child. As a result Tim was neglected within the family, and was showing his distress through stealing. The work we contracted to do involved helping Tim's parents to identify at what point they joined forces in the view that Tim was a difficult child and that the best course of action was to ignore him. This work took several months but eventually it transpired that his mother had had an affair and both parents believed Tim to be the child of a different father. A DNA test proved their 'belief' to be wrong, which meant we were then in a position to work on his mother's guilt and his father's rage about the affair and to negotiate a different place for Tim within the family. This negotiation took the form of revising the original contract, unpacking the 'beliefs' that Tim's parents had, some of which Tim had internalized, and carefully negotiating a new place for him in his family.

The second arena where negotiation skills are important is in relation to services. It is estimated that about one-third of our work involves face-to-face contact with service users (Coulshed 1991: 62). The remaining time is spent on indirect service provision, such as negotiating with our own agency and other organizations, or other parties who hold key resources or positions. This figure is likely to be higher where resources are scarce and/or the demands for professional accountability excessive, or for practitioners employed in certain settings, such as community work. For example, as a field worker arguing for resources, I have spent many hours trying to negotiate residential placements, both for children and for older people. It took me some time to realize that I was more likely to be successful in my negotiations if I made sure there was a correct 'fit' between the resources being sought and the needs of the service user. This is very important. Where resources seemed to be withheld for no apparent reason, it sometimes helped to address the reservations of those individuals responsible for resource allocation. For example, many managers worry that, once a place has been allocated the social worker will 'disappear' from the life of the child, young person or older person and fail to maintain links with their family and other significant contacts (Millham et al. 1986). Although residential care is now a less favoured option in relation to children and young people, these concerns about maintaining links remain (Aldgate 1997: 143), and can require that we have sound negotiating skills.

The time and effort involved in mobilizing resources is considerable and can require our having to use collaborative, competitive or combative tactics depending on the situation and our response (Coulshed 1991: 62–4). Combative skills may be particularly important when we are dealing with injustice or inequalities in resource provision, and one way to see campaigning is as a form of political negotiation. However, our success in these and other endeavours is more likely to depend on how well we prepare and present our case, particularly factual information, and how carefully we have thought through where key figures in the negotiation are coming from. It may also be important to know where to enlist further support or leverage so that the same negotiation is being played from several sides. In addition, it is essential to be in a position to highlight the advantages that a negotiated decision could bring to those who would normally be uninterested. One way to achieve this may involve appealing to a person's sense of fairness. According to Jordan, social work is 'crucially concerned with fairness, both in redistributing resources to people in need . . . and in negotiations over problems in relationships in families, neighbourhoods and communities' (1990: 178). To enlist people's sympathy or sense of fairness – perhaps by asking them to imagine how they might feel in the same situation – can come across as manipulative and the lines between being strategic, determined and manipulative can be difficult to draw. Honesty is an important safeguard. So too is the ability to acknowledge a respect for the other person's point of view, at the same time believing that we can 'change their mind', and do so in ways that retain a sense of personal integrity for all parties concerned.

Finally, it can be easy to give up in our efforts to negotiate if we are immediately unsuccessful, yet our success may depend on our being able to withstand rejection and failure. Resilience, determination and the skills of persuasion are the hallmarks of a successful negotiator.

Contracting skills

Drawing up contracts provides an opportunity to formalize and structure the nature of the contact between ourselves and service users in relation to the purpose of the work and the roles, responsibilities and expectations of those concerned. The process involved in arriving at this working agreement is as important as the task itself and acts as 'a tangible manifestation of working in partnership' (Aldgate 1997: 143). The contract must be based on the needs of service users and, for this reason, may be agreed verbally or in writing, sometimes in the form of a letter. Failing to keep a written record of agreements reached is dangerous; reliance on memory alone can be highly problematic, not least because we all hear through our histories and, as the game Chinese Whispers reveals, we can hear the same information quite differently. In some situations, however, perhaps where literacy is a problem, written agreements or contracts may not be appropriate.

Whatever the format, care should be taken to ensure that a shared understanding has been reached, and in a language that is clear, explicit and accessible, with sufficient information for the task at hand. Confusion and anxiety act as barriers to effective action. For example, contracts may specify the time and length of sessions, location, duration, ground rules, confidentiality and recording procedures. They can also state who is invited to attend, a summary of the major concerns, the purpose of the work in terms of objectives and the approaches to be used, emergency cover arrangements and how any breakdown of the agreement might be dealt with. It helps to build in some flexibility so that the contract can be revised if required.

Drawing up an action plan is an example of how a contract or working agreement might be used in practice (Hanvey and Philpot 1994: 17–20). Action plans can take different forms. For example, I once ran a group for severely depressed women where suicidal thoughts and intentions were very much in evidence. In order to address the anxieties that this threat posed both to the workers and other women in the group, we drafted a plan of action in the event of accident or crisis, whether self-inflicted or not. When drafting individual plans, everyone in the group was asked to lay down in detail what steps we had to take, and in what order, should a crisis occur. We even included details of the next-of-kin. Fortunately, these plans never needed to be put into action.

Contracts provide the opportunity to formalize the relationship and the purpose of the work in ways that can bring people together to work in partnership. This structured approach towards a common purpose enables sensitive issues to be addressed at the outset, such as differences in status, authority, knowledge and experience that we, and service users, bring to the partnership and how these will be worked with. This can demystify the helping process, ensuring that as practitioners we are open about how much power service users and others have, and where our accountability lies (Preston-Shoot 1994: 185). It also provides an opportunity to build on service users' strengths and to provide help when needed.

On the other hand, some writers believe that drawing up contracts or written agreements can be oppressive because they assume a freedom of choice that has little bearing on service users' everyday experiences of social inequalities and injustices (Rojek and Collins 1988: 205). Are they contracts or 'con tricks' (Corden and Preston-Shoot 1987)? Similarly, our choices as practitioners are limited by agency policy, our legal responsibilities and scarcity in terms of resources and services. To enable 'mutuality and exchange' (Smale and Tuson 1993) between service users and practitioners, with 'users as equal partners in problem definition and negotiation about solutions' (Braye and Preston-Shoot 1995: 116), a fundamental shift is needed in the extent to which service users' views are allowed to determine problem definition and the solutions sought. Certainly at present, and probably in the foreseeable future, 'social workers and clients do not have equal power in their professional contact' (Lishman 1994: 91).

Finally, the term 'contract culture' describes the introduction of internal markets into health and social services in the 1990s and the commissioning of services by a purchaser from a provider. This approach to service delivery has been severely criticized, particularly for failing to increase user choice and involvement (Braye and Preston-Shoot 1995: 22), and for its emphasis on individualism, which is 'antithetical to mutual help, collaboration and co-operation' (Adams 1998: 256).

Networking skills

According to Seed, a network is a 'system or pattern of links . . . which have particular meaning' (1990: 19). These can be divided into:

- formal networks – such as planned formal support groups; and
- informal or natural networks – such as those made up of 'natural' carers who help others: family members, friends and neighbours.

In its recommendation for decentralized community based services, the Barclay Report recognized the importance of 'local networks of formal and informal relationships' and their 'capacity to mobilize individual and collective responses to adversity' (1982: xiii). Also, the importance of informal networks and caring resources was acknowledged in the Griffiths Report (1988) and built into the NHS and Community Care Act 1990, but in ways that were felt by many to be an appropriation by government of 'natural' support systems (Reigate 1997: 216). Whereas it is appropriate for statutory services to support existing 'natural' networks, 'attempting to replace formal provision with informal care or to change the existing patterns of informal care is likely to be unsuccessful' (Payne 1997: 152).

According to Coulshed and Orme (1998: 224) networking can involve three 'strategies':

- *network therapy* uses groupwork skills to help families in crisis by bringing together their network to act as the 'change agents' (e.g. Family Group Conferences used in child protection work);

- *problem-solving network meetings* bring together formal and informal carers, often to unravel who is doing what; and
- *network construction* is how to build new networks and sustain or change existing networks.

All of these involve mediating, advocating and organizing skills (1998: 149) and also the ability to assess the capabilities of the individual in question and of the social networks that are in existence and what these can sustain. Again, assessment skills are used when attempting to establish a 'personalized support network', perhaps for someone leaving residential care, where the work involves identifying key figures, described as 'central figures' (Collins and Pancoast 1976) or 'competent others' (Atkinson 1986: 84), to form part of a personalized support network, where this needs to be created.

The importance of networking in social work is to strengthen the links and connections that exist for people within a particular community or geographical area. This support is particularly important when there is the danger of people becoming isolated. For example, research indicates that people discharged from psychiatric hospital who have social support are less likely to be re-admitted (Huxley 1997: 136; Sheppard 1997: 214). The debilitating impact of isolation also exists for people with learning disabilities (Atkinson 1986), and for elderly people (Phillipson 1997: 163). However, it is important to see social support networks as complementing other services, and not replacing the obligations of the state and social services to provide key services. Other forms of help, such as a 'close personal working relationship in order to sustain community living' (Huxley 1997: 136), are also crucial for individuals who have difficulty relating or those whose situation leaves them vulnerable to stigma and social exclusion.

Within this work, our knowledge of black networks may not be built on a 'proper understanding' of black people's experience and, as a result, we may fail to help black people to link to the networks that exist (Shah 1989: 179). The dangers here are many. For example, our failure to understand the complex nature of African-Caribbean and Asian cultures can mean that we focus on the problems or 'defects' rather than their resilient and supportive characteristics (Ahmed 1986: 141; Robinson 1995: 12). Although it is always important to locate people within their cultural context, there can be a pull to rely on cultural explanations at the expense of exploring other relevant factors, particularly structural influences and limitations (Ahmed 1986: 140). What is described as 'normal' and, therefore, acceptable for any culture, including aspects of working-class culture, needs to be analysed carefully. For example, it can be thought of as 'normal' and acceptable for working-class people to use physical force, or the threat of violence, to restrain and control their children. These assumptions need to be challenged and so-called 'normal' behaviour carefully scrutinized.

Working in partnership

Partnership, and the principles of participation and 'user involvement', inform current legislation in relation to health and social care, having found favour with both the political left and right, but for different reasons. 'Where the left saw empowerment of the poor and disadvantaged, the right saw growth in personal responsibility, independence and individual choice' (Howe 1996: 84). Similarly, it is possible for both left and right to share a commitment to empowerment and its emphasis on 'people taking control of their own lives and having the power to shape their own future' (Shardlow 1998: 32). This joint ownership might help to explain why partnership is considered to be 'very misleading without qualification' (Stevenson and Parsloe 1993: 6) and 'used to describe anything from token consultation to a total devolution of power and control' (Braye and Preston-Shoot 1995: 102).

The point to be stressed is that positive practice must involve service users if it is to achieve agreed objectives (empowerment and personal responsibility) and that within this process, service users must be seen not only in terms of the 'problems' they bring, but as 'whole people' and 'full citizens' (Dalrymple and Burke 1995: 64) who have an important contribution to make in terms of their knowledge and perception of the situation, personal qualities and problem-solving capabilities. This differs from those approaches where there is a 'topdown hierarchical bureaucracy' (Braye and Preston-Shoot 1995: 116), dominated by agency policies and procedures, or an approach where the practitioner is seen to be the expert who diagnoses the problem and prescribes a cure.

One of the most helpful accounts of the principles and skills involved in working in partnership can be found in *The Challenge of Partnership in Child Protection: Practice Guide* (DoH 1995b). Under four headings, this publication identifies the reasons for working in partnership with parents. These headings have been adapted to include other service user groups:

- *Effectiveness* More is likely to be achieved through an approach that is co-operative and collaborative (Howe 1987: 7; Sheldon 1995: 126; Thoburn et al. 1995; Roberts and Taylor 1996).
- *Clients as a source of information* It is important to build on the detailed knowledge and understanding that service users have of their situation and the problems they face (Sheldon 1995: 125), and to take as our starting point the priorities that they consider most urgent (Lishman 1994: 100).
- *Citizens' rights* Service users should have the right to know what is being said about them and to contribute to decisions that affect their lives.
- *Empowering parents* Involving service users in decision-making helps to build self-esteem and confidence, and to enable clients to feel more in control of their lives.

(DoH 1995b: 9–10)

The knowledge, values and skills required for working in partnership are described by the Department of Health (1995b: 14) under the heading 'Fifteen essential principles for working in partnership' (see Appendix 7). Many of the values and skills included in that list are described here, such as the importance of good communication, listening skills and observation skills; being respectful, caring, competent in our approach; clear in our purpose and intentions, our professional boundaries and responsibilities including the language we use; sensitive to the issue of power and power imbalances; mindful of the importance of the strengths and potential that service users possess, as well as addressing 'weaknesses, problems and limitations'; aware of our own 'personal feelings, values, prejudices and beliefs'; being able to acknowledge our mistakes and to use supervision to ensure the quality of our work and its effectiveness (DoH 1995b: 14).

This summary serves as a reminder that we have still much to learn about how to work in partnership in ways that enhance service users' capacity to consolidate and extend their self-knowledge, decision-making and problem-solving abilities. This work is much more complex than is sometimes described, particularly where this involves working across differences (Smale et al. 2000) and trying to understand the power differentials that exist between practitioners and service users from different cultural, ethnic and racial groups (DoH 1995b: 24). For example, the contribution that service users feel they can give – and the knowledge they can actually access and communicate – may, in fact, be quite limited. Some may feel too depleted or have too little confidence to take on the responsibilities implied within the concept of partnership. This can result in an imbalance that must be worked through if service users are to continue to feel engaged and their contribution valued, no matter how limited this might be.

I recall working with a family where the children, aged 2, 3 and 5, were severely neglected. Both parents had been diagnosed as having learning difficulties, although what part this played in their ability to parent their children was never clear, because both were known to have had impoverished childhoods, moving in and out of care. Their deep sense of mistrust and their fear of social workers made any attempt to find a common purpose a seemingly impossible task. For a long time a stultifying silence and apparent lack of interest dominated the communication. In desperation, I took the issue to supervision and set about the task of analysing the blocks to communication and to establishing a rapport. One of the problems identified by my supervisor was that my agenda – the protection of the children – was getting in the way of establishing a rapport. I had failed to ask these parents what help they felt they most needed from social services and, in particular, from me. When I did ask this question, I found they wanted my help to press the housing department to mend their leaking roof. The other mistake I had made was that I had failed to reframe their actions and behaviour in positive terms. For example, they were always in when I visited and always allowed me to have contact with the children. They were also committed parents, determined not to see their children 'dumped into care' as they themselves had been. I had not seen their

commitment; only their mistrust and lack of cooperation. By re'
actions in this way, new possibilities emerged (Watzlawick *et al.*
also 'reframing' pp. 130–1). We were able to find 'mutual agreemem.
1994: 92): a common purpose. Together, our purpose was to ensure tha.
did not lose custody of their children. With this aim in mind, we negotiateu
different tasks, where control of the decision-making process was more equitable (O'Sullivan 1999: 49). I agreed to address the problem about the housing
repairs, thereby hoping to bring about some improvement in the quality of
their lives and, in this process, to gain some trust, but on condition that both
parents attended parenting classes at the local health centre. In other words, I
attended to their primary concern and, in return, they attended to mine.

This example highlights the fact that the partnerships created can take
many forms. It can be helpful to stress this at the beginning of the contact and
also the fact that partnership does 'not imply an equality of power, nor an
equality of work' (Marsh 1997: 199). Addressing issues of this kind is a complex activity, requiring sophisticated communication skills. This is particularly
true in the area of child protection where research findings indicate that
greater parental involvement has been linked to better outcomes (Thoburn
et al. 1995; Waterhouse and McGhee 1998: 286). The ability to create a climate
of inclusion and collaboration, based on a recognition of the importance of
everyone's contribution to the partnership process, is a key skill within this
process.

The main concern that critics highlight in relation to the notion of partnership centres around the inequalities that exist in terms of power and control.
This has been described as 'conflicting imperatives' with regard to 'rights
versus risks, care versus control, needs versus resources, professionalism versus
partnership with users, professional versus agency agendas' (Braye and Preston-Shoot 1995: 63). Where these conflicts and tensions are not addressed
honestly and openly, the partnership can feel hollow, and users' experience of
involvement can feel 'stressful, diversionary and unproductive' (Croft and
Beresford 1997: 275). This is particularly the case where service users are
invited to 'participate in decisions over which they have no control' (Langan
1998: 215), thereby being rendered powerless. Equally, unless adequate
resources are made available for the objectives being pursued, partnerships can
become strained and vulnerable to being overtaken by events and the unwel-
come intrusion of greater problems and desperate solutions (Howe 1996: 96).
A final concern relates to where our professional responsibilities lie as practitioners in relation to working in partnership. If we are to act as gatekeepers
to resources (Phillips 1996: 141), our power and authority need to be made
explicit. But if our role is, as Jordan suggests, to exercise 'moral reasoning' and
to use our 'judgement, discretion and skill' to highlight choice and resource
inequalities (1990: 4), then this too needs to be made clear and also the fact
that little progress may be possible without this kind of agitation. How much
service users feel able to become involved in this form of political negotiation
should be discussed as part of the partnership agreement.

Despite these concerns, working in partnership can provide an important framework for us to work closely with service users. This is likely to involve the skills of working across differences, including cultural and racial differences:

> In order to achieve successful partnerships with families in child protection work, professionals must give special consideration to the different cultural, ethnic and racial origins of families and their different religious beliefs and languages. The many different ethnic and cultural variations in our society require all professionals to develop a personal and organisational commitment to equality and to meeting the needs of families and children as well as understanding the effects of racial discrimination, and cultural misunderstanding or misinterpretation.
>
> (DoH 1995b: 24)

From this place, we can learn a great deal about the hardships experienced by service users and encounter first-hand the barriers and obstacles that block the way forward. This may require extending the remit of our role, and the objectives of the partnership, to include working with social or environmental factors that hinder progress, drawing on skills described in this and other chapters, such as negotiating skills, advocacy, and so forth.

Mediation skills

Ensuring that different parties communicate with one another is an important skill within social work. Within this process, mediation skills have a particular part to play 'in disputes between parties to help them reconcile differences, find compromises, or reach mutually satisfactory agreements' (Barker 1995: 228). Although often grouped with advocacy skills, where our role is to represent, defend or to speak for another person, mediation involves taking up 'a neutral role between two opposing parties (members of families, for example) rather than taking up the case of one party against another' (Thompson 1997: 314). Common situations where mediation skills may be called for are disputes between neighbours in conflict, or between divorcing parents. One approach to mediation would be to try to find some common ground. In the case of neighbours at 'war', what they might share could be the desire to live in peace. For parents in dispute, the common ground may be their desires for their children's future: to want the best for them and to protect them from harm. To be a successful 'go-between' involves being able to gain a degree of trust from both or all parties to represent their point of view. This may or may not involve bringing people together into one setting. Mediation, conciliation and arbitration skills all belong to the same negotiating skills 'family'. To define these terms may be important if it helps to identify the focus of our work. For example, conciliation skills can involve attempting to pacify, whereas in some situations, to act as a mediator may look more like being a referee.

This neutrality required of a mediator can be a difficult role to sustain in situations where one party is more articulate and powerful than the other. It can feel as if we are condoning the browbeating or bullying of another person.

However, to be drawn outside the role, most commonly into the role of advocate, can have disastrous consequences because, once lost, neutrality may never be regained. One way to avoid this danger is to stay active. For example, we may ask both parties to direct their comments to one another through us, perhaps in the first instance suggesting or insisting they discuss issues likely to be less contentious and more amenable to agreement. Our role is then to address the comments of one party to the other and to feed replies back in the same way and to do so until it seems possible for both parties to speak directly. Within this process it may be helpful to reframe some comments, to keep the same 'frame' but to take some of the 'sting' out of what is being said. This is only possible where people feel comfortable about having the sense of what they are saying reframed in this way. If these efforts fail and we still feel we are being drawn out of role, it is wise to call the session to a halt so that we can reflect on events, seek help if necessary, and review what other steps we (or others) need to take to move the situation forward to a satisfactory resolution. As these examples indicate, mediation is a 'highly skilled activity' (Smith 1998: 341).

'Mediation' is a term used in other situations. For example, mediators play an important role within cognitive-behavioural approaches as 'people in the client's surroundings who can record, prompt and reinforce appropriate behaviour' (Hudson and MacDonald 1986: 69; Sheldon 1995: 127). In this context, mediators may be family members, friends or volunteers. Mediation can also be found in divorce court welfare services where its role is to reduce conflict and to work with parents to agree the arrangements for the upbringing of their children (James 1997: 340). Whereas conciliation was once the term used in divorce court proceedings, mediation is now the preferred term (Home Office 1994). The fact that these terms are sometimes used interchangeably highlights the importance of being clear ourselves in relation to our purpose and role in different situations.

Advocacy skills

CCETSW identify advocacy as a central skill within social work (1995a: 16), linking it to other human and civil rights issues such as citizen's charters, empowerment, partnership, collaboration and participation. Advocacy involves representing the interests of others when they are unable to do so themselves (Thompson 1998: 314). Central to this work is an acknowledgement of differences in power that disadvantage certain groups of people, denying access to certain resources or opportunities, including the right to participate as full members of society (Townsend 1993: 36). Advocacy aims to ensure that the voices and interests of service users are heard and responded to in ways that affect attitudes, policy, practice and service delivery. The mandate for this undertaking can be found in the objectives of the NHS and Community Care Act 1990 which is 'to give people a greater say in how they live their lives and the services they need to help them to do so' (DoH 1989).

A key concept within advocacy is that of representation, which can involve:

- supporting clients to represent themselves;
- arguing clients' views and needs;
- interpreting or representing the views, needs, concerns and interests of clients to others;
- developing appropriate skills for undertaking these different tasks such as listening and negotiating skills, empathy, assertiveness skills, being clear and focused; and so on.

Advocacy can involve speaking, writing, acting or arguing on behalf of others. According to Payne (1997: 269) this representation can take different forms:

- *Case advocacy* Advocating on behalf of another person for resources, services or opportunities. This may be undertaken by a professional, volunteer or peer.
- *Cause advocacy* Arguing for changes in policies or procedures and other forms of reform (e.g. entitlement to health services or welfare benefits).
- *Self-advocacy* People finding ways to speak for themselves in order to protect their rights and to advance their own interests. This links to self-help, group and peer advocacy. This type of advocacy is used by 'mental health system survivors' and people with learning disabilities.
- *Peer advocacy* This describes people working together to represent each other's needs. Many self-help groups undertake this kind of advocacy and some are also actively involved in campaigning to influence public opinion and government policies.
- *Citizen advocacy* This 'involves volunteers in developing relationships with potentially isolated clients, understanding and representing their needs'.

For advocacy to be seen as a legitimate element of the social work role, it is essential that adequate training, supervision and support are provided. To act as an advocate for another person requires considerable professional confidence and standing on the part of practitioners, particularly when confronted with officialdom and authority figures (Kadushin 1990: 388–90). Some practitioners have neither the confidence nor the body of knowledge needed to be an effective advocate. This knowledge includes how to use the law, government guidance and regulations, agency policy and practices to act as an advocate for the rights and needs of service users (Braye and Preston-Shoot 1995: 65).

For example, many years ago I was involved in advocating on the behalf of a service user and her two children who were homeless and 'squatting' and had been threatened with eviction by the local authority. A telephone call to a squatter's rights organization in London revealed that the local authority had failed to provide three days' notice, which was then required for an eviction order. I passed this information on to the barrister representing this family, who duly presented this information to the judge. The case was adjourned, with the judge chastising the local authority for failing to prepare their case properly and requiring them to offer alternative accommodation before the next hearing. There was no legal requirement on the part of the local authority to adhere to the judge's requirement. This example highlights the fact that we are more likely to be successful in our role as advocate where we have gathered accurate, detailed and relevant facts, including those relating to the law or legal expectations.

As a final point, an important concept within advocacy work relates to the concept of normalization. This is often used to describe a commitment to provide an environment that gives people with disabilities the kind of social roles and lifestyle that other citizens enjoy. It is also sometimes used in relation to the rights and needs of people in residential care (Payne 1997: 271). Another way to see the concept of normalization would be to see it as a description of what all human beings need: 'It contains, in prototype, a framework of minimum requirements for the good life' (Clark 2000: 130). We may be called to act as an advocate in relation to any of the five interdependent needs identified by Clark (2000: 130–1), which are similar to those identified by Maslow (1954), described in Chapter 2. They include:

- safety and psychological security (physical care, security and safety)
- means of life (basic needs such as food, shelter)
- opportunity for creativity (rewarding work, personal growth)
- social participation and status (recognition and respect)
- power and choice (to participate in society, to make choices)

Describing the different forms of advocacy is relatively straightforward. However, advocacy is a subject that remains bound by qualification and, sometimes, a mistrust about the intentions of practitioners and their skills to undertake this task well. Some writers express the danger of professionals taking over in such a way that a service user's ability to represent themself – or to learn to represent themself – is undermined or disempowered through 'pressurizing or persuading' (Dalrymple and Burke 1995: 69). Others state that focusing solely on equalizing power imbalances between service users and others more powerful is not enough, and that practitioners should also 'challenge those inequalities within the system which contribute to or which cause difficulties' (Phillipson 1993: 183). However, it is not clear how this can be achieved and whether this form of advocacy is likely to be a priority for social work agencies constrained by other imperatives. Certainly, there is a need for some form of advocacy in areas where our involvement is both sanctioned and greatly needed, namely in relation to welfare rights, but this is an area increasingly neglected by social workers, partly due to the development of specialist welfare rights agencies (Burgess 1992: 175), and partly because addressing the issue is not considered a priority for some social workers (Jones 1998: 124; Walker and Walker 1998: 47).

Assertiveness skills

Ongoing experiences of defeat, oppression and exploitation can leave people feeling powerless and unable to protect themselves properly. This inability can include being unable to protect others in their care. Social workers, as well as service users, can find it difficult to be assertive, particularly when dealing with higher status professionals, such as psychiatrists, solicitors or higher management. One way to understand the lack of assertiveness is to analyse the issue of powerlessness, defined as 'the inability to manage emotions, skills, knowledge and/or material resources in a way that effective performance of valued social roles will lead to personal gratification' (Solomon 1976: 16), and to link this to concepts such as learned helplessness (Seligman 1975) and locus of control (Lefcourt 1976; Cigno and Bourn 1998: 102–5). These concepts help us to map the degree to which people feel in charge of their lives and able to influence their circumstances and future.

Passivity is seen to be the opposite of assertiveness or self-efficacy (Egan 1990: 99), and can lead to worrying consequences: 'Failure to act assertively often results in submission, exploitation and resentment or in aggression, misunderstanding and negative consequences' (Feltham and Dryden 1993: 12). Yet it can be very difficult for people to risk exploring other options, mainly because their view of themselves – their sense of worth as a human being – has taken too many blows and they cannot sustain the confidence or belief in themselves necessary to begin to effect change. Assertiveness skills can be an important starting point and are recognized as crucial in relation to concepts of empowerment, partnership and participation. Where service users lack necessary skills and confidence, it is assumed that practitioners should help them to acquire these skills (Croft and Beresford 1997), so that 'the possibilities for effective collaboration can be maximized' (Thompson 1998: 317).

This transition can be difficult to achieve. Central to the task involves encouraging service users to challenge self-defeating statements and helping them to substitute these with more positive and hopeful viewpoints. These self-defeating statements can be in the form of attitudes or beliefs, both about themselves, other people, or future possibilities and opportunities likely to improve their situation. It also involves helping to address and contain the fears and anxieties that are holding service users back, and encouraging and supporting them to risk taking small steps forward (Egan 1990: 99). This focus on the importance of assertiveness skills is one that has been used a great deal in the USA, particularly in relation to women (Gilligan 1993) but also as a key empowerment strategy for other oppressed groups (Gitterman 1991).

Assertiveness training

There may be times where a more formal teaching approach to assertiveness skills is required. Assertiveness training involves teaching people how to stand up for themselves without being aggressive, threatening, punishing, manipulative, or over-controlling, and without demeaning other people. Drawing on learning theory and other cognitive-behaviourist approaches, including modelling, rehearsal and operant reinforcement (Sheldon 1995: 202), assertiveness training is designed to identify and replace submissive and self-denying messages with statements that more accurately reflect what the individual feels, needs or wants for themselves. Assertiveness training encourages people to learn to say no, to defend themselves and to complain in ways that are likely to be beneficial and successful in terms of outcomes. Sheldon (1995: 203) identifies a range of skills and tasks associated with assertiveness training:

- *assessment* to gain an understanding of the extent of the problem;
- *discrimination training procedures* to help clients to learn the difference between assertiveness, false or compulsive compliance and aggression;
- *a modelling and rehearsal component* to show the client, step-by-step, the degree of assertiveness appropriate in different circumstances and to encourage the skills to be rehearsed, offering encouragement and validation;
- *a desensitization component* to help to remove the fears by exposing clients to frightening situations; and
- *generalization* to ensure that the skills learned can be generalized to everyday experiences and problems by relating them to real situations.

The importance of people being able to assert their thoughts, feelings, choices or needs openly and directly cannot be overstated, but its importance is not confined to service users. As practitioners we too need to be able to assert and represent the needs and rights of others and also our own views and perspectives, personal and professional needs.

Being challenging and confrontative

There are times when it is important to challenge or confront certain kinds of behaviour. This includes being able to manage conflict and bear confrontations (O'Sullivan 1999: 78). It also includes the right to be allowed to challenge our own agency policies and practices without the fear of reprisal (Mitchell 1996). The skill is to know when and how to do this in ways that help to move the situation forward. Some authors view 'challenging' as virtually synonymous with 'confrontation' (Feltham and Dryden 1993: 26; Lishman 1994: 121), whereas Egan associates confrontation with 'unpleasant experiences' (1990: 184), and close to bullying and coercion. It is for this reason that the terms are included together here.

Challenging

Within this text, 'challenging' describes a low level, gentle yet firm invitation to face service users with 'contradictions, distortions, inconsistencies or discrepancies and inviting or stimulating them to reconsider and resolve the contradictions' (Lishman 1994: 121), where they may otherwise be reluctant to do so. The timing of challenges, and how they are undertaken, can be as important as what is actually said because challenges should come at a point where it is clear that the service user is unlikely to pick up on the 'lack of fit', and needs us to intervene in order to move the situation forward. For example, some service users do not understand how they come across; the extent to which some of their behaviours are off-putting or set people against them. A well timed challenge should strengthen our relationship, whereas one that is premature or inopportune, perhaps because it is too forceful, persistent or moves too far ahead of a service user, could damage the relationship and threaten progress, sometimes irreparably. Millar *et al.* (1992) see challenging as a form of feedback and stress the tentative nature of the communication as a means of aiding further self-reflection and understanding: 'What interviewees need is a chance to consider what behaviours they display, how they "come across". What appear to be less helpful are attempts to present analyses of underlying meanings, interpretations or evaluative statements' (Millar *et al.* 1992: 97).

Confronting

Egan identifies a range of different behaviours that may warrant challenging:

- Failure to own problems.
- Failure to define problems in solvable terms.
- Faulty interpretations of critical experiences, behaviours, and feelings.
- Evasion, distortions, and game playing.
- Failure to identify or understand the consequences of behaviour.
- Hesitancy or unwillingness to act on new perspectives.

(Egan 1990: 187)

Similarly, Kadushin writes of confrontation as 'pulling the interviewee up short . . . By acting contrary to the usual social expectation that inconsistencies will be ignored, the interviewer sets up a new situation which requires resolution' (Kadushin 1990: 161). For Egan, it is 'all too common for clients to refuse to take responsibility for their problems and lost opportunities' (1990: 186). Service users must own their part in whatever problems they have because, without this ownership, they cannot own the solutions. Defining problems in terms of the past means that they cannot be solved because the past cannot be changed. For Egan, confronting clients is not to strip them of their defences, which could be dangerous because these are needed for survival, 'but to help them to overcome blind spots and develop new strategies' (1990: 194).

The ability to confront people without making them more defensive and guarded is a skilled activity, involving the qualities of tolerance, patience and acceptance, remembering that the ultimate goal 'is action and change' (Lishman 1994: 121). Nelson-Jones offers the following practice guidelines:

- start with reflective responding
- where possible, help speakers to confront themselves
- do not talk down
- use the minimum amount of 'muscle'
- avoid threatening voice and body language

- leave the ultimate responsibility with the speaker
- do not overdo it

(Nelson-Jones 1990: 135–6)

It is important that we think beforehand about the kind of reaction that our challenge is likely to produce and what our response might be. Reactions can range from anger, rage and pain to a sense of relief. Also, challenging others can be a stressful undertaking, which may call for additional peer and supervision support.

As a final point, a word of warning is needed in relation to being challenging or confrontational. People who have experienced too many 'put-downs' or too much humiliation in their lives can be extremely sensitive to challenges of any kind and, where this is the case, can experience the mildest rebuke as quite devastating. Sometimes merely asking a particular kind of question can be construed as a form of criticism. This can be expressed in different ways. Some may become more withdrawn and silent, while others may become agitated, or even aggressive. It is often hard to guess the kind of reaction criticism will elicit and even if it does bring about some kind of positive outcome, the ends never justify the means. It is possible that the same outcome could have been achieved by adopting a more caring and sensitive intervention. Also, some people can easily turn criticism against themselves or against others. In my experience, bullying and self-harm among young people can be triggered by criticism, or other 'put-downs', as can aggressive behaviour (Howe *et al.* 1999: 138).

This is not to ignore the importance of being able to challenge the difficult and sometimes abusive behaviour that some people demonstrate, particularly when we or others are being targeted. It is not possible to avoid feeling critical of some kinds of behaviour: it is part of being human. Some people justify unacceptable behaviour as being natural to a particular culture or group. This may be true and leave us feeling unable to challenge certain behaviours. In relation to child abuse, this can have serious consequences (Modi *et al.* 1995: 99; Trowell and Bower 1995). Some behaviour may still fall outside the realms of acceptable behaviour and need to be challenged. Where the unacceptable behaviour is extreme, the law should be our 'defining mandate' (Blom-Cooper 1985). Before these extremes are reached, it is important to use our interpersonal skills to help people to find appropriate ways to give vent to feelings of upset, anger and frustration that are not harmful to themselves or others.

Dealing with hostility, aggression and violence

Violence against social workers is increasing (Kemshall and Pritchard 1999; Pringle and Thompson 1999: 135–44; Littlechild 1996). For example, research indicates that 25 to 30 per cent of social workers have been physically assaulted at some point in their careers (Rey 1996). Clearly, it is important that we avoid hostile situations as much as possible and minimize the likelihood of being the victims of violence. This section explores the skills involved in dealing with aggressive and violent behaviour.

Sound organizational arrangements can help to keep our fears in check and avoid violent confrontations. The ideal location should be a room that cannot be locked from inside, which has an alarm/panic button, is within easy reach of others and has a window for colleagues to keep an unobtrusive yet watchful eye. The seating should be arranged so that it is easy for us or the service user to get to the door and leave. If a service user is known to be violent, it is important to work out a contingency plan beforehand. Our attempts to minimize the risk of violence need to be undertaken in ways that do not exacerbate the situation. Some practitioners easily fall into a 'siege mentality'. Visible protection devices, such as closed-circuit television, buzzers and combination locks, are important but it is essential to remember that most service users are not violent (Lishman 1994: 17) and that excessive preoccupation with self-protection among practitioners can interfere with our being able to establish a trusting rapport with service users. Clearly, we must protect ourselves, but our best protection is our skill and capacity to avoid or to deal with aggressive and potentially violent encounters because, once we have acquired these skills, they travel with us into all situations.

For example, situations that involve depriving people of their liberty are the most likely to produce aggressive and violent reactions (Nathan 1997: 236). Given this fact, we need to reflect beforehand whether our intervention is justified in a situation where the person may be a danger to themselves (suicide or deliberate self-harm), or to others (child abuse, domestic violence or attacks on others). We then need to consider what the person's reaction might be and to prepare our response (Lishman 1994: 59). For example, we might decide not to undertake a home visit or, if this is essential, take a colleague with us (although to outnumber the service user may be counter-productive). We may also need to be clear how we intend to deal with actual violent attacks perpetrated against us or others. In my opinion, all violent attacks have to involve the police because, despite convincing justifications, violence goes beyond the realms of acceptable behaviour. If it is known that all attacks will be reported to the police, then this boundary is clear. People who choose violence know the consequences and that it will lead to police involvement. We may feel we played some part in provoking the attack. This too needs to be brought out into the open and our actions need to be seen in context. Some people are very frightening and this can affect our capacity to read situations accurately and our skills become lost because much of our thinking is taken up working out how to protect ourselves. If the threat is this serious, we need to find ways to leave or, if that is not possible, to ensure that the person in question can leave. Barring the door is unwise.

One of the best ways to defuse the situation is to try to engage the person in a dialogue. This cannot be forced but most people want to be understood. Many have serious grievances about the unfair way they have been treated, and their current behaviour may be some form of retaliation. It is important to listen to their story and to allow ourselves to be influenced by this, but not to the point where we make inappropriate promises. It also helps to remember that most people who are threatening or violent are frightened of themselves and of their own reactions. Many have suffered terrible experiences of violence and know what it is like to be terrified. To reveal how frightened we feel – and the fact that we mean them no harm – can sometimes help to establish a point of contact and help to defuse the situation (Jordan 1990: 185). We may also need to offer a gentle reminder that their current behaviour is unlikely to bring about the outcome they most desire and, indeed, can lead to negative consequences – but caution is needed. To stress negative consequences too much can be experienced as a threat and escalate the situation. To find a way for an individual to back down, but with honour and self-respect, is essential.

7 PROFESSIONAL COMPETENCE AND ACCOUNTABILITY

It is important to understand professional accountability in context and to attempt to differentiate between professionalism, professionalization and 'technicist' solutions. 'Professionalism' is defined by Barker as 'The degree to which an individual possesses and uses the knowledge, skills, and qualification of a profession and adheres to its values and ethics when serving the client' (1995: 297). On the other hand, 'professionalization' involves the 'control of knowledge' (Payne 1997: 30), thereby excluding service users. Similarly, 'technicist' solutions also fail service users by applying techniques 'regardless of wider debates about values and underlying social relations' (Mayo 1994: 70). Anti-oppressive practice calls for 'a redefinition of professionalism, with expertise being rooted in more power-sharing egalitarian directions and making explicit the value system to which the profession subscribes' (Dominelli 1998: 8).

What this means in practice, in terms of the day-to-day experiences of practitioners and service users, is not clear. Most service users do not come to social services asking for 'power-sharing' or to be informed of the 'value system' of the agency, but they regularly request quality services, delivered in ways that are respectful and caring. Our value base and our desire to create more equitable relationships need to be linked more directly to practice and the context within which social work currently exists in terms of 'managerial categories of cost, efficiency and risk' (Clarke 1996: 58). They also need to be linked to the requirements of government, which for Social Services departments too involves meeting specific targets, such as those laid down in *Quality Assurance and Best Value*, and for practice to be based on 'the best evidence of what works' (DoH 1998b: 93). Linking our value base to an analysis of effectiveness is part of the challenge we face and, to some extent, this is already happening. For example, research findings indicate that our chances of success are likely to be enhanced if our skills include 'accurate empathy, warmth and genuineness which have long been known to be associated with effective practice' (Thoburn 1997: 295).

However, as social workers our accountability to service users is only one of 'multiple accountabilities':

> Social workers are engaged in complex webs of social and institutional relationships, embracing multiple accountabilities: to the state, to their employers who provide social work services, to colleagues, to professional values and not least toward the service user and the wider community.
>
> (Adams 1998: 269)

This can lead to conflicting demands as we attempt to balance the best interests of one group against those of another. For example, in children's services this can lead to tensions as we attempt to balance children's needs and the requirement to protect parents' rights (Hollis and Howe 1990: 549). Yet these themes are linked because the central task of social work involves problem solving across these conflicting interests and competing needs. In this work, it is probably true to say that social work is 'crucially concerned with fairness' (Jordan 1990: 178) but the extent to which the pursuit of 'fairness' or, more particularly, redressing injustices, is considered to be a legitimate part of our social work role is a controversial issue. Again, we are caught in a double-bind: we are being asked to be 'empowering' yet not political. It may not always be possible, or effective, to separate the two.

Practitioners who see their professional competence and accountability primarily in terms of their accountability to service users are likely to view their work and priorities differently from those who place agency accountability at the forefront. Some authors are clear that addressing underlying causes, such as poverty and discrimination, is not the main priority of social work. Other demands dominate; 'Social workers and their agencies are already very over-pressed with current commitments, many of them statutory, and cannot afford the resources for excursions into areas outside social work proper' (Clark 2000: 198). Other authors would take issue with this view and argue that the way social work is organized and managed is itself problematic and potentially oppressive (Mullender and Perrott 1998: 67). If professional competence means the ability to 'do the job', this raises the question, what is the 'job'? What is the role or task of social work and social workers and how can effectiveness be measured? Whatever our views, most writers, practitioners, managers, policy makers and politicians are clear that social work accountability, competence and effectiveness are centre stage.

These different views of practice are likely to be mirrored in the practice orientations, approaches and perspectives we use within our work, and to influence how we view professional competence and accountability. For more detailed coverage on competence and competencies, see Chapter 1. These differences need to be borne in mind in the following account, which analyses in general terms the following skills:

* providing protection and control
* managing professional boundaries

- record keeping skills
- reflective and effective practice
- using supervision creatively.

Providing protection and control

One of the tasks of social work is to provide appropriate levels of 'protection and control' (CCETSW 1995a: 16). This can be seen as a manifestation of our dual role as carers and as 'agents of social control' (Coulshed and Orme 1998: 93). It is difficult to generalize about how these protection and control powers are used. Much depends on the situation, on our practice orientation and on the fact that there is a degree of discretion about the extent to which practitioners or agencies exercise the power that statute gives (Dalrymple and Burke 1995: 32), although it has been argued that this discretion is becoming increasingly bound in 'managerial imperatives', as well as 'statutory or legal framings' (Clarke 1996: 58).

This discussion links back to the nature and task of social work. For example, Blom-Cooper (1985) stated in the Beckford Report that the law should be social work's defining mandate, while others have challenged this narrow view and insisted that the defining mandate is our ethical duty to care, within which the law is centrally important but only one component (Stevenson 1988). The decision to adopt a more 'holistic' approach, which avoids the dangers of 'a narrow procedural legalistic approach' (O'Sullivan 1999: 170), is important, but so too is the need to have an in-depth knowledge of the law and legal procedures, including agency policy and procedures. This is our statutory responsibility. However, a knowledge of the law – or how to use the law – is also important because local authorities have a duty to provide certain services (see Chapter 2, Johns and Sedgwick 1999). Social workers can also use the law to protect children 'likely to suffer significant harm' (Children Act 1989, s47) and, under the Mental Health Act 1983, to safeguard the 'interests of the patient's health and safety, or the safety of others'; not, as frequently misquoted, to protect patients from being a danger to themselves or others (Pringle and Thompson 1999: 141).

In relation to our direct work with service users, concepts such as protection and control are important because they define a framework within which the relationship between service user and social worker, the individual and the state, is located. To cross over an invisible line into the realms of 'dangerous' behaviour brings into play certain 'safeguards'. Although these safeguards are designed to protect the individual or others from harm, it is not always clear – nor the case – that the protection given is warranted, as in the case of the compulsory sectioning under the Mental Health Act 1983 of people from ethnic minorities, nor that the type of protection offered is in any sense appropriate to that individual, empowering or enabling. This can lead to a moral dilemma because to fail to act can increase risk and threaten our professional credibility, yet to use our powers of protection and control could result in our being 'an active accessory to that exploitation and domination . . . those constraints, exclusions and coercions which entrap and disempower clients' (Jordan 1990: 58). For these reasons, notions of protection and control have been scrutinized in recent years with the introduction of anti-discriminatory/anti-oppressive perspectives within social work where the emphasis is on ensuring that people's rights are not violated (Dalrymple and Burke 1995: 30). An important focus has been to question who decides what protection and control are required and what part service users play in this decision-making process. This relates to earlier accounts in this text on empowerment and partnership.

The most common use of the term 'protection' relates to the concepts of 'risk' and 'vulnerability' to exploitation, neglect and/or abuse. Child protection services are the best known examples but the concept of protection also extends to other vulnerable groups, such as some people with learning disabilities, emotional problems or older people. The concept of vulnerability is important. At present there is no law relating to vulnerable adults, but there is for children under the Children Act 1989. However, the Law Commission (1993) has drafted proposals on this theme, defining vulnerability as indicating 'people who are for various reasons unable to take care of themselves or protect themselves from others' (Johns and Sedgwick 1999: 2). A differentiation is made between vulnerability and incapacity, with the latter referring to people who are unable to understand information in relation to a particular issue (Law Commission 1993).

Where children, or other vulnerable groups, are unable to articulate their needs, it can be difficult to gauge the necessary level of protection. This can lead to too much or too little protection, or to protection of the wrong kind, all of which could lead to negative outcomes. A different tension exists where people present a threat or danger to themselves and/or to others, such as the threat of suicide. Here we have a professional obligation to protect and control. If persuasion does not work, and if the person's life is to be saved and a breathing space provided from which other, better solutions can be sought, then an external control – sectioning under the Mental Health Act 1983 – may be the only alternative available.

Managing professional boundaries

Boundaries are important in social work, as in all other areas of professional activity, because they are a way of marking the responsibilities that lie within a particular role or task, and differentiating these from other activities or aspects of social work. The notion of boundaries can include work with individuals, groups, families, communities and organizations:

> This concept helps us to look at ways of marking off and establishing the identity of something, by differentiating it from other entities and from its surroundings. It is also concerned with setting limits, as we do in

everyday life, for example whenever we delineate what is acceptable from what is not. Boundary definition gives enhanced understanding of the types of relationship and interchange that occur between one entity and another.

(Brearley 1995: 49)

For example, an interview kept within clear boundaries will start and end on time. This clarity allows us to measure whether the service user is late or not. Similarly, we can learn a great deal about a service user's capacity to let go – to leave one experience and move on to another – if we set a time for the appointment or session to end and they try to extend this on a regular basis, perhaps with 'doorknob revelations'. Without these boundaries, which act as markers, we can fail to pick up on a range of behaviours that may be relevant. Service users who are trying to find employment but are always late for appointments with us may be at risk of losing any job they find due to poor timekeeping. To be able to help them, we have to know what they find difficult.

If we were to meet this same service user away from our agency, say at the local shops, our conversation would not need to be bound by time or other constraints because we are in a different role. It is important to strike the right balance. Too loose a boundary can result in insecurity and a loss of identity, whereas too rigid a boundary can feel too controlling or unnecessarily withholding.

This highlights that within any discussion of boundaries, there are areas of overlap. For this reason, Brearley suggests that it is better to think in terms of boundary regions rather than boundary lines. This helps to avoid taking up rigid inflexible positions but instead allows us to explore this overlap based on an acknowledgement of 'common ground and shared territory and concerns between one group or activity and another' (1995: 49).

There are several advantages for laying down and working within clear boundaries:

- Boundaries ensure that we keep to the task and roles designated and agreed, thereby ensuring that we are not drawn into other areas or issues. For example, some service users may like to become our friends (or we may want to become their friend). In work settings, this may actually contravene agency policy, as well as blurring professional boundaries.
- Boundaries ensure the economic use of time and resources. For example, if an interviewing room has been booked for an hour, it can disrupt and frustrate other practitioners if the session is allowed to extend beyond the allocated time so that it encroaches on their work.
- Practical arrangements can be formalized and the contact put on a professional footing. Some practical negotiations are similar to ground rules and can include identifying the purpose of the work or the nature of the task and contract (written or otherwise); the frequency and location of the sessions; who is eligible to attend; agreement about record keeping; transport/child-care arrangements; expectations about punctuality; smoking prohibitions; how crises or emergencies will be dealt with; behaviour

expectations (no alcohol, drug-taking, spitting or violence); communication rules (no swearing or interrupting); and so on.

The above categories are sometimes summarized as the three 'Ts': time, territory and task. It is usual for practitioners to ensure that these three elements or other boundary issues are adhered to.

Limits of confidentiality

One of the most problematic boundary problems in social work is the issue of confidentiality. Confidentiality is essential to create a climate of trust and to protect service users' rights. The general rule is that no information will be disclosed without the service users' consent. Barker differentiates between absolute confidentiality, where no information is disclosed regardless of circumstances without consent, and relative confidentiality, indicating the circumstances where it is our ethical or professional responsibility to disclose information (1995: 74). Some situations may warrant absolute confidentiality. However, in addition to the needs of service users, our role is dictated by agency and legal requirements, as well ethical and moral considerations. Although the 'precept of professional ethics [is] that the professional should not divulge the content of the client's communication unless the client clearly authorize otherwise' (Clark 2000: 184), in some circumstances this is not possible. The two suggestions put forward by Clark (2000: 191–2) to help clarify our professional boundaries in relation to confidentiality are:

- for agencies to make their confidentiality policy available, in written form, as a guide for practitioners and service users, including the recording policy of each agency; and
- for the confidentiality policy to be translated, individualized and negotiated with every service user, thereby making it 'appropriate to the client's understanding, ability and emotional capacity to deal with them' (Clark 2000: 192).

It is important to remember the record keeping policy of the agency, particularly in relation to inter-agency collaboration or multi-professional work. This may include service users' rights to see and contribute to their records, stipulating who has access to these records and under what circumstances (typists, supervisors, line managers, colleagues, other outside agencies or professional contacts), security arrangements, and so forth. It may also include service users being informed of information that is being passed between one agency and another.

One area where a boundary tension exists in relation to confidentiality is in the boundary between counselling and other social work tasks, particularly the use of interviewing skills. For a helpful account of this tension, see Seden (1999) and Brearley (1995).

Record keeping skills

Record keeping is an essential skill within social work and can be an intervention in its own right. However, record keeping is an area most criticized in the findings of the 45 public inquiries into child deaths held in Britain between 1973 and 1994. According to Munro (1998), who analysed these findings, the main criticism centred on the lack of information:

> Lack of information was particularly demonstrated by the poverty of social work records. Twenty-six reports (fifty-five per cent) criticize the standard of record keeping and conclude that it adversely affected the way the case was handled. Sometimes, records were inaccurate. Heidi Koseda's records contained falsely reassuring information that she had been seen in good health by the health visitor in September, even though, by this time, she would already have been showing signs of starvation.
>
> (Munro 1998: 94)

Other criticisms included: a lack of baseline details, making it difficult to assess improvement or deterioration; records failing to state who had been seen during visits or to record a child's absence; and a failure to collate and to link information. Evidence suggests that there has been no marked improvement. A Social Services Inspectorate report of all six local authorities noted that 'recording was below standard . . . the content of the records was inadequate, making it difficult to understand what had been achieved through the investigation and post-case conference work' (Social Services Inspectorate 1993: 34).

Had sound record keeping formed a central part of the work mentioned above, it is likely that some errors of judgement could have been avoided. Given these findings, it is important to restate why record keeping is essential to the social work task. Its primary purpose is to enhance service delivery in relation to effectiveness, accountability and confidentiality but it is also a crucial learning tool because record keeping provides an opportunity for analytical reflection and evaluation, particularly in relation to decision making, to formulating hypotheses and evolving collaborative ways of working. It provides an opportunity to step back and to think things through. The following is a helpful summary of the multi-purpose nature of record-keeping that can be used:

- as learning and teaching material
- for supervision purposes
- for administrative purposes, e.g. budgeting
- to ensure accountability
- for research and evaluation
- to illustrate shortfalls or absence of services
- to 'cover' the worker for work done
- to provide continuity when workers change
- to aid planning and decision making
- to monitor progress

- as an *aide mémoire*
- to facilitate client participation, as indicated.

(Coulshed 1991: 41–2)

One of the greatest tensions within record keeping is how much information to record and how best to do this in ways that are accurate, objectively critical and sufficiently detailed yet also succinct. Much depends on how the records might be used. For example, as already implied, records in relation to legal proceedings need to be detailed. The four main methods used within social work include:

- process recording (sometimes called verbatim recording)
- diagnostic recording (often used in therapy)
- problem-centred (sometimes called task-centred) recording
- proforma (often computerized) recording.

All have advantages and disadvantages, but in recent years more structured, systematized forms of recording have been encouraged as a way of ordering information, checking its validity, drawing up and testing hypotheses, ensuring that facts can be differentiated from opinion or hearsay, relating information to a knowledge base and using this to inform future practice. For Coulshed, records should 'register significant facts, evidence, feelings, decisions, action taken and planned, monitoring, review, evaluation and cost ing information' (1991: 40). Sheldon recommends summarizing statements to represent 'the best-informed judgements' but that these should be tentative and open to refutation as new information emerges (1995: 123). However, structuring information does not in itself ensure good practice nor effectiveness. This is more likely to be achieved when service users have open access to their records and play an active part in the recording process as an integral part of the work. One way to symbolize this participative effort would be for service users to countersign their records (Neville and Beak 1990).

It is important to note that the Data Protection Act 1984 gave people the right to access information recorded about them on computer. This right was extended to manual records held by housing and social services departments by the Access to Personal Files Act 1987. Since 1 April 1989, people have the right to see their manual records. Notice must be given to the authorities, who are allowed 40 days to respond. Information about third parties, excluding professionals, cannot be divulged without their consent (Neville and Beak 1990).

Reflective and effective practice

According to Shaw, 'social work works' (1996: 166). Similarly, Cheetham *et al.* state that in some areas 'social work can now claim to be cost effective' (1992: 4). However, these statements call us to define what effectiveness means and how we measure success. One answer could be to say that 'social work is effective in so far as it achieves intended aims' (Cheetham *et al.* 1992: 10).

However, we then must question whether these aims are too high, too low or appropriate to the situation, given the existence of other constraints and variables operating at the time. These variables over which we may have little or no control, together with the fact that we often encounter problems that are complex, multidimensional, and intractable, make the task of evaluating effectiveness fraught. This difficulty is made worse by the fact that we know very little about what actually happens in practice in terms of the impact of particular interventions or services. Evidence of positive or beneficial outcomes is not enough to tell us what factors did or did not play a part in bringing about a particular outcome.

Yet despite these difficulties, it is important that we provide quality services and find ways to evidence effectiveness (Macdonald and Macdonald 1995). This is demanded of us in a climate, in terms of government policy, of 'what works is what counts'. 'Professionals must seek to ensure that their interventions are not only carried out with due competence and in good faith, but are effective in the sense that they lead to the desired outcomes' (Clark 2000: 56). It is also essential because mistakes can be very costly in terms of human lives, as the errors in child abuse cases and public inquiries reveal. Reflective practice provides an opportunity to review our decisions and decision-making processes, and to learn from the lessons of the past. An analysis of 45 inquiry reports into the death of children known to social services shows that in 42 per cent of reports, social workers were not criticized but other concerns prevail:

> The analysis however also reveals one persistent error: social workers are slow to revise their judgements. Psychology research indicates that this error is widespread and by no means peculiar to social workers but it means that misjudgements about clients that may have been unavoidable on the limited knowledge available when they were made continue to be accepted despite a growing body of evidence against them. Social workers need a greater acceptance of their fallibility and a willingness to consider that their judgements and decisions are wrong. To change your mind in the light of new information is a sign of good practice, a sign of strength not weakness.
>
> (Munro 1996: 793)

As well as arriving at decisions based on 'best evidence', reflective practice provides a vital link between theory and practice. This is particularly important for complex situations where, as a result of conflicting values and purposes, there is no guarantee that agreed tasks and objectives can be effectively implemented on the basis of theories, 'technical rationality' (Schön 1991: 338) or undertaking. Reflection involves more than thinking things out carefully. It allows us to acknowledge that we are experiencing the situation we seek to understand and are a part of the interventions we are involved in providing. This creates a crucial link between task and process, and makes it important to 'look underneath the surface relationships and events which are presented to us' (Payne 1998: 122), in order to locate ourselves, and others, within the overall picture.

Reflective practice involves developing the capacity for flexible and creative thinking. This Schön describes as the 'unprecedented requirement for adaptation' (1991: 15), where we constantly need to engage in drawing up working hypotheses and testing these out by acting temporarily as if they were true. This means being involved in a process where thinking itself, and its attendant activities, are subject to critical scrutiny so that we are always open to looking again and to observing carefully the factors that influence the direction and content of our actions, and those of others.

Although reflective practice of this kind may fit uneasily with more rationalist approaches encouraged with social work, Schön's concept of *reflection-in-action* and *reflective conversation with the situation* provide a way of building on our knowledge base so that we can observe and attend to the uniqueness of every situation and human experience in order to link 'understanding, action and effect' (England 1986: 154). In terms of practice, Schön's concepts can help us to formulate a more rigorous approach to our judgements in deciding what practice orientation, approach, perspective and interventions should be used in relation to certain kinds of problems. These can then be tested, using different evaluative approaches. These can be broadly divided into an analysis of service user based or service based outcomes (O'Sullivan 1999: 163). For an account of different approaches to evaluation – managerialist, academic and participative – see Marsden *et al.* (1994).

Using supervision creatively

The purpose of supervision within social work is to facilitate the professional development of practitioners to ensure that our work is effective, efficient, accountable and undertaken in ways that sensitively address the needs of service users (Pritchard 1995). For this reason, regular supervision is recognized as an essential feature of social work practice. In general terms, supervision consists of three main components (Hawkins and Shohet 1989: 41–4):

- a management or an accountability component
- an educational component
- a supportive component.

The weight given to certain functions over others depends on a range of different factors such as the nature of the work, agency requirements, the practice orientation of the supervisor and practitioner and the particular features of the work at hand. For example, one definition of the purpose of supervision is 'to establish the accountability of the worker to the organization and to promote the worker's development as a professional person' (DHSS 1978: 200). Lishman disagrees with the first purpose and sees supervision as 'different from management control and accountability' because it is built on a 'professional-to-professional relationship rather than a superior-to-subordinate one' (1994: 39). Others endorse the importance of providing support but within a framework which 'offers challenges, professional in character, to an apparently fixed view of risk or fixed ideas about the appropriateness of therapeutic practitioners' decisions' (Sheldon 1995: 120). This emphasis is on how judgements are formed, and particularly how to reduce worker bias (Coulshed 1991: 31) and to review decisions made (Munro 1996: 973; Milner and O'Byrne 1998: 174; O'Sullivan 1999: 167–70). For example, Hollis and Howe remind us that 'good intentions and keeping to the procedures' are not enough and that 'well judged risks sometimes lead to bad outcomes' (1990: 548–9). Where practitioners encounter this degree of uncertainty, one of the major functions of supervision can involve containing or managing anxiety and helping to cope with the demands that the work entails (Brearley 1995: 93). Given the lack of uniformity, it is essential that the purpose of the supervision relationship between practitioners and supervisors is clarified in the early stages of the relationship.

Most supervision takes place on a regular one-to-one basis with a line manager, although other forms can also exist alongside, or instead of, individual supervision, such as peer, group and team supervision and also inter-agency supervision structures. 'Live' supervision, which may involve inviting a manager or colleague to sit-in on a session in order to give their observations, can be particularly valuable to add another dimension to our appraisal. Similarly, the range of information made available for supervision can also vary and include written case notes or reports, tape or video recordings, feedback from colleagues, service users, and others who have direct experience of the work at hand and/or the practitioner's particular strengths and weaknesses, and so forth. The range of issues that can form a part of the supervision session can also vary and include:

- an opportunity to reflect on the content of a particular session or details of an encounter;
- an analysis of the different practice choices adopted; that is, the practice orientation (work with individuals, families, groups and communities), theories, practice approaches, perspectives, interventions and skills, their impact and overall effectiveness in terms of achieved and desired outcomes;
- exploring the service user–practitioner relationship, its strengths and weaknesses; and how any of the feelings we or others have might enhance/detract from the work;
- looking at the supervision session and what is happening in the here and now, particularly with a view to seeing if issues in relation to the service user are being replayed in the supervision session (Mattinson 1975); and
- looking at practitioners' professional development, such as training opportunities and how to enhance our knowledge, value base and practice skills (Lishman 1998: 89–103).

Supervision sessions that are carefully planned beforehand by all parties tend to be more supportive, informative and creative. Responsibility for establishing a rapport based on shared learning and exploration lies with both parties. However, to be able to use supervision creatively is a real skill (Brearley 1995: 92–8). For some practitioners supervision is not a creative or comfortable experience, perhaps due to personality clashes or because exposing our work to scrutiny in this way feels threatening. If the supervision is to be effective and a support, it is important that these 'blocks' are addressed (Hawkins and Shohet 1989: 21–7). Where workload pressures are an inhibiting factor, these tensions need to be fed back into the agency or organizational structure so that accountability is not seen as a one-way process (Macdonald 1990a: 542).

CONCLUSION

As social workers we work with some of the most vulnerable people in society, often dealing with intractable, complex, severe and enduring problems. This work requires that we are skilled and knowledgeable across a broad range of areas. As well as linking people to services, I believe we have an important part to play in helping service users deal with the impact of the trauma, deprivation and discrimination so that they can begin the work of reparation: to 'mend' themselves and take their lives forward. Social work is well positioned to do this because of our history, as a profession, of working with people who are struggling to cope; people who find themselves marginalized within society. We are also well positioned because of our long-standing commitment to social justice. People at the edge of life rarely have a voice and I believe it is possible and important for us to speak up for this group of people more than we do at the moment.

I have argued in this book that social work is a highly skilled activity. I have also argued that practitioners invariably find themselves having to deal with difficult situations and complex problems that are enduring, severe and multifaceted. These problems call for the development of specialist skills and a degree of creativity and imagination. These skills extend beyond the individual and involve addressing social, environmental and policy restraints that inhibit progress and the opportunity for effective action. I see social work as having a major part to play in creating and maintaining a link between vulnerable individuals, society and the welfare state to ensure these come together and 'join up', in ways that open up new opportunities and enhance an individual's quality of life where this has become threatened. This work involves linking people to services and to each other. Here, the role of groupwork in social work is important. It also involves working creatively with people who are powerless, hopeless, helpless and despairing, who lack the energy or resilience to sort out and work through the problems they face. This area requires that we develop our skills in motivating others; that we learn creative ways of helping people to get up, move on and to keep going (Miller and Rollnick 1991). This skill may be as valuable in relation to the demoralization that our colleagues sometimes feel as it is for service users. A connected yet separate area where our expertise is required involves working creatively with the impact of unwantedness. Children and adults who are unwanted are some of the most vulnerable individuals in society. They risk being abused in a range of different ways, often living in harsh worlds, with no one to protect them. Adults who have grown up in an environment where they were not wanted often carry with them a deep sense of 'not counting'. This can seriously inhibit their ability to create the life that they want to live, and to embrace the opportunities that they deserve to have. I hope that the direction that social work takes allows this creative work to happen. As an example of the kind of work we can engage in, with appropriate training, support and supervision, I would like to end this book by describing my experiences of working with Michael.

Michael

In telling this story, my aim is to describe how we might work more creatively with the suffering and anguish that is brought to us for 'mending'. I once worked with a 13-year-old, Michael, whose behaviour was so negative and self-destructive that it was almost impossible not to feel rejected by this individual. We were 'forced together' in a residential setting, and whenever we had to meet, he refused to speak, preferring to use his body language to communicate. He would arrive late and then need to go to the toilet, where he would linger until I came to find him. Once inside the room, he would refuse to sit down, but instead spent the time shuffling from one foot to the other, with his arms crossed and his eyes cast to the ceiling. His two consistent comments beyond ignoring me could be summarized as 'don't know' and 'can I go now?'. One regular point of contact was police stations, as we waited for hours while his latest episode of damaging and dangerous behaviour was recorded and processed.

Over a period of months, Michael gradually began to reveal why his behaviour was so dismissive. It came from a profound belief in the pointlessness and futility of his life. He appeared not to care whether he lived or died: life had no meaning for him. The immediate causes for this terrible despair were many, but for Michael they stemmed from the fact that throughout his young life he felt that he had never been wanted. Michael had spent most of his life in care, having been rejected and abandoned by his parents. He managed to deal with this rejection by blaming social services for 'taking him away' from his parents, thereby protecting himself from his sense of unwantedness. Then one day, the story bubble burst when his mother, in a heated argument, said she had tried to abort him when she was pregnant and that she wished he had never been born. From that time, the meaning he ascribed to his experience was not only that he was not wanted but that he would never be wanted. From this place, he felt there was no point in living. No one could replace the mother he wanted to love him, and his clearest message to those who came into his life was that he did not want them. I believe that not being wanted is one of the most devastating experiences that any human being can be asked to endure and one that is very difficult to overcome (Jacobs 1995). This was certainly the case for Michael.

My approach to this terrible dilemma was to add another element to the story of his conception and creation. I added the fact that providence wanted him. I did this by reminding Michael that a baby is not always made every time two people make love. Therefore, for conception to occur, there have to be three elements present: the mother and father, and that third element – providence (had Michael been religious, I may have described God as the third element). Even if his parents did not want him, the fact that he was conceived and born meant that providence wanted him; that providence had set aside a place for him on this earth and that he had a right to take up this place.

Fortunately, I had the opportunity to work with Michael over a long period. This allowed us to address, slowly and carefully, his feelings of unwantedness. In time, we worked together to create a new and different meaning about his conception based on the idea of a 'providence parent', whom he nicknamed 'PP' to protect himself from outside intrusion or ridicule. In the story he created, he made himself an only child and described different imaginary exchanges with his PP. He imagined doing things and saying things to his PP. Sometimes his PP was his companion, someone to talk to when he felt lonely and uncared for. Other times his PP acted as a source of encouragment or chastisement. He regularly switched the gender of his PP, depending on what role he wanted them to play. Interestingly, his imaginary parents were quite stereotypical in terms of the gendered roles he gave them.

I do not think that it would have been possible for this young man to embrace this imaginary realm had he not had some hope and trust that we could build on. This suggests that he had experienced some degree of stability and security in his early life (Winnicott 1971: 1–25; Winnicott 1986: 150–66; Dockar-Drysdale 1990). It always felt that he was building on some positive experiences. Maybe some hardship or adversity interfered with his parents' ability to care for him: it was never clear why the family break-up occurred. Whichever way, he managed to create an imaginary parent who wanted him and who gave his life a sense of meaning and purpose. I think that life will always be a struggle for Michael but I hope he continues to feel less alone in that struggle.

APPENDIX 1

Client-centred approaches

Description/definition

Client-centred/person-centred approaches are usually attributed to the work and writings of Carl Rogers and are based on the humanist belief that people have an innate motivation to grow and to develop their capacities as human beings (i.e. to self-actualize – see Maslow's triangle, p. 32). In order to achieve this, Rogers (1951) argued that people need a non-directive stance, where their thoughts, feelings and actions are not subject to advice, interpretation, criticism, confrontation or challenge beyond encouraging people to try as hard as possible to clarify what they see to be happening. This non-directive, non-judgemental, accepting, warm and caring stance forms part of the 'facilitative conditions', which Rogers summarized as involving empathy, unconditional positive regard and congruence:

- *empathy* – caring, warmth. 'It means entering the private perceptual world of the other and becoming thoroughly at home in it' (Rogers 1975: 2);
- *unconditional positive regard* – respect, non-possessive warmth, acceptance and non-judgementality even if the social worker personally does not approve of or condone the person's actions;
- *congruence* – genuineness, authenticity, acting in a human way as a real person and not someone hiding behind a mask or professional role.

Client-centred approaches assume a non-directive stance and the social worker usually does not offer advice, interpretations, criticism or challenges because these would be seen to contravene people's innate ability to be their own change agents. Because of its accessibility and flexibility as a theory and practice, this is one of the most popular approaches used by social workers, but it is also an approach that is vulnerable to being misunderstood and misapplied, sometimes being used to stress the rights of service users to be treated with respect and dignity rather than as a distinct theory and practice. Also, confusion can emerge about the difference between acceptance and approval. Some behaviour is intolerable, such as child abuse, and it can be difficult to reconcile this fact with adopting an approach that encompasses unconditional positive regard.

Rogers's seven stages of change

Carl Rogers provides a clear framework for understanding change, describing the 'stages of progress' as running through seven stages. His 'necessary and sufficient conditions of therapeutic personality change' are located in the therapeutic relationship between the client and therapist, with the process of change leading not only to changes in behaviour but a fundamental shift in the way an individual relates to themself. The change being mapped relates to service users becoming increasingly involved in their inner worlds, which McLeod (1998) summarizes as follows:

1 *Communication is about external events.* Feelings and personal meanings are not 'owned'. Close relationships are construed as dangerous. Rigidity in thinking. Impersonal, detached. Does not use first-person pronouns.
2 *Expression begins to flow more freely in respect of non-self topics.* Feelings may be described but not owned. Intellectualization. Describes behaviour rather than inner feelings. May show more interest and participation in therapy.
3 *Describes personal reactions to external events.* Limited amount of self-description. Communication about past feelings. Beginning to recognize contradictions in experience.
4 *Descriptions of feelings and personal experiences.* Beginning to experience current feelings, but fear and distrust of this when it happens. The 'inner life' is presented and listed or described, but not purposefully explored.
5 *Present feelings are expressed.* Increasing ownership of feelings. More exactness in the differentiation of feelings and meanings. Intentional exploration of problems in a personal way, based on processing of feelings rather than reasoning.
6 *Sense of an 'inner referent, or flow of feeling which has a life of its own.* 'Physiological loosening', such as moistness in the eyes, tears, sighs or muscular relaxation, accompanies the open expression of feelings. Speaks in present tense or offers vivid representation of past.
7 *A series of felt senses connecting the different aspects of an issue.* Basic trust in own inner processes. Feelings experienced with immediacy and richness of detail. Speaks fluently in present tense.

(McLeod 1998: 103)

Advantages
- This is an accessible approach that is easily understood (though not always easy to achieve).
- It values all forms of experience for itself and allows people to find their own way in their own time.
- It resists the temptation to criticize people or to see events in a negative light.
- It encourages the development of an equal, non-authoritarian relationship where both service user and social worker work together to establish a significant and meaningful relationship.

Limitations
- It is difficult for social workers to demonstrate a sense of empathy, unconditional positive regard and congruence in their everyday work and, because of this, this client-centred approach has to be adapted.
- Client-centred approaches involve a great deal of motivation on the part of the client and are, as a result, difficult to use when working with reluctant people who are destructive and dangerous.
- It focuses strongly on the individual and individual change, with little recognition of societal influences and pressures.

APPENDIX 2

Cognitive-behavioural approaches

Description/definition

Unlike 'insight-based therapies', cognitive-behavioural approaches involve:

> Approaches to treatment and to helping people resolve specific problems using selected concepts and techniques from behaviourism, social learning theory, action therapy, functional school in social work, task-centred treatment, and therapies based on cognitive models.
>
> (Barker 1995: 65)

According to Sheldon, 'behaviour therapy and applied behavioural psychology have undergone a "cognitive revolution" in the past decade' (1995: xii) with the development of cognitive-behavioural approaches, which attempt to link behaviour with how human beings organize and understand their worlds and how these beliefs become known, perceived and understood. The four major behaviourist techniques include systemic *desensitization, aversion therapy, operant conditioning* and *modelling*. Therapists may use or combine these interventions differently.

Gambrill's (1995) 'indicators of behavioral practice'

The clarity that behaviourism brings to a cognitive-behavioural approach is highlighted in Gambrill's 'indicators of behavioral practice':

A What will be found
1 A focus on altering complaints of concern to clients and significant others
2 Translation of complaints into specific behaviors (including thoughts and feelings) that if altered would remove complaints
3 Reliance on basic behavioral principles and related learning theory to guide assessment and intervention
4 Descriptive analysis of problems and related circumstances based on observation (i.e. clear description of problem-related behaviors and related setting events, antecedents, and consequences)

5 Functional analysis: identification of factors that influence problem-related behaviors by rearranging environmental factors and observing the effects

6 Identification of client assets that can be put to good use in attaining desired outcomes

7 Involvement of significant others

8 Selection of intervention programs based on what research suggests is effective and what clients find acceptable

9 Ongoing evaluation of progress using both subjective and objective measures; comparison of data gathered during intervention with baseline data when feasible

10 Clear description of assessment, intervention, and evaluation methods

11 A concern for social validity: (i.e. outcomes attained are valued by clients and significant others; procedures used are acceptable to clients)

12 Inclusion of procedures designed to enhance generalization and maintenance of positive gains

B What will not be found

1 Appeals to thoughts or feelings as sole causes of behavior

2 Appeals to personality dispositions as sole causes of behavior

3 Use of uninformative diagnostic labels (they provide neither information about problem-related causes nor guidelines for selecting intervention plans)

4 Reliance on self-report alone for assessment, evaluation, or both

5 Vague statements of outcome, problems, or progress indicators

6 Claims of success based on questionable criteria such as testimonials, and anecdotal experience

(Gambrill 1995: 462)

Case example: Mr Brooks' wife died suddenly

Ellis's ABC theory of emotions A→B→C (Ellis and Greiger 1977)

A *Activating* event or situation
Mr Brooks' wife died suddenly

B *Beliefs* or thoughts about the event or situation
iB, irrational belief *Had I called the doctor earlier, my wife would not have died.*

C emotional *consequence* of the thoughts or beliefs
iC, irrational emotional consequence *I deserve to suffer for what I have done.*

D *Disputation*
D by exploring the implicit thoughts and dysfunctional emotions and/or behaviours with the guidance of the therapist or practitioner the service user is taught to replace irrational beliefs (iB) with rational beliefs (rB)

E

The process of disputation (D) should produce an *evaluation* (E) of the activating (A) event or situation

Full sequence $A→B→C→D→E$

Advantages
• Cognitive-behavioural therapies are brief, widely applicable, highly structured, relatively easy to learn and effective.

- Where the focus of the work is towards teaching skills or correcting deficits, practitioners have found that behavioural performance based interventions particularly successful.
- Cognitive-behavioural therapies can offer a strategy and an approach to complex social problems.
- Combining two important approaches can build on the strengths of each approach and compensate for limitations.

Limitations

- It is directive with relatively high expectations of service users and their commitment to the programme.
- It is focused solely on the presenting problem and not on understanding causes and/or underlying problems.
- Some of the language of cognitive-behavioural approaches can be very abstract, mechanistic and detached.
- It can be hard for some service users to do homework because some do not have the capacity or emotional energy to undertake a task of this kind (some selection processes would try to select out such service users).

APPENDIX 3

Task-centred work

Description/definition

A model of short-term social work intervention in which the social worker and client identify specific problems and the tasks needed to change these problems, develop a contract in which various activities are to occur at specified times, establish incentives and a rationale for their accomplishment, and analyse and resolve obstacles as they are identified. The client may also be helped to accomplish tasks by simulation and guided practice in the social worker's office before performing them independently during the week. The social worker also facilitates a contextual analysis by helping the client identify, locate, and utilize resources and modify distorted perceptions or unrealistic expectations.

(Barker 1995: 378)

The mission of the task-centred project for the field of practice was to develop technologies that could be learned efficiently and could increase effectiveness of direct services in social welfare.

(Epstein 1980: vi)

All approaches involve undertaking a range of activities, or task. Task-centred work differs from other social work approaches, such as client-centred or cognitive-behavioural approaches, because it does not have a distinct theoretical base (Marsh 1997: 194). It also differs in the systematic way tasks are undertaken and the rigorous link made to a specific goal or outcome. This involves working in close collaboration with service users, and others, in order to agree specific goals or outcomes and to identify what steps, task, or 'building blocks', need to be undertaken to achieve those goals. Focusing on tasks in this way is one of the best ways we have of identifying whether an individual is motivated and whether s/he has the necessary skills, knowledge, confidence and resources to undertake and complete a particular task or to achieve a specific goal or outcome. This helps us to see what role we might need to play in this collaborative endeavour. This may involve teaching specific skills, such as how to make a telephone call or providing vital information, such as where to go to ask for help. It may also involve our taking responsibility for specific tasks appropriate to our professional role, such as liaison with other agencies. At the heart of task-centred work lies the importance of utilizing, extending and consolidating service users' strengths and abilities to address key issues, 'and developing ideas that reflect the actual reality of the users' relationships and lives' (Marsh 1997: 199).

The target problem

The task of the worker is to identify the target problem and to help bring about collaborative change by:

- establishing a mandate for the work
- exploring problems
- drawing up a written agreement
- formulating a task developmental sequence
- ending the work.

Advantages

- Tasks and goals are discreet and chosen because they are achievable. This enhances the likelihood of success and builds confidence because its focus is on enhancing people's capacities and strengths.
- Task-centred approaches are time-limited, usually within three months and outcomes and effectiveness are easy to evaluate.
- Task-centred approaches are person-centred and based on close collaboration between the worker and service user and a recognition of the importance of service user self-determination in the decision-making process.
- They can be oriented to alleviate the most pressing problems, as defined by the person seeking help and not by others.

Limitations

- This approach cannot be easily used when working with reluctant service users who are not prepared to collaborate in this way.
- The more difficult or underlying problems may never be identified to be worked on.
- Some people are overwhelmed by the problems they face and may not have the emotional energy to commit themselves to this approach, which involves a great deal of effort on the service users' part.
- Task-centred approaches can easily lose a political/social dimension. This is particularly important when problems are due to social causes such as poverty, unemployment and bad housing, where the problem may not be easy to overcome without social or political change.

APPENDIX 4

Crisis intervention

Crisis can be seen as:

- a hazardous event
- decision making (Greek)
- danger and opportunity (Chinese).

Description/definition

Crisis intervention as a theory was developed by Caplan (1964) who defined a crisis as a situation where an individual is thrown for a time into an upset in a steady state (Rapoport 1967) and, as a result, finds her/himself unable to benefit from their normal methods of coping with such problems. A sense of helplessness is produced and 'we fail to adjust either because the situation is new to us, or it has not been anticipated, or a series of events become too overwhelming' (Coulshed 1991: 68).

Caplan (1964) described a three-stage model, based on the view that people act as self-regulating systems to try to maintain an internal state of equilibrium. These phases of a crisis are:

- *impact* recognizing a threat to the equilibrium;
- *recoil* attempting to restore the equilibrium but being unable to do so, leaving the individual physically or psychologically exhausted, defeated and showing signs of stress or crisis; and
- *adjustment/adaptation* or *breakdown* – where the individual begins to move through to a higher level of functioning or to a lower level

The approach is based on the perspective that crises are time-limited and usually last no longer than six weeks. It draws from psychoanalytic theory, particularly ego psychology, and emphasizes that people's capacity to deal with problems – to be able to return to a steady state from an upset in the steady state – is based on three factors:

- people's internal psychological strengths and weaknesses (ego strength)

- the nature of the problem being faced
- the quality of help being given.

Keiran O'Hagan's criticism of Caplan's model

the style and 'tone' of classical crisis literature conveys nothing of the harsh realities of crisis intervention in social services: the atmosphere of chaos, panic and fear; the acute poverty and appalling living conditions; the sprawling decaying council estates; the numerous crisis; the worker's uneasy awareness of the possibility of being overwhelmed by the crisis.

(O'Hagan 1986: 39)

Advantages

- Where people can develop new adaptive ways of coping, they can function at a higher level.
- Help is time-limited (1–6 weeks) and therefore effective in terms of effort/resources.
- Crisis intervention relates internal crises to external changes (i.e. people's internal and external worlds).
- It is relevant and useful across a range of short-term crises (especially bereavement and loss, depression, traumatic experiences such as accidents and other situations of sudden change).

Limitations

- The term 'crisis intervention' is often used by practitioners to describe more general crisis (emergency) work or to describe the interventions adopted when working with people living in a chronic state of crisis. This makes it difficult to differentiate between crisis intervention as a specific approach rather than as an intervention used in crisis situations.
- It can be costly in terms of the amount of resources needed for new adaptive states to be developed (as opposed to maladaptive states).
- It may not be possible, because of limited resources or time, to assemble all the elements necessary for positive change to occur. As a result, this can mean that this approach is not viable as an option in most social work departments or settings.
- It can involve workers being highly intrusive and directive, which can raise important ethical issues, particularly in terms of the notion of empowerment and service users' rights to be at the centre of the decision-making process.

Interestingly, new texts such as *The Blackwell Companion to Social Work* (Davies 1997) and *Social Work: Themes, Issues and Critical Debates* (Adams *et al.* 1998) do not have a chapter on crisis intervention, probably because it is so little used within social work and some of its strengths have been superseded by time-limited, brief or focused social work approaches.

APPENDIX 5

Psychoanalytic concepts

Description/definition

Any line of investigation, no matter what its direction, which recognizes transference and resistance, and takes them as the starting point of its work may call itself psychoanalysis, though it arrives at results other than my own.

(Freud 1914: 3)

Central concepts

The unconscious

Central to the concepts of transference and resistance is the notion of the unconscious that is 'mental processes of which the subject is not aware'.

(Rycroft 1968: 172)

Defence mechanism

Defences are strategies which a person employs either knowingly or unknowingly, in order to avoid facing aspects of the self which are felt to be threatening.

(Jacobs 1988: 79–80)

Resistance

Resistance, which takes different forms, describes those times when clients cannot or will not talk freely, or are unable to acknowledge thoughts and feelings, because they are afraid of what will emerge, and of their or their counsellor's reactions.

(Jacobs 1988: 15)

Transference

A concept . . . that refers to emotional reactions that are assigned to current relationships but originate in earlier, often unresolved and unconscious experiences.

(Barker 1995: 385)

Transference occurs in every human relationship in that it involves passing on or 'transferring' an emotion or pattern of relating from one person onto another person or object. Feelings of mistrust, dislike, love and care can be in response to the practitioner's particular qualities but can also be a reflection of earlier feelings, fears and anxieties being activated. In this situation it is important not to collude or to allow ourselves to be manipulated by these positive and negative feelings, but instead to help the individual to understand what the feelings represent and what we have become for them. For example, a young person who is refusing to attend school may experience her social worker as blaming her or as judging her critically, when in fact the social worker has neither felt nor indicated such unsympathetic reactions.

Within social work, psychoanalysis has been influential in the development of other theories such as the psychosocial approach to social casework (Hollis 1977), ego psychology, ecological systems, crisis intervention, Bowlby's attachment theory, Erikson's eight stages of man, group therapy and within some developments within systems theory and family therapy. Hollis summarizes the main elements of the psychosocial approach: 'It is . . . an attempt to mobilize the strengths of the personality and the resources of the environment at strategic points to improve the opportunities available to the individual and to develop more effective personal and interpersonal functioning' (Hollis 1977: 1308).

Advantages
- Concepts such as the unconscious, transference, counter-transference, attachment and emotional development are important in helping us to understand human behaviour – it is 'the "bread and butter" of our job' (Coulshed 1991: 112).
- It is a theory that can explain all human behaviour, including complex, difficult behaviour and what meaning individuals place on events.
- Its recognition of good and bad elements within human nature and neutrality about emotions encourages understanding and avoids the danger of judging people.
- It has inspired the development of many other theories and practices and continues to do so, including transactional analysis, crisis intervention, and approaches based on ego psychology.

Limitations
- As a therapy, it is elitist, expensive to access and lacks clear time boundaries. As a theory, its concepts are difficult to grasp. In the past, practitioners working from psychoanalytic perspectives have been accused of being out of touch with 'bread and butter' issues.
- It can create an unhealthy dependency in the therapist–patient relationship.
- It has a tendency to ignore the importance of external factors, such as social causes and cultural influences and, therefore, for the most part has no political perspective.
- Its benefits and outcomes are hard to evaluate in terms of effectiveness because of its emphasis on quality of life issues, such as the capacity to relate to oneself and to others in ways that feel more personally satisfying.

APPENDIX 6

Twenty point interview preparation checklist

Preparation beforehand

1 1–2 weeks before proposal planned appointment send a letter or reminder to the interviewee stating:

  - date ☐
  - time ☐
  - location (if needed, send a map and bus details of how to get there) ☐
  - purpose of the interview ☐
  - any information or leaflets relevant to the interview. ☐

2 Book the interviewing room. ☐
3 Refer to records relating to the individual being interviewed (e.g. case notes, referral forms, etc.) and think about how to incorporate relevant information and queries into the interview. Check the status of the records in relation to confidentiality and agency policy in practice. ☐
4 Send off for any leaflets or information required for the interview. ☐
5 Make or plan relevant phone calls that need to be undertaken before the interview (i.e. liaison with other agencies). ☐

On the day

6 • Inform the receptionist of the interview and what help, if any, might be needed from him or her. ☐
   • If away from your desk prior to the interview, tell the receptionist where you are likely to be and how you can be contacted when the individual arrives. ☐
   • Tell the receptionist whether or not you can be disturbed, and under what circumstances, during the interview. ☐
   • If appropriate, let the receptionist know what help the individual might

need on arrival (e.g. wheelchair access, space for a pushchair). If the individual is likely to be upset, suggest how the receptionist might handle this situation.   ☐

7   Prepare the interviewing room paying attention to:
   • comfort and the overall appearance of the room (too formal/informal, untidy, over decorated, cluttered? Does it reflect the cultural diversity of the people using your office?)   ☐
   • seating arrangements and whether these suit the purpose of the interview   ☐
   • temperature (where possible find additional heat for cold rooms because people who get upset or frightened can easily become cold)   ☐
   • lighting (particularly important for people with poor sight)   ☐
   • security/safety arrangements, if needed   ☐
   • availability of a telephone, if needed   ☐
   • pens, paper and other information or equipment, if needed   ☐
   • agency guidelines in relation to smoking (ashtray?)   ☐
   • the room's set-up if children are being interviewed or present, in terms of their safety and what toys, crayons, books, magazines, etc. are available.   ☐

8   Check other activities taking place in the agency to ensure minimum disruption.   ☐
9   Consider any other difficulties or obstacles, e.g. the accessibility of the interviewing room in terms of wheelchair access.   ☐
10   When the interviewee arrives think about:

   • being punctual   ☐
   • your welcome   ☐
   • how you intend to introduce yourself and whether you will offer tea or coffee   ☐
   • what questions you will ask that allow the individual to express any immediate problems or queries they have, e.g. parking restrictions.   ☐

During the Interview

11   Think about how you intend to induce the purpose of the interview and how you will link this to earlier events (the referral, your letter, your last contact, other incidents that have happened).   ☐
12   Consider how you intend to use open and closed questions and other specific interviewing skills in order to communicate clearly and openly what you see to be the purpose, aims and objectives of the interview. Similarly, think about how you intend to use the same skills to elicit what the individual may want from the interview.   ☐
13   What notes or records, if any, do you intend to take during this interview, how do you intend to explain their purpose and what access will the interviewee and others have to these notes/records?   ☐
14   As part of the content and process of the interview, keep your focus on:

   • the time   ☐
   • the task at hand   ☐
   • how to protect the interview (territory) so that you are not being distracted by extraneous noises or demands. (It is helpful to put a sign on the door saying that an interview is in progress and must not be disturbed.)

Remember, it is fine to change what you planned to cover in the interview in order to address current concerns   ☐

15 How do you intend to end the interview and what future contact, if any, do you propose?   ☐

16 How do you intend to take your leave and to show people out?   ☐

After the interview

17 What record keeping/recording/forms need to be completed? (It helps to do this immediately after the interview when your thoughts are still fresh in your mind.)   ☐

18 What follow-up work needs to be done, and how do you intend to communicate and liaise with other interested parties and agencies?   ☐

19 It can be valuable to write a follow-up letter to the interviewee thanking them for attending and running through the main points covered or agreed. If the contact is ongoing, you could include the date and time of the next appointment or, if the contact is to cease, you could offer your best wishes for the future.   ☐

20 What follow-up work needs to be done to round off the interview or to take the work to the next stage (e.g. liaison with other agencies)?   ☐

APPENDIX 7

The challenge of partnership in child protection

Fifteen essential principles for working in partnership

1 Treat all family members as you would wish to be treated, with dignity and respect
2 Ensure that family members know that the child's safety and welfare must be given first priority, but that each of them has a right to a courteous, caring and professionally competent service
3 Take care not to infringe privacy any more than is necessary to safeguard the welfare of the child
4 Be clear with yourself and with family members about your power to intervene, and the purpose of your professional involvement at each stage
5 Be aware of the effects on family members of the power you have as a professional, and the impact and implications of what you say and do
6 Respect confidentiality of family members and your observations about them, unless they give permission for information to be passed to others or it is essential to do so to protect the child
7 Listen to the concerns of the children and their families, and take care to learn about their understanding, fears and wishes before arriving at your own explanations and plans
8 Learn about and consider children within their family relationships and communities, including their cultural and religious contexts, and their place within their own families
9 Consider the strengths and potential of family members, as well as their weaknesses, problems and limitations
10 Ensure that children, families and other carers know their responsibilities and rights, including the right to services, and their right to refuse services and any consequences of doing so

11 Use plain, jargon-free, language appropriate to the age and culture of each person. Explain unavoidable technical and professional terms
12 Be open and honest about your concerns and responsibilities, plans and limitations, without being defensive
13 Allow children and families time to take in and understand concerns and processes. A balance needs to be found between appropriate speed and the needs of people who may need extra time in which to communicate
14 Take care to distinguish between personal feelings, values, prejudices and beliefs, and professional roles and responsibilities, and ensure that you have good supervision to check that you are doing so
15 If a mistake or misinterpretation has been made, or you are unable to keep to an agreement, provide an explanation. Always acknowledge the distress experienced by adults and children and do all you can to keep it to a minimum.

(Department of Health 1995b: 14)

REFERENCES

Adams, R. (1998) *Quality Social Work*. Basingstoke: Macmillan.

Adams, R., Dominelli, L. and Payne, M. (1998) *Social Work: Themes, Issues and Critical Debates*. Basingstoke: Macmillan.

Ahmed, S. (1986) Cultural racism in work with Asian women and girls, in S. Ahmed, J. Cheetham and J. Small (eds) *Social Work with Black Children and their Families*. London: Batsford.

Ainsworth, M. D. S., Blehar, M., Walters, F. and Wall, S. (1978) *Patterns of Attachment: A Psychological Study of the Strange Situation*. Hillsdale, NJ: Lawrence Erlbaum.

Aldgate, J. (1997) Family breakdown, in M. Davies (ed.) *The Blackwell Companion to Social Work*. Oxford: Blackwell.

Aldgate, J., Tunstill, J. and McBeth (1994) *Implementing Section 17 of the Children Act – the First 18 Months*. Leicester: University of Leicester.

Angelou, M. (1994) *Wouldn't Take Nothing for my Journey Now*. London: Virago.

Applegate, J. S. and Bonovitz, J. M. (1995) *The Facilitating Partnership: A Winnicottian Approach for Social Workers and other Helping Professionals*. Northvale, NJ: Jason Aronson.

Atkinson, D. (1986) Engaging competent others: a study of the support networks of people with mental handicap, *British Journal of Social Work*, supplement, 16: 33–101.

Audit Commission (1992) *Community Care: Managing the Cascade of Change*. London: HMSO.

Bagley, C. and King, K. (1990) *Child Sexual Abuse*. London: Tavistock/Routledge.

Ball, C. (1996) *Law for Social Workers*, 3rd edn. Aldershot: Arena.

Bandura, A. (1969) *Principles of Behavior Modification*. New York: Holt, Rinehart and Winston.

Bandura, A. (1977) *Social Learning Theory*. Englewood Cliffs, NJ: Prentice-Hall.

Barclay Report (1982) *Social Workers: Their Roles and Task*. London: Bedford Square Press.

Barker, R. L. (1991) *The Social Work Dictionary*, 2nd edn. Silver Spring, MD: NASW Press.

Barker, R. L. (1995) *The Social Work Dictionary*, 3rd edn. Washington, DC: NASW Press.

Bee, H. (1995) *The Developing Child*. New York: Harper Collins.

Benjamin, J. (1990) *The Bonds of Love*. London: Virago.

Benjamin, J. (1995) *Like Subjects, Like Objects*. London: Yale University Press.

Biestek, F. P. (1961) *The Casework Relationship*. London: Allen & Unwin.

Birdwhistell, R. (1970) *Kinesics and Context*. Philadelphia, PA: University of Pennsylvania.

Blom-Cooper, L. (1985) *A Child in Trust: A Report of the Panel of Inquiry into Circumstances Surrounding the Death of Jasmine Beckford*. London: London Borough of Brent.

Boswell, G. (1997) The role of the practice teacher, in M. Davies (ed.) *The Blackwell Companion to Social Work*. Oxford: Blackwell.

Boushel, M. (1994) The protective environment of children: towards a framework of anti-oppressive, cross-cultural and cross-national understanding, *British Journal of Social Work*, 24: 173–90.

Bowlby, J. (1979) *The Making and Breaking of Affectional Bonds*. London: Tavistock.

Bowlby, J. (1980) *Attachment and Loss, Vol. III: Loss, Sadness, and Depression*. London: Hogarth.

Bowlby, J. (1988) *A Secure Base: Clinical Applications of Attachment Theory*. London: Routledge.

Brandon, M., Schofield, G. and Trinder, L. (1998) *Social Work with Children*. Basingstoke: Macmillan.

Braye, S. and Preston-Shoot, M. (1995) *Empowering Practice in Social Care*. Buckingham: Open University Press.

Brearley, J. (1991) A psychodynamic approach to social work in J. Lishman (ed.) *Handbook of Theory for Accredited Practice Teachers in Social Work*. London: Jessica Kingsley.

Brearley, J. (1995) *Counselling and Social Work*. Buckingham: Open University Press.

British Association for Counselling (1992) *16th Annual Report 1991/92*. Rugby: BAC.

Broverman, I., Broverman, D., Clarkson, F., Rosenkrantz, P. and Vogal, S. (1970) Sex-role stereotypes and clinical judgements of mental health, *Journal of Consulting and Clinical Psychology*, 34: 1–7.

Brown, G. (1986) Explaining, in O. Hargie (ed.) *A Handbook of Communication Skills*. London: Routledge.

Brown, H. C. (1998) Counselling, in R. Adams, L. Dominelli and M. Payne (eds) *Social Work: Themes, Issues and Critical Debates*. Basingstoke: Macmillan.

Burgess, P. (1992) Welfare rights, in C. Hanvey, and T. Philpot (eds) *Practising Social Work*. London: Routledge.

Burnham, J. B. (1986) *Family Therapy*. London: Routledge.

Bywaters, P. (1986) Social work and the medical profession – arguments against unconditional collaboration, *British Journal of Social Work*, 16: 661–7.

Bywaters, P. (1999) Social work and health inequalities, *British Journal of Social Work*, 29: 811–16.

Caplan, G. (1964) *Principles of Preventative Psychiatry*. New York: Basic Books.

CCETSW (Central Council for Education and Training in Social Work) (1989) *Requirements and Regulations for the Diploma in Social Work – Paper 30*. London: CCETSW.

CCETSW (Central Council for Education and Training in Social Work) (1991) *DipSW: Rules and Requirements for the Diploma in Social Work*, CCETSW Paper 30, 2nd edn. London: CCETSW.

CCETSW (Central Council for Education and Training in Social Work) (1995a) *Assuring Quality in the Diploma in Social Work – 1: Rules and Requirements for the DipSW* (revised). London: CCETSW.

CCETSW (Central Council for Education and Training in Social Work) (1995b) *DipSW: Rules and Requirements for the Diploma in Social Work – Paper 30*, revised edition. London: CCETSW.

CCETSW (Central Council for Education and Training in Social Work) (1996) *Assuring Quality in the Diploma in Social Work – 1: Rules and Requirements for the DipSW* (2nd revision). London: CCETSW.

Cheetham, J., Fuller, R., McIvor, G. and Petch, A. (1992) *Evaluating Social Work Effectiveness*. Buckingham: Open University Press.

Cheetham, J. (1997) The research perspective, in M. Davies (ed.) *The Blackwell Companion to Social Work*. Oxford: Blackwell.

Chodorow, N. J. (1978) *The Reproduction of Mothering: Psychoanalysis and the Sociology of Gender*. Berkeley, CA: University of California Press.

Chodorow, N. J. (1989) *Feminism and Psychoanalytic Theory*. London: Yale University Press.

Chodorow, N. J. (1994) *Femininities Masculinities Sexualities: Freud and Beyond*. London: Free Association.

Chodorow, N. J. (1999) *The Power of Feelings: Personal Meaning in Psychoanalysis, Gender and Culture*. London: Yale University Press.

Cigno, K. (1998) Cognitive behavioural practice, in R. Adams, L. Dominelli and M. Payne (eds) *Social Work: Themes, Issues and Critical Debates*. Basingstoke: Macmillan.

Cigno, K. and Bourn, D. (1998) *Cognitive-behavioural Social Work in Practice*. Aldershot: Arena.

Clandinin, D. and Connelly, F. (1994) Personal experience methods, in N. Denzin and Y. Lincoln (eds) *Handbook of Qualitative Research*. London: Sage.

Clark, C. L. (2000) *The Political Ethics of Social Work: Towards Welfare Citizenship*. Basingstoke: Macmillan.

Clarke, J. (ed.) (1993) *A Crisis in Care: Challenges to Social Work*. London: Sage.

Clarke, J. (1996) After social work, in N. Parton (ed.) *Social Theory, Social Change and Social Work*. London: Routledge.

Coleman, J., Lyon, J. and Piper, R. (1995) *Teenage Suicide and Self-harm*. London: Trust for the Study of Adolescence.

Collins, A. H. and Pancoast, D. L. (1976) *Natural Helping Networks*. Washington, DC: NASW.

Copley, B. and Forryan, B. (1997) *Therapeutic Work with Children and Young People*. London: Cassell.

Corby, B. (1993) *Child Abuse: Towards a Knowledge Base*. Buckingham: Open University Press.

Corden, J. and Preston-Shoot, M. (1987) Contract or con trick? A reply to Rojek and Collins, *British Journal of Social Work*, 17: 535–43.

Corney, R. (ed.) (1991) *Developing Communication and Counselling Skills*. London: Routledge.

Coulshed, V. (1990) *Management in Social Work*. Basingstoke: Macmillan/BASW.

Coulshed, V. (1991) *Social Work Practice: An Introduction*. Basingstoke: Macmillan/BASW.

Coulshed, V. and Orme, J. (1998) *Social Work Practice: An Introduction*, 2nd edn. Basingstoke: Macmillan/BASW.

Craib, I. (1989) *Psychoanalysis and Social Theory: The Limits of Sociology*. Hemel Hempstead: Harvester Wheatsheaf.

Croft, S. and Beresford, P. (1997) Service users' perspectives, in M. Davies (ed.) *The Blackwell Companion to Social Work*. Oxford: Blackwell.

Dalrymple, J. and Burke, B. (1995) *Anti-oppressive Practice: Social Care and the Law*. Buckingham: Open University Press.

Dartington Social Research Unit (1995) *Child Protection and Child Abuse: Messages from Research*. London: HMSO.

Davies, M. (1981) *The Essential Social Worker: A Guide to Positive Practice*. Aldershot: Arena.

Davies, M. (ed.) (1997) *The Blackwell Companion to Social Work*. Oxford: Blackwell.

Davis, A. and Ellis, K. (1995) Enforced altruism in community care, in R. Hugman and D. Smith (eds) *Ethical Issues in Social Work*. London: Routledge.

Department of Health (1988) *Protecting Children: A Guide for Social Workers Undertaking a Comprehensive Assessment* [Orange Book]. London: HMSO.

Department of Health (1989) *The Care of Children: Principles and Practice in Regulations and Guidance.* London: HMSO.

Department of Health (1995a) *Child Protection: Messages from Research.* London: HMSO.

Department of Health (1995b) *The Challenge of Partnership in Child Protection.* London: HMSO.

Department of Health (1998a) *Quality Protects Circular: Transforming Children's Services.* London: The Stationery Office.

Department of Health (1998b) *Modernising Health and Social Services: National Priorities Guidance.* London: The Stationery Office.

Department of Health (2000) *Assessing Children in Need and their Families: Practice Guidance.* London: The Stationery Office.

Department of Health and Social Security (1978) *Social Services Teams: The Practitioner's View.* London: HMSO.

Department of Health and Social Security (1982) *Child Abuse: A Study of Inquiry Reports, 1973–81.* London: HMSO.

Dockar-Drysdale, B. (1990) *The Provision of Primary Experience: Winnicottian Work with Children.* London: Free Association Books.

Doel, M. (1994) Task-centred work, in C. Hanvey and T. Philpot (eds) *Practising Social Work.* London: Routledge.

Doel, M. (1998) Task-centred work, in R. Adams, L. Dominelli and M. Payne, (eds) *Social Work: Themes, Issues and Critical Debates.* Basingstoke: Macmillan.

Dominelli, L. (1998) Anti-oppressive practice in context, in R. Adams, L. Dominelli and M. Payne (eds) *Social Work: Themes, Issues and Critical Debates.* Basingstoke: Macmillan.

Dominelli, L. and McLeod, E. (1989) *Feminist Social Work.* Basingstoke: Macmillan.

Doyle, C. (1997) *Working with Abused Children.* Basingstoke: Macmillan/BASW.

Egan, G. (1990) *The Skilled Helper: A Systematic Approach to Effective Helping.* Pacific Grove, CA: Brooks/Cole.

Eichenbaum, L. and Orbach, S. (1982) *Outside In: Inside Out. Women's Psychology: A Feminist Psychoanalytic Approach.* Harmondsworth: Penguin.

Eichenbaum, L. and Orbach, S. (1984) *What do Women Want?* London: Fontana.

Ellis, A. and Greiger, R. (1977) *Handbook of Rational-Emotive Therapy.* New York: Springer.

England, H. (1986) *Social Work as Art: Making Sense of Good Practice.* London: Allen & Unwin.

Epstein, L. (1980) *Helping People: The Task-centered Approach.* St. Louis, Missouri: C. V. Mosby.

Erikson, E. (1965) *Childhood and Society.* London: Fontana.

Ernst, S. and Maguire, M. (eds) (1987) *Living With the Sphinx: Papers from the London Women's Therapy Centre.* London: Women's Press.

Everitt, A. and Hardiker, P. (1996) *Evaluating Good Practice.* Basingstoke: Macmillan/BASW.

Fahlberg, V. (1991) *A Child's Journey Through Placement.* London: BAAF.

Fawcett, M. and Lewis, K. (1996) Competence in conciliation work, in K. O'Hagan (ed.) (1996) *Competence in Social Work Practice: A Practical Guide for Professionals.* London: Jessica Kingsley.

Feltham, C. and Dryden, W. (1993) *Dictionary of Counselling.* London: Whurr.

Finkelhor, D. (1984) *Child Sexual Abuse: New Theory and Research.* New York: Free Press.

Finkelhor, D. (1990) Early and long-term effects of child sexual abuse, *Professional Psychology: Research and Practice,* 21: 325–30.

Fischer, J. (1973) Is casework effective? A review, *Social Work*, 1: 107–10.

Fisher, M. (ed.) (1983) *Speaking of Clients*. Sheffield: Social Services Research.

Flax, J. (1981) The conflict between nurturance and autonomy in mother–daughter relationships and within feminism, in E. Howell and M. Bayes (eds) *Women and Mental Health*. New York: Basic Books.

Flax, J. (1991) *Thinking Fragments: Psychoanalysis, Feminism and Postmodernism in the Contemporary West*. Berkeley, CA: University of California Press.

Flax, J. (1993) *Disputed Subjects: Essays on Psychoanalysis, Politics and Philosophy*. London: Routledge.

Freud, S. (1914) On the history of the psycho-analytic movement, *Standard Edition*. Penguin Freud Library.

Freud, S. (1924) *Collected Papers* (Vol. 11). London: Hogarth.

Fuller, R. and Petch, A. (1995) *Practitioner Research: the Reflective Social Worker*. Buckingham: Open University Press.

Gambrill, E. D. (1985) Behavioral approach, in J. B. Turner (ed.) *Encyclopedia of Social Work*, Volume 1. Washington, DC: National Association of Social Workers.

Gambrill, E. D. (1995) Behavioural social work: past, present and future, *Research on Social Work Practice*, 5(4): 460–84.

Garbarino, J., Stott, F. M. and Faculty of the Erikson Institute (1992) *What Children can Tell Us? Eliciting and Evaluating Critical Information from Children*. San Francisco, CA: Jossey-Bass.

Gilligan, C. (1993) *In a Different Voice: Psychological Theory and Women's Development*, 2nd edn. Cambridge, MA: Harvard University Press.

Gitterman, A. (ed.) (1991) *Handbook of Social Work Practice with Vulnerable Groups*. New York: Columbia University Press.

Gough, D. (1993) *Child Abuse Investigations: A Review of the Literature*. London: HMSO.

Gould, L. J. (1999) A political visionary in mid-life: notes on leadership and the life cycle, in R. French and R. Vince (eds) *Group Relations, Management and Organization*. Oxford: Oxford University Press.

Griffiths, R. (1988) *Community Care: Agenda for Action*. London: HMSO.

Guntrip, H. (1977) *Psychoanalytic Theory, Therapy and the Self*. London: Hogarth.

Gutiérrez, L. M. (1990) Working with women of color: an empowerment perspective, *Social Work*, 35(2): 149–53.

Hague, G. and Malos, E. (1998) *Domestic Violence: Action for Change*, 2nd edn. Cheltenham: New Clarion Press.

Hanks, P. (ed.) (1979) *Collins Dictionary of the English Language* (1979) London: Collins.

Hanvey, C. and Philpot, T. (eds) (1994) *Practising Social Work*. London: Routledge.

Hardiker, P. and Barker, M. (1994) *The 1989 Children Act – Significant Harm. The Experience of Social Workers Implementing New Legislation*. Leicester: University of Leicester School of Social Work.

Hardiker, P. and Barker, M. (eds) (1981) *Theories of Practice in Social Work*. London: Academic Press.

Hartmann, F. (1958) *Ego Psychology and the Problem of Adaptation*. New York: International Universities Press.

Hawkins, P. and Shohet, R. (1989) *Supervision in the Helping Professions*. Milton Keynes: Open University Press.

Hawton, K., Fagg, J. and Simkin, S. (1996) Deliberate self-poisoning and self-injury in adolescents: a study of characteristics and trends in Oxford. 1976–1993, *British Journal of Psychiatry*, 169: 741–7.

Hayes, N. (1994) *Foundations of Psychology*. London: Routledge.

Hayman, V. (1993) Re-writing the job: a sceptical look at competences, *Probation Journal*, 40(4): 180–3.

Haynes, K. and Holmes, K. (1994) *Invitation to Social Work*. New York: Longman.

Hester, M., Kelly, L. and Radford, J. (eds) (1996) *Women, Violence and Male Power*. Buckingham: Open University Press.

Hibbert, J. and van Hesswyk, D. (1988) Black Women's Workshop, in S. Krzowski and P. Land (eds) *In Our Experience: Workshops at the Women's Therapy Centre*. London: Women's Press

Hill, M. (1990) The manifest and latent lessons of child abuse inquiries, *British Journal of Social Work*, 20: 197–312.

Hollis, F. (1964) *Casework: A Psychosocial Therapy*. New York: Random House.

Hollis, F. (1977) Social casework: the psychosocial approach, in *Encyclopaedia of Social Work*, 17 edn.: 1300–7. Washington DC: NISW Press.

Hollis, M. and Howe, D. (1990) Moral risks in the social work role: a response to Macdonald, *British Journal of Social Work* 20: 547–52.

Holman, R. (1993) *A New Deal for Social Welfare*. Oxford: Lion.

Holmes, J. (1997) Attachment, autonomy, intimacy: some clinical implications of attachment theory, *British Journal of Medical Psychology*, 70: 231–48.

Home Office (1994) *National Standards for Probation Service Family Court Welfare Work*. London: Home Office.

Howe, D. (1987) *An Introduction to Social Work Theory*. Aldershot: Gower.

Howe, D. (1993) *On Being a Client: Understanding the Process of Counselling and Psychotherapy*. London: Sage.

Howe, D. (1994) Modernity, post modernity and social work, *British Journal of Social Work*, 24: 513–32.

Howe, D. (1995) *Attachment Theory for Social Work Practice*. Basingstoke: Macmillan.

Howe, D. (1996) Surface and depth in social-work practice, in N. Parton (ed.) *Social Theory, Social Change and Social Work*. London: Routledge.

Howe, D. (1997) Relating theory to practice, in M. Davies (ed.) *The Blackwell Companion to Social Work*. Oxford: Blackwell.

Howe, D. (1998) Psychosocial work, in R. Adams, L. Dominelli and M. Payne, (eds) *Social Work: Themes, Issues and Critical Debates*. Basingstoke: Macmillan.

Howe, D. (ed.) (1999) *Attachment and Loss in Child and Family Social Work*. Aldershot: Ashgate.

Howe, D. and Fearnley, S. (1999) Disorders of attachment and attachment therapy, *Adoption and Fostering*, 22(3).

Howe, D., Brandon, M., Hinings, D. and Schofield, G. (1999) *Attachment Theory, Child Maltreatment and Family Support*. Basingstoke: Macmillan.

Howell, E. and Bayes, M. (eds) (1981) *Women and Mental Health*. New York: Basic Books.

Huber, N. (1999) Milburn demands 'excellence not excuses' from local authorities, *Community Care*, 4–10 November.

Hudson, B. L. and MacDonald, G. (1986) *Behavioural Social Work: An Introduction*. London: Macmillan.

Huxley, P. (1997) Mental illness, in M. Davies (ed.) *The Blackwell Companion to Social Work*. Oxford: Blackwell.

Issac, B., Minty, E. and Morrison, R. (1986) Children in care: the association with mental disorder in the parents, *British Journal of Social Work*, 16: 325–39.

Jacobs, M. (1988) *Psychodynamic Counselling in Action*. London: Sage.

Jacobs, M. (ed.) (1995) *Charlie: an Unwanted Child?* Buckingham: Open University Press.

James, A. L. (1997) Divorce court welfare, in R. Adams, L. Dominelli and M. Payne (eds) *Social Work: Themes, Issues and Critical Debates*. Basingstoke: Macmillan.

Jewett, C. (1997) *Helping Children Cope with Separation and Loss*. London: Free Association Books.

Johns, R. and Sedgwick, A. (1999) *Law for Social Work Practice: Working with Vulnerable Adults*. Basingstoke: Macmillan.

Jones, C. (1996) Anti-intellectualism and the peculiarities of British social work, in N. Parton (ed.) *Social Theory, Social Change and Social Work*. London: Routledge.

Jones, C. (1997) Poverty, in M. Davies (ed.) *The Blackwell Companion to Social Work*. Oxford: Blackwell.

Jones, C. (1998) Social work and society, in R. Adams, L. Dominelli and M. Payne, (eds) *Social Work: Themes, Issues and Critical Debates*. Basingstoke: Macmillan.

Jordan, B. (1990) *Social Work in an Unjust Society*. London: Harvester Wheatsheaf.

Jordan, J. V. (ed.) (1997) *More Writings from the Stone Center*. New York: Guilford Press.

Jordan, J. V., Kaplan, A. G., Miller, J. B, Stiver, I. P. and Surrey, J. L. (eds) (1991) *Women's Growth and Connection: Writings from the Stone Center*. New York: Guilford Press.

Kadushin, A. (1990) *The Social Work Interview*, 3rd edn. New York: Columbia University Press.

Karpman, S. (1968) Fairy tales and script drama analysis, *Transactional Analysis Bulletin*, 7: 39–48.

Kemshall, H. and Pritchard, J. (1996) *Good Practice in Risk Assessment and Risk Management*. London: Jessica Kingsley.

Kemshall, H. and Pritchard, J. (1999) *Good Practice in Working with Violence*. London: Jessica Kingsley.

Kendall, P. C. *et al.* (1992) *Anxiety Disorders in Youth: Cognitive Behavioural Interventions*. London: Allyn & Bacon.

Kernberg, O. F. (1976) *Object Relations Theory and Clinical Psychoanalysis*. New York: Jason Aronson.

Kernberg, O. F. (1984) *Severe Personality Disorders: Psychotherapeutic Strategies*. New Haven, CT: Yale University Press.

Klein, M. (1975) *Envy and Gratitude*. London: Hogarth Press.

Kohlberg, L. (1969) *Stages in the Development of Moral Thought and Action*. New York: Holt, Rinehart and Harcourt Brace.

Kohlberg, L. (1984) *The Psychology of Moral Development: The Nature and Validity of Moral Stages*. New York: Harper Row.

Kohon, G. (1988) *The British School of Psychoanalysis: The Independent Tradition*. London: Free Association Books.

Kohut, H. (1971) *The Analysis of Self*. London: Hogarth Press.

Kohut, H. (1977) *The Restoration of Self*. Madison, CT: International University Press.

Kroger, J. (1996) *Identity in Adolescence: The Balance between Self and Other*. London: Routledge.

Kuhn, T. (1970) *The Structure of Scientific Revolutions*. Chicago: Chicago University Press.

Land, H. and Rose, H. (1985) Compulsory altruism for some or an altruistic society for all, in P. Bean, J. Ferris and D. Whynes (eds) *In Defence of Welfare*. London: Tavistock.

Langan, M. (1998) Radical social work, in R. Adams, L. Dominelli and M. Payne (eds) *Social Work: Themes, Issues and Critical Debates*. Basingstoke: Macmillan.

Langan, M. and Lee, P. (eds) (1989) *Radical Social Work Today*. London: Unwin Hyman.

Law Commission (1993) *Mentally Incapacitated and other Vulnerable Adults: Public Law Protection*, Consultation Paper 130, London: HMSO.

Lefcourt, H. M. (1976) *Locus of Control: Current Trends in Theory and Research*. Hillsborough, NJ: Lawrence Erlbaum.

Levinson, D. J. (1978) *The Seasons of a Man's Life*. New York: Alfred A. Knopf.

Levinson, D. J. (1996) *The Seasons of a Woman's Life*. New York: Alfred A. Knopf.

Lindon, J. (1993) *Child Development from Birth to Eight*. London: National Children's Bureau.

Lishman, J. (1991) *Handbook for Practice Teachers in Social Work*. London: Jessica Kingsley.

Lishman, J. (1994) *Communication in Social Work*. Basingstoke: Macmillan/BASW.

Lishman, J. (1998) Personal and professional development, in R. Adams, L. Dominelli and M. Payne (eds) *Social Work: Themes, Issues and Critical Debates*. Basingstoke: Macmillan.

Littlechild, R. (1996) Risk and older people, in H. Kempshall and J. Pritchard (eds) *Good Practice in Risk Assessment and Risk Management*. London: Jessica Kingsley.

Lloyd, M. and Taylor, C. (1995) From Hollis to the Orange Book: developing a holistic model of assessment in the 1990s, *British Journal of Social Work*, 25: 691–710.

London Borough of Brent (1985) *A Child in Trust: the Report of the Panel of Inquiry into the Circumstances Surrounding the Death of Jasmine Beckford*. London: London Borough of Brent.

MacDonald, G. (1990a) Allocating blame in social work, *British Journal of Social Work*, 20: 525–46.

MacDonald, G. (1990b) Moral risks? A reply to Hollis and Howe, *British Journal of Social Work*, 20: 553–6.

MacDonald, G., Sheldon, B. and Gillespie, J. (1992) Contemporary studies of the effectiveness of social work, *British Journal of Social Work*, 22: 615–43.

Macdonald, G. and Macdonald, K. (1995) Ethical issues in social work research, in R. Hugman and D. Smith (eds) *Ethical Issues in Social Work*. London: Routledge.

Mahler, M. S., Pine, F. and Bergman, A. (1975) *The Psychological Birth of the Human Infant*. New York: Basic Books.

Main, M. (1995) Recent studies in attachment: overview, with selected implications for clinical work, in S. Goldberg, R. Muir and J. Kerr (eds) *Attachment Theory: Social, Developmental and Clinical Perspectives*. Hillside, NJ: Analytic Press.

Major, E. L. (2000) Simply impossible, *Guardian Higher Education*, 1 February.

Marris, P. (1996) *The Politics of Uncertainty: Attachment in Private and Public Life*. London: Routledge.

Marsden, D., Oakley, P. and Pratt, B. (1994) *Measuring the Process: Guidelines for Evaluating Social Development*. Oxford: Intrac Publications.

Marsh, P. (1997) Task-centred work, in M. Davies (ed.) *The Blackwell Companion to Social Work*. Oxford: Blackwell.

Marsh, P. and Triseliotis, J. (1996) *Ready to Practise? Social Workers and Probation Officers: Their Training and First Year at Work*. Aldershot: Avebury.

Marshall, G. (1994) *Oxford Concise Dictionary of Sociology*. Oxford: Oxford University Press.

Marziali, E. (1988) The first session: an interpersonal encounter, *Social Casework*, 69(1): 23–7.

Maslow, A. H. (1954) *Motivation and Personality*. New York: Harper and Row.

Mattinson, J. (1975) *The Reflection Process in Casework Supervision*. London: Institute of Marital Studies.

Mayer, J. E. and Timms, N. (1970) *The Client Speaks*. London: Routledge and Kegan Paul.

Mayo, M. (1994) Community Work, in C. Hanvey, and T. Philpot (eds) *Practising Social Work*. London: Routledge.

McLaughlin, J. (1996) Competence in conciliation work, in K. O'Hagan (ed.) *Competence in Social Work Practice: A Practical Guide for Professionals*. London: Jessica Kingsley.

McLeod, J. (1993) *An Introduction to Counselling*. Buckingham: Open University Press.

McLeod, J. (1998) *An Introduction to Counselling*, 2nd edn. Buckingham: Open University Press.

Mehrabian, A. (1972) *Nonverbal Communication*. Chicago, IL: Aldine.

Millar, R., Crute, V. and Hargie, O. (1992) *Professional Interviewing*. London: Routledge.

Miller, J. B. (ed.) (1973) *Psychoanalysis and Women*. Harmondsworth: Penguin.

Miller, J. B. (1976) *Toward a New Psychology of Women*. Harmondsworth: Penguin.

Miller, W. R. and Rollnick, S. (1991) *Motivational Interviewing: Preparing People to Change Addictive Behavior*. London: Guilford Press.

Millham, S., Bullock, R., Hosie, K. and Haak, M. (1986) *Lost in Care*. Aldershot: Gower.

Milner, J. and O'Byrne, P. (1998) *Assessment in Social Work*. Basingstoke: Macmillan.

Minuchin, S. (1979) Constructing a therapeutic reality, in E. Kaufman and P. N. Kaufman (eds) *Family Therapy of Drug and Alcohol Abuse*. New York: Gardner Press.

Mitchell, D. (1996) Fear rules, *Community Care*, 14–20 March: 18–19.

Mitchell, J. (1974) *Psychoanalysis and Feminism*. Harmondsworth: Penguin.

Mitchell, J. (1984) *Women: the Longest Revolution: Essays in Feminism, Literature and Psychoanalysis*. London: Virago.

Modi, P., Marks, C. and Watley, R. (1995) From the margin to the centre: empowering the child, in C. Cloke and M. Davies (eds) *Participation and Empowerment in Child Protection*. London: Pitman.

Mruk, C. J. (1999) *Self-Esteem: Research, Theory and Practice*, 2nd edn. London: Free Association Books.

Mullender, A. and Perrott, S. (1998) Social work and organisations, in R. Adams, L. Dominelli and M. Payne (eds) *Social Work: Themes, Issues and Critical Debates*. Basingstoke: Macmillan.

Munro, E. (1996) Avoidable and unavoidable mistakes in child protection work, *British Journal of Social Work*, 26: 793–808.

Munro, E. (1998) Improving social workers' knowledge base in child protection work, *British Journal of Social Work*, 28: 89–105.

Murray, L. and Cooper, P. (1994) Clinical application of attachment theory and research: change in infant attachment with brief psychotherapy, in J. Richer (ed.) *The Clinical Application of Ethnology and Attachment Theory*. Occasional paper no. 9. London: Association for Child Psychotherapy and Psychiatry.

Myers, L. L. and Thyer, B. A. (1997) Should social work clients have the right to effective treatment?, *Social Work*, 42(3): 288–98.

Nathan, J. (1997) Psychoanalytic theory, in M. Davies (ed.) *The Blackwell Companion to Social Work*. Oxford: Blackwell.

Nelson-Jones, R. (1990) *Human Relationship Skills*. London: Cassell.

Nelson-Jones, R. (2000) *Introduction to Counselling Skills: Text and Activities*. London: Sage.

Neville, D. and Beak, D. (1990) Solving the case history mystery, *Social Work Today*, 28 June.

O'Hagan, K. (1986) *Crisis Intervention in Social Services*. London: Macmillan.

O'Hagan, K. (1994) Crisis intervention: changing perspectives, in C. Hanvey and T. Philpot (eds) *Practising Social Work*. London: Routledge.

O'Hagan, K. (ed.) (1996) *Competence in Social Work Practice: A Practical Guide for Professionals*. London: Jessica Kingsley.

O'Hare, T. (1991) Integrating research and practice: a framework for implementation, *Social Work*, 36(3): 220–23.

O'Sullivan, T. (1999) *Decision-making in Social Work*. Basingstoke: Macmillan.

Oliver, M. (1990) *The Politics of Disablement: A Sociological Approach*. London: Macmillan.

Oliver, M. (1996) *Understanding Disability: From Theory to Practice*. London: Macmillan.

Parad, H. J. (1958) *Ego Psychology and Dynamic Casework*. New York: Family Service Association of America.

Parad, H. J. and Parad, L. G. (1990) Crisis intervention: an introductory overview, in H. J. Parad and L. G. Parad *Crisis Intervention Book 2: The Practitioner's Sourcebook for Brief Therapy*. Milwaukee, WI: Family Service Association of America.

Parsloe, P. (1988) Developing interviewing skills, *Social Work Education*, 8(1): 3–9.

Parton, N. (ed.) (1996) *Social Theory, Social Change and Social Work*. London: Routledge.

Pavlov, I. P. (1927) *Conditional Reflexes*. London: Oxford University Press.

Payne, M. (1991) *Modern Social Work Theory*. Basingstoke: Macmillan.

Payne, M. (1997) *Modern Social Work Theory*, 2nd edn. Basingstoke: Macmillan.

Payne, M. (1998) Social work theories and reflective practice, in R. Adams, L. Dominelli and M. Payne (eds) *Social Work: Themes, Issues and Critical Debates*. Basingstoke: Macmillan.

Perlman, H. H. (1986) The problem-solving model, in F. J. Turner (ed.) *Social Work Treatment: Interlocking Theoretical Approaches*, 3rd edn. New York: Free Press.

Phillips, J. (1996) The future of social work with older people in a changing world, in N. Parton (ed.) *Social Theory, Social Change and Social Work*. London: Routledge.

Phillipson, C. (1993) Approaches to advocacy, in R. Adams, L. Dominelli and M. Payne (eds) *Social Work: Themes, Issues and Critical Debates*. Basingstoke: Macmillan.

Phillipson, C. (1997) The frailty of old age, in Martin Davies (ed.) *The Blackwell Companion to Social Work*. Oxford: Blackwell.

Piaget, J. (1932) *The Moral Judgement of the Child*. London: Routledge and Kegan Paul.

Piaget, J. (1959) *The Language and Thought of the Child*. London: Routledge and Kegan Paul.

Pinker, R. (1990) *Social Work in an Enterprise Society*. London: Routledge.

Portnoy, D. (1999) Relatedness: Where humanistic and psychoanalytic psychotherapy converge, *Journal of Humanistic Psychology*, 39(1): 19–34.

Preston-Shoot, M. (1994) Written agreements: a contractual approach to social work, in C. Hanvey and T. Philpot (eds) *Practising Social Work*. London: Routledge.

Preston-Shoot, M. and Agass, D. (1990) *Making Sense of Social Work*. Basingstoke: Macmillan.

Pringle, N. N. and Thompson, P. J. (1999) *Social Work, Psychiatry and the Law*. Aldershot: Arena.

Pritchard, J. (ed.) (1995) *Good Practice in Supervision*. London: Jessica Kingsley.

Prochaska, J. O. and DiClemente, C. C. (1984) *The Transtheoretical Approach*. Homewood, IL: Dow Jones-Irwin.

Ramon, S. (1991) *Beyond Community Care: Normalization and Integration Work*. London: Macmillan.

Rapoport, L. (1967) Crisis-orientated short term casework, *Social Services Review*, 41: 31–44.

Reber, A. S. (1985) *Dictionary of Psychology*. Harmondsworth: Penguin.

Reid, W. J. (1978) *The Task-centred System*. New York: Columbia University Press.

Reigate, N. (1997) Networking, in R. Adams, L. Dominelli and M. Payne (eds) *Social Work: Themes, Issues and Critical Debates*. Basingstoke: Macmillan.

Rey, L. D. (1996) What social workers need to know about client violence, *Families in Society*, 77(1): 33–9.

Roberts, J. and Taylor, C. (1996) Sexually abused children and young people speak out, in L. Waterstone (ed.) *Child Abuse and Child Abusers: Protection and Prevention*. London: Jessica Kingsley.

Robinson, L. (1995) *Psychology for Social Workers: Black Perspective*. London: Routledge.

Rogers, C. R. (1951) *Client-centred Therapy*. Boston, MA: Houghton Mifflin.

Rogers, C. R. (1957) The necessary and sufficient conditions of therapeutic personality change, *Journal of Consulting Psychology*, 21: 95–103.

Rogers, C. R. (1961) *On Becoming a Person*, Boston, MA: Houghton Mifflin.

Rogers, C. R. (1975) Empathic: an unappreciated way of being, *Counseling Psychologist*, 5: 2–10.

Rojek, C. and Collins, S. (1988) Contact or con trick?, *British Journal of Social Work*, 18(6): 11–22.

Ruber, A. S. (1985) *The Penguin Dictionary of Psychology*. London: Penguin.

Rutter, M. (1991) A fresh look at maternal deprivation, in P. Bateson (ed.) *The Development and Integration of Behaviour*. Cambridge: Cambridge University Press.

Rutter, M. and Rutter, M. (1993) *Developing Minds: Challenge and Continuity Across the Life Span*. Harmondsworth: Penguin.

Ryan, J. and Trevithick, P. (1988) Lesbian workshop, in S. Krzowski and P. Land (eds) *In Our Experience: Workshops at the Women's Therapy Centre*. London: Women's Press.

Rycroft, C. (1968) *A Critical Dictionary of Psychoanalysis*. Harmondsworth: Penguin.

Sainsbury, E. (1987) Client studies: their contribution and limitations in influencing social work practice, *British Journal of Social Work*, 17: 635–44.

Sainsbury, E., Nixon, S. and Phillips, D. (1982) *Social Work in Focus; Clients' and Social Workers' Perceptions of Long Term Social Work*. London: Routledge and Kegan Paul.

Salzberger-Wittenberg, I. (1970) *Psycho-analytic Insight, and Relationships*. London: Routledge.

Schön, D. (1991) *The Reflective Practitioner: How Professionals Think in Action*. Aldershot: Arena.

Seden, J. (1999) *Counselling Skills in Social Work*. Buckingham: Open University Press.

Seed, P. (1990) *Introducing Network Analysis in Social Work*. London: Jessica Kingsley.

Seligman, M. E. P. (1975) *Helplessness*. San Francisco, CA: Freeman.

Seu, I. B. and Heenan, M. C. (eds) (1998) *Feminism and Psychotherapy: Reflections on Contemporary Theories and Practices*. London: Sage.

Shah, N. (1989) It's up to you sisters: black women and radical social work, in M. Langan and P. Lee (eds) *Radical Social Work Today*. London: Unwin Hyman.

Shardlow, S. (1998) Values, ethics and social work, in R. Adams, L. Dominelli and M. Payne (eds) *Social Work: Themes, Issues and Critical Debates*. Basingstoke: Macmillan.

Shaw, I. (1996) *Evaluating in Practice*. Aldershot: Arena.

Shaw, I. and Shaw, A. (1997) Keeping social work honest; evaluating as profession and practice, *British Journal of Social Work*, 27: 847–69.

Sheldon, B. (1995) *Cognitive-behavioural Therapy: Research, Practice and Philosophy*. London: Routledge.

Sheppard, M. (1997) The psychiatric unit, in M. Davies (ed.) *The Blackwell Companion to Social Work*. Oxford: Blackwell.

Shulman, L. (1984) *The Skills of Helping: Individuals and Groups*, 2nd edn. Itasca, IL: Peacock.

Sinason, V. (1988) Smiling, swallowing, sickening and stupefying: the effect of sexual abuse on the child, *Psychoanalytic Psychotherapy*, 3(2): 97–111.

Skinner, B. F. (1974) *About Behaviourism*. London: Jonathan Cape.

Smale, G. and Tuson, G. with Biehal, N. and Marsh, P. (1993) *Empowerment, Assessment, Care Management and the Skilled Worker*. London: HMSO.

Smale, G. and Tuson, G. with Biehal, N. and Statham, D. (2000) *Social Work and Social Problems*. Basingstoke: Macmillan.

Smith, D. (1998) Social work with offenders, in R. Adams, L. Dominelli and M. Payne (eds) *Social Work: Themes, Issues and Critical Debates*. Basingstoke: Macmillan.

Smith, V. (1986) Listening, in O. Hargie (ed.) *A Handbook of Communication Skills*. London: Routledge

Social Services Inspectorate (1991) *Getting the Message Across: A Guide to Developing and Communicating Policies, Principles and Procedures on Assessment*. London: HMSO.

Social Service Inspectorate (1993) *Evaluating Child Protection Services: Findings and Issues*. London: Department of Health.

Solomon, B. B. (1976) *Black Empowerment: Social Work with Oppressed Communities*. New York: Columbia University Press.

Stern, D. N. (1985) *The Interpersonal World of the Infant: A View for Psychoanalysis and Developmental Psychology*. New York: Basic Books.

Stevenson, O. (1988) Law and social work education: a commentary on the 'Law Report', *Issues in Social Work Education*, 8(1): 37–45.

Stevenson, O. and Parsloe, P. (1993) *Community Care and Empowerment*. York: Joseph Rowntree Foundation.

Sugarman, L. (1986) *Life-Span Development: Concepts, Theories and Interventions*. London: Methuen.

Surrey, J. (1991) Relationships and empowerment, in J. V. Jordan, A. G. Kaplan, J. B. Miller, I. P. Stiver, and J. L. Surrey, (eds) *Women's Growth and Connection: Writings from the Stone Center*. New York: Guilford Press.

Susser, M. (1968) *Community Psychiatry: Epidemiologic and Social Themes*. New York: Random House.

Thoburn, J. (1997) The community child care team, in M. Davies (ed.) *The Blackwell Companion to Social Work*. Oxford: Blackwell.

Thoburn, J., Lewis, A. and Shemmings, D. (1995) *Paternalism or Partnership? Family Involvement in the Child Protection Process*. London: HMSO.

Thompson, N. (1995) *Theory and Practice in Health and Social Welfare*. Buckingham: Open University Press.

Thompson, N. (1997) Anti-discriminatory practice, in M. Davies (ed.) *The Blackwell Companion to Social Work*. Oxford: Blackwell.

Thompson, N. (1998) Social work with adults, in R. Adams, L. Dominelli and M. Payne (eds) *Social Work: Themes, Issues and Critical Debates*. Basingstoke: Macmillan.

Thorne, B. (1992) *Carl Rogers*. London: Sage.

Thorne, B. (1997) Person-centred counselling, in M. Davies (ed.) *The Blackwell Companion to Social Work*. Oxford: Blackwell.

Townsend, P. (1993) *The International Analysis of Poverty*. Hemel Hempstead: Harvester Wheatsheaf.

Trevithick, P. (1988) Unconsciousness raising with working class women, in S. Krzowski and P. Land (eds) *In Our Experience: Workshops at the Women's Therapy Centre*. London: Women's Press.

Trevithick, P. (1993) Surviving childhood sexual and physical abuse: the experience of two women of Irish-English parentage, in H. Ferguson, R. Gilligan and R. Torode (eds) *Surviving Childhood Adversity: Issues for Policy and Practice*. Dublin: Social Studies Press.

Trevithick, P. (1995) 'Cycling over Everest': groupwork with depressed women, *Groupwork*, 8(1): 5–33.

Trevithick, P. (1998) Psychotherapy and working class women, in I. B. Seu and

M. Colleen Heenan (eds) *Feminism and Psychotherapy: Reflections on Contemporary Theories and Practices*. London: Sage.

Trotter, C. (1999) *Working with Involuntary Clients: A Guide to Practice*. London: Sage.

Trowell, J. and Bower, M. (1995) *The Emotional Needs of Young Children and their Families*. London: Routledge.

Trower, P., Casey, A. and Dryden, W. (1988) *Cognitive-behavioural Counselling in Action*. London: Sage.

Truax, C. B. and Carkhuff, R. R. (1967) *Towards Effective Counselling and Psychotherapy*. Chicago, IL: Aldine.

Vygotsky, L. S. (1932) *Thought and Language*. Cambridge, MA: MIT Press.

Walker, C. and Walker, A. (1998) Social policy and social work, in R. Adams, L. Dominelli and M. Payne (eds) *Social Work: Themes, Issues and Critical Debates*. Basingstoke: Macmillan.

Waterhouse, L. and McGhee, J. (1998) Social work with children and families, in R. Adams, L. Dominelli and M. Payne (eds) *Social Work: Themes, Issues and Critical Debates*. Basingstoke: Macmillan.

Watson, J. B. (1970) *Behaviourism*. New York: Norton.

Watzlawick, P., Weakland, J. and Risch, R. (1974) *Change: Principles of Problem Formation and Problem Resolution*. London: Norton.

Winnicott, D. W. (1971) *Playing and Reality*. London: Routledge.

Winnicott, D. W. (1975) *Through Paediatrics to Psychoanalysis*. London: Hogarth.

Winnicott, D. W. (1986) *Home is Where We Start From*. Harmondsworth: Penguin.

Winnicott, D. W. (1990) *The Maturational Process and the Facilitating Environment: Studies in the Theory of Emotional Development*. London: Karnac and the Institute of Psychoanalysis (first published Hogarth Press 1965).

Wise, S. (1995) Feminist ethics in practice, in R. Hugman and D. Smith (eds) *Ethical Issues in Social Work*. London: Routledge.

Wolfensberger, W. (1984) A reconceptualization of normalization as social role valorization, *Mental Retardation*, 34: 22–5.

Wolff, S. (1989) *Childhood and Human Nature*. London: Routledge.

Wootton, B. (1959) Daddy knows best, *Twentieth Century*, 166: 248–61.

Yelloly, M. (1980) *Social Work Theory and Psychoanalysis*. New York: Van Nostrand.

INDEX

CL

361.
32
TRE

6000609850